OLYMPICS

Copyright: North Parade Publishing
Published by: North Parade Publishing
4 North Parade, Bath, England

First Published: 2011

Designed and packaged by
Q2AMEDIA
Printed in China

OLYMPICS

1896 – 2012

CONTENTS

Introduction

The Olympic Games are eagerly anticipated all over the world. They are truly great sporting events, covering everything from archery to wrestling, and today involve almost every nation in the world.

Evolution of the Olympic Games

The origins of the Games go back to ancient Greece, when people from all over the Greek world would gather to watch and take part in various athletic, combat and chariot racing events. These were staged every four years in the valley of Olympia and were held in honour of Zeus, the king of the gods. The Olympic Games were only one of a number of religious games held in ancient Greece, but they became the most important. However, with the coming of the Romans, their popularity declined and eventually they stopped altogether.

The modern Olympic Games were revived in 1894 by a Frenchman named Baron Pierre de Coubertin, who was fascinated by ancient Greece and believed that sport could build great moral and social strength. De Coubertin brought together a group of like-minded individuals and in 1896 the first modern Olympic Games were held in Athens in Greece.

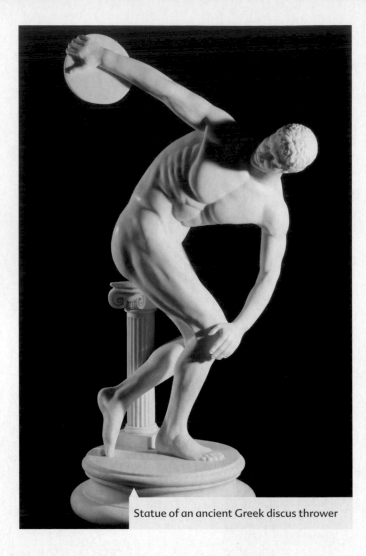
Statue of an ancient Greek discus thrower

As in ancient Greek times, it was decided that the Olympics would be held once every four years: in the first year of an Olympiad, which is a period of four years beginning in a year divisible by four (ie 1896, or 2012).

It was determined that they could only ever be held in the first year of the Olympiad and that they could not be postponed. It was also decided that the Games should be international and would therefore be held in different countries throughout the world — although the Greek contingency lobbied strongly for them being held always in Greece!

Crowds walking around the Olympic stadium in Athens, during the first modern Olympic Games

6

Over the years, the popularity of the Olympic Games has soared. From 241 participants representing 14 nations in Athens in 1896, the Games have grown to nearly 11,000 competitors from 204 countries at the 2008 Summer Olympics in Beijing, China. Initially, only men were allowed to enter, but now women compete in almost every event. In 1896 there were 43 events held altogether, including swimming, cycling, artistic gymnastics, Greco-Roman wrestling, athletics, fencing, shooting, tennis and weightlifting. For the London Olympics in 2012 there are over 300 events planned, covering a wide range of disciplines.

The modern Olympic Games welcome competitors from all countries, following the motto '*Faster, Higher, Stronger,*' all hoping to do themselves and their country proud. Many icons and legends have emerged from the Olympic Games. They have allowed individuals to shine on an international stage.

Games have been held in every continent — the first Games were in Greece, in Europe, but since then they have been held all over the world, from Barcelona to Beijing, from Atlanta to Amsterdam, from Mexico City to Montreal and from Sydney to Seoul. The Olympic Games are truly international in a way that possibly no other sporting competition can match — they belong to the whole world.

Today, the Games are big business — the Beijing Olympics in 2008 allegedly cost around £20 billion — yet the fundamental values of the Olympic Movement are still paramount: excellence, friendship and respect.

The Opening Ceremony of the Beijing Paralympic Games, 2008

History

As far as records can tell, the Olympic Games started in ancient Greece in about 776 BC. They were held in the valley of Olympia in southwestern Greece. Thousands of spectators would gather in the main stadium to watch the lighting of a flame at the altar of Zeus, the supreme god. They would join in the religious ceremonies and watch the single sporting event that made up the original Games — a running race for one length of the stadium (about 210 yards).

Ruins at ancient Olympia. This is where the first Olympic Games were held to honour Zeus

The Events and the Winners

Over time, more events were added and soon athletes came from all over the Greek world — from the city-states and from Greek colonies — for the honour of competing in a range of events that were held over five days. Events included dangerous chariot races; bareback horse races; a pentathlon made up of five events including discus, javelin, jumping, running and wrestling; long-distance running; sprints; contact sports such as wrestling, boxing and the *pankration;* and a race in armour. The *pankration* was an all-in wrestling competition almost without rules, where only biting and gouging with the fingers were forbidden! Strangling your opponent was perfectly acceptable!

War was part of the way of life for ancient Greeks and their sports illustrated that: the *hoplitodromos*, where competitors had to run a race in armour and carrying a shield to demonstrate their fitness and strength, was also used as a training exercise for Hoplite soldiers. Sport helped them to achieve and maintain fitness.

On the final day of the Games, the victors would be presented with olive leaf crowns (a sign of hope and peace), and after feasting and celebrations would return home to a hero's welcome. Winners might marry rich women, enjoy free meals, invitations to parties, and the best seats in the theatre!

Map of ancient Greece

The Truce

In ancient Greece, the city states were often at war with one another. Because the Games were essentially religious affairs, when it was time for the Games, local rulers would send out messengers all over Greece and to the Greek colonies around the Black Sea and the Mediterranean. They declared a truce throughout the Greek world for a month to ensure the safety of all the competitors and spectators travelling to or from Olympia. This sacred truce was known as the *hieromenia*.

Women at Olympia

To begin with, only men were allowed to compete in the Olympic Games. Married women were not even allowed into the Olympic Games as spectators. Unmarried women did, however, have their own festival at Olympia every four years. This was the *Heraia*, held in honour of Hera, wife of Zeus. Women could compete in running races, though only unmarried girls took part. Winners were awarded crowns of sacred olive branches, the same as men.

The one thing that women could do in the Olympic Games was own horses that ran in the chariot race. In this way they could be declared Olympic champions , as the owners of the winning horses were declared victors, even though they did not compete!

Facts

- The very first Olympic champion was a cook named Coroebus who won the *stadion* or foot race.
- The Olympic Games included competitions for trumpeters and choirs.
- Spectators were not allowed to wear big sunhats, because they blocked other people's view.
- Competitors were naked — the only thing they might have on was perhaps a coating of oil!
- A famous wrestler of the time named Milo reportedly trained by carrying a calf every day. As the calf grew heavier, his muscles got stronger.

The End of the Games

The Games were held every four years for over 1,100 years. Athletes began to specialise in certain events and trained intensively, even hiring coaches. But gradually the Games decreased in importance and lost their reputation, especially after AD 67 when the Roman Emperor Nero competed personally in a chariot race and was declared the winner even though he fell from his chariot! (He had also altered the timing of the Games to suit his own schedule!) In AD 393, the Roman Emperor Theodosius I, a Christian, abolished the Games because of their pagan influences. It would be another 1,500 years before the Games were revived.

The Revival

The modern Olympic Games were recreated by a Frenchman, Baron Pierre de Coubertin, almost 1,500 years after they were abolished in 393 AD. In 1894, the International Olympic Committee (IOC) was established in Paris. Two years later, in 1896, the first modern Olympic Games were held in Athens as a tribute to the Greek origins of the Games.

Baron Pierre de Coubertin

Pierre de Coubertin

Towards the end of the nineteenth century, archaeologists began excavating the site of the ancient Olympics. This, together with the growing interest of the day in sports of all kinds, led to a revival of interest in the ideals of the original Games.

Baron Pierre de Coubertin, a young Frenchman, was not the first to try to revive the Olympic Games, but he was the most successful. When he was young, Coubertin was a very keen sportsman. He believed that exercise, and most especially sport (he was particularly impressed with sport at British public schools such as Rugby School), helped to make a person well-rounded and energetic. He was also influenced by Dr William Penny Brookes, a British doctor who firmly believed that regular exercise was the best way to prevent illness. Furthermore, de Coubertin passionately believed that sport could play a major role in encouraging peace and bringing people together from all over the world.

He was greatly inspired by the ancient Olympic Games and travelled to many countries to promote his theories. In 1894 he managed to gather together representatives of several countries in Paris, and the Olympic Movement was born. With dedication and hard work, Coubertin organised the international sporting competition in Athens in 1896 that became known as the first modern Olympic Games.

Boys playing rugby in the early 20th century

Not the Winning . . .

Coubertin felt strongly that it was competition itself that was most important, rather than winning. In his words, which are now the Olympic Creed:

"L'important dans la vie ce n'est point le triomphe, mais le combat, l'essentiel ce n'est pas d'avoir vaincu mais de s'être bien battu."

("The important thing in life is not the triumph but the struggle, the essential thing is not to have conquered but to have fought well.")

Pierre de Coubertin wanted the Games to encourage competition between amateur athletes (rather than between paid professionals) and hoped that they would promote understanding between cultures, encouraging peace.

The Olympic Movement

The Olympic Games are a part of a broader network, the Olympic Movement, which aims to bring together sports, culture and education harmoniously with body, will and mind. Three core values are emphasised:

- *Excellence*: To give one's best, on the field of play or in life, focusing not just on winning but on taking part and on making progress against personal goals.
- *Friendship*: To encourage understanding between people of different genders, nationalities and races, overcoming all political, economic and regional barriers to build a peaceful and better world through solidarity, team spirit, joy and optimism in sport.
- *Respect*: To respect oneself and one's body, as well as to respect others. To respect the rules and regulations of the game and to respect one's environment.

The International Olympic Committee (IOC)

The management head of the modern Games is the International Olympic Committee or IOC which looks after all the organisation and operational activities of the Games.

IOC headquarters, Lausanne, Switzerland

Symbols

There are various symbols associated with the Olympic Games. Among these are the rings, the motto and the flame. These help to give the Games and the Olympic Movement an identity and are very familiar to many people.

The five rings of the Olympic symbol represent the union of five continents in the Games

The Olympic Rings

In 1913, Baron Pierre de Coubertin came up with the idea for the symbol most closely associated with the Olympics: the Olympic rings. The five rings stand for the five continents (Antarctica is excluded and North America and South America are considered one). The connection of the rings symbolises the connection of the continents and the coming together of athletes from all over the world during the Games and the ideal of peace and brotherhood of the whole planet.

The Olympic Flag

One of the most commonly known symbols of the Games is its flag. The flag has five intertwined Olympic rings in different colours — blue, yellow, black, green and red — shown on a white background. Combined in this way, the six colours of the flag represent universality, for every country's national flag has at least one of these colours.

The Olympic flag

The flag was first flown at the 1920 Olympic Games in Belgium. Ever since the Opening Ceremony of the 1972 Munich Games, the flag has been carried into the stadium by athletes and then hoisted on the flagpole. It is lowered during the Closing Ceremony, marking the end of the Games. At this stage, the flag is passed on to the next host nation. The original Olympic flag was used until 1984, when Seoul presented a new flag made of Korean silk to the IOC.

Facts

- Although de Coubertin always intended the modern Olympic Games to be an international event, it wasn't until the 1912 Games in Stockholm in Sweden that there were participants from all five continents.
- In 1913, the five rings appeared at the top of a letter written by de Coubertin. He had drawn the rings and coloured them in by hand.
- De Coubertin also came up with the idea for the Olympic flag comprising the rings, which he presented in June 1914 in Paris at the Olympic Congress.

The Olympic Flame

The ancient Greeks believed that fire was stolen from Mount Olympus, the home of the gods, and given to mankind by Prometheus, and they considered fire to have sacred qualities. Eternal flames burned in front of Greek temples, and the Olympic torch was lit months before the start of the Games.

A flame was first lit at a modern Olympic Games in Amsterdam in 1928. It was kindled on site and remained lit throughout the Games. This was repeated in Los Angeles in 1932, but in 1936 a torch was ignited with a flame borne directly from Olympia, Greece, and was then carried by a team of relay runners to Berlin in what has become an Olympic tradition.

The Olympic flame and cauldron during the Summer Olympics at the 'Bird's Nest' Stadium in Beijing

The Olympic flame is lit in front of the ruins of the Temple of Hera in Olympia. An actress playing a high priestess uses a special mirror to light the flame using the rays of the sun. (A backup flame, also lit from the sun's rays, is ready in case of bad weather!)

The flame is then carried by relay from Olympia to the host city of the Games, crossing different regions, countries and continents. A new torch is created for each edition of the Games. Each relay runner carries his or her own torch, and the flame is passed from runner to runner. The runners are usually special members of the local communities, celebrities or athletes, and it is seen as a great honour to help carry the flame. In this way the Games are announced throughout the world, and many people have a chance to feel a part of them.

The Olympic Motto

The motto of the Games is '*Citius, Altius, Fortius.*' It is a Latin expression meaning '*Faster, Higher, Stronger*' and epitomises the idea that the key thing is to strive to do one's best, not just to win.

The motto was proposed on the creation of the IOC by Pierre de Coubertin, who had heard it used by his friend Henri Didon, a Dominican priest. The motto was first introduced in 1924 at the Games in Paris.

Olympic Values Through the Symbols

These symbols are used to express the values held by the Olympic Movement:

The **motto** embodies **excellence** by encouraging athletes to strive to do their personal best.

The **flame** symbolises **friendship** between people of different lands and cultures, with the torch relay usually travelling through different countries on its way from Olympia to the host city.

The **rings** represent **respect**, bringing all nations and all five continents together without discrimination. The principles shown are universality and humanism.

Traditions

The Olympic Games are steeped in ceremony, from the lighting of the flame at the Opening Ceremony, to national anthems being played as winners receive their medals on the podium.

Doves being released at the Opening Ceremony of the 1968 Games in Mexico

Opening and Closing Ceremonies

The Opening and Closing Ceremonies of the Olympics have become increasingly grand and elaborate events. They usually feature music, singing, dancing and elaborate fireworks. They are an opportunity for the host country to showcase their creative talent before millions of viewers and spectators. Indeed, this is in keeping with the tradition started by the ancient Greek Olympic Games, when there were competitions for choirs and trumpeters, and sculptors and artists would gather to show their work to prospective patrons.

To begin with, the modern ceremonies took whatever form the host nation desired, but since the Antwerp Games in Belgium in 1920 there have been clear guidelines to shape the events.

The Opening Ceremony

Athletes from all the participating countries march into the stadium holding their flags. The athletes from Greece enter first, in memory of the tradition behind the Games, followed by other countries in alphabetical order. The host nation is the last to enter the stadium.

After some speeches by the head of state of the host country and the president of the IOC, the Olympic anthem is played and the Olympic flag is raised. Then the relay runners bring the Olympic flame into the stadium and the last runner lights the cauldron, so that the flame may burn throughout the Games. Following this, doves are released — nowadays these are symbolic — and then the Olympic oath is taken. The final part of the official ceremony before the artistic programme commences is the playing of the host country's national anthem.

Muhammad Ali holds the torch before lighting the Olympic flame during the Opening Ceremony of the 1996 Centennial Olympic Games in Atlanta, Georgia

Release of Doves

From 1920, part of the Olympic tradition, after the lighting of the cauldron, was to release doves into the sky, as a symbol of peace. However, in the 1988 Games in Seoul, birds were released before the cauldron was lit, and tragically some were caught in the flames. As a result, the last time live doves were released at an Opening Ceremony was in 1992 in Barcelona, hours before the flame was lit. Balloon doves were released in 1994 at the Lillehammer Winter Games and paper doves were used at the Atlanta Ceremonies in 1996, while in Beijing in 2008 images of doves flying into the sky were projected onto the stadium rim, along with images of people from around the world making an animated flying dove symbol with their crossed hands.

Britain's Wing Commander Donald Finlay takes the Olympic oath at the Opening Ceremony of the 1948 Games in London

The Olympic Oath

The Olympic oath is taken by one athlete and one judge from the home nation, acting on behalf of all the competitors and judges. Athletes have taken the oath since 1920, although the wording has changed over the years, whilst the oath was first taken by a judge in 1972. Since 1984, the person taking the oath holds a corner of the Olympic flag.

The flag-bearers of all the delegations form a semicircle, while the athlete from the host country mounts the rostrum to take the oath:

The Olympic Anthem

The Olympic anthem or hymn was written for the first modern Games in 1896. It was composed by Spyros Samaras to lyrics written by Kostis Palamas. However, until 1960, each subsequent Olympics host nation commissioned its own specific hymn to be played during the Games.

In Tokyo in 1958, the IOC agreed to adopt the piece by Samaras and Palama as the official anthem, and since then it has been used at every Games.

Olympic Anthem
(English Translation)

Immortal spirit of antiquity,
Father of the true, beautiful and good,
Descend, appear, shed over us thy light
Upon this ground and under this sky
Which has first witnessed thy unperishable fame

Give life and animation to those noble games!
Throw wreaths of fadeless flowers to the victors
In the race and in the strife!
Create in our breasts, hearts of steel!

In thy light, plains, mountains and seas
Shine in a roseate hue and form a vast temple
To which all nations throng to adore thee,
Oh immortal spirit of antiquity!

"In the name of all the competitors I promise that we shall take part in these Olympic Games, respecting and abiding by the rules which govern them, committing ourselves to a sport without doping and without drugs, in the true spirit of sportsmanship, for the glory of sport and the honour of our teams."

Then the judge takes the following oath:
"In the name of all the judges and officials, I promise that we shall officiate in these Olympic Games with complete impartiality, respecting and abiding by the rules which govern them, in the true spirit of sportsmanship."

The Closing Ceremony of the Summer Olympic Games in Sydney

The Closing Ceremony

The Closing Ceremony takes place in the main stadium at the end of the competitions. (Today, the Olympic Games cannot extend to more than 16 days, officially.) During the Summer Olympics, the medal ceremony for the men's marathon is traditionally held during the Closing Ceremony, but the timing of this can change depending on the wishes of the organising committee. The flag-bearers of the participating countries and the name-board-bearers enter the stadium first, and behind them march the athletes, without any distinction or grouping by nationality, in keeping with the philosophy of friendship and peace that the Olympics embody. The Greek national anthem is played and the Greek flag and those of the current and future host countries are raised, each accompanied by their national anthems.

The Games end with these words, spoken by the president of the IOC: *"I declare the Games of the ... Olympiad closed and, in accordance with tradition, I call upon the youth of the world to assemble four years from now at ... to celebrate with us there the Games of the ... Olympiad."*

A fanfare then sounds, the Olympic flame is extinguished, and while the Olympic anthem is being played, the Olympic flag that was raised in the Opening Ceremony is lowered from the flagpole and carried out of the stadium. The mayor of the host city then returns a special Olympic flag to the president of the IOC, who entrusts it to the mayor of the next host city. A farewell song resounds.

Since 1976, the next host nation then has the opportunity to introduce itself with a short artistic and creative display.

Choosing the Host City

The IOC elects host cities following a two-stage process. The host city for an Olympic Games is usually chosen seven years in advance. The IOC elects host cities following a two-stage process that spans a two-year period. Cities wishing to stage the Games in question become '*Applicant Cities.*' From these, the IOC selects a number to be considered '*Candidate Cities,*' from which one is chosen by a vote of the IOC session.

The Medal Ceremony

After each event a medal ceremony is held. During the Summer Games this is usually held immediately after the event at the venue, but during the Winter Games the medals are usually presented at a nightly ceremony held at a medal plaza.

A three-tiered rostrum is used for the three medal winners, with the gold medal winner stepping onto the highest platform. The medals are awarded by a member of the IOC. After medals are distributed, the flags of the nations of the three medalists are raised, with that of the country of the gold medalist raised the highest, and at the same time the national anthem of the gold medalist is played. According to the Olympic Charter, the athletes who win the gold medal will have their names engraved on the walls of the main stadium.

Interestingly, it was not until 1904 that gold medals were awarded — in 1896, at the first modern Games, the winner was awarded a silver medal along with an olive wreath, while the runners-up were awarded bronze medals and a laurel wreath.

Jade was used for the first time in the Olympic medals in the Beijing Olympic Games. The medals symbolise nobility, virtue and honour

Women athletes in the 100 m hurdles in Beijing (Lolo Jones of the US in the lead)

The Games

Nowadays, there are four Olympic events: the Summer Olympics, the Winter Olympics, the Paralympics and, the latest addition, the Youth Olympics.

The Summer Games

The Summer Games are held in the first year of an Olympiad (a period of four years). If, for any reason, the Games cannot be held, as happened during the First and Second World Wars, they cannot be rescheduled, but are cancelled.

The Summer Games include a range of indoor and outdoor sports. Swimming and athletics are major attractions, but many sports are included and are constantly reviewed. To make it onto the Olympic programme, a sport must be administered by an International Federation which ensures that the sport's activities follow the Olympic Charter. It also has to be widely practised around the world and meet a number of criteria established by the IOC.

The Winter Games

The Winter Olympics Sports are arranged into three main categories: ice sports; alpine, skiing and snowboarding events; and Nordic events. In each of these sports there are more events. From a total of 7 sports, split into 15 disciplines, there were over 80 individual events at the 2010 Winter Olympics. Skating, skiing and ice hockey are sports keenly awaited in the Winter Olympiad.

The move toward a winter version of the Olympics began in London in 1908 when a figure skating event was held. This was repeated in 1920 in Antwerp, when ice hockey was also added.

The IOC (against the wishes of Pierre de Coubertin and despite the resistance of the Scandinavian countries, which staged their own Nordic championships) decided to hold a winter sports week (it was actually 11 days) in Chamonix, France to enable other winter

Épée fencing is one of the five events in the Olympics modern pentathlon contest

Cyclists during the men's Olympic sprint at the Sydney Olympic Games in 2000

sports to be featured. The event, which included Nordic skiing, speed skating, figure skating, ice hockey, and bobsledding, proved very successful and was retrospectively known as the first Olympic Winter Games.

Gold medalist Giorgio di Centa of Italy in the men's cross country skiing 50km mass start final at the 2006 Turin Winter Olympic Games

Until 1992, the Winter Olympics were staged in the same year as the Summer Olympics. However, after this it was decided to alternate the two events. Thus, since Lillehammer, Norway, in 1994, the Winter Games have been held during the third year of an Olympiad, while the Summer Games are celebrated during the first year.

Paralympics

In 1948, Sir Ludwig Guttmann, a German doctor living in England, was trying to promote the rehabilitation of soldiers after World War II. He organised a multi-sport event between several hospitals to coincide with the 1948 London Olympics. Known as the Stoke Mandeville Games, this became an annual sports festival. Over the next twelve years, Guttman and others continued their efforts to use sports to aid healing. In 1960, when the Olympic Games were held in Rome, Guttman brought 400 athletes to compete in the 'Parallel Olympics,' which became known as the first Paralympics. Since then, the Paralympics have been held in every Olympic year.

During the 1988 Summer Games in Seoul, the city hosted the Paralympic Games too, and today, any city hosting the Summer Olympics also has to host the Paralympics. Lord Coe, the Chairman of the London Organising Committee for the 2012 Summer Olympics and Paralympics in London, England, has stated: *"We want to change public attitudes towards disability, celebrate the excellence of Paralympic sport and to enshrine from the very outset that the two Games are an integrated whole."*

Players in a game of basketball at the 2008 Paralympics, Beijing

Participants at the Youth Olympics, Singapore

have been created specifically for young athletes to compete. In Singapore, a total of 3,531 athletes between 14 and 18 years of age from 204 National Olympic Committees competed in 201 events in 26 sports. The first gold medal of the Games was awarded to 18 year old Japanese triathlete Yuka Sato.

There will also be a Winter Games for young athletes, and the first will be hosted in Innsbruck, Austria, in early 2012.

The Youth Games will be shorter than the senior Games — the Summer Games will last twelve days, while the Winter Games will last ten days. The sports to be contested will coincide with those scheduled for the traditional Games, although there will be a reduced number of disciplines and events.

Youth Olympic Games

In August 2010 the very first Youth Summer Games was held in Singapore. The concept was introduced in 2001 by the IOC President Jacques Rogge and was approved during the 119th Congress of the IOC. The Youth Games

The first Summer Youth Olympic Games were held in Singapore

Women in the Games

Women were not allowed to compete in the ancient Olympic Games. Even in the early days of the modern Olympics, women were not well represented.

It was in Paris in 1900 that women first competed in the Games, in lawn tennis and golf. Female athletes had to face severe prejudices against their participation. After a tough struggle they made their first mark in athletics in the Amsterdam Games in 1928.

Homare Sawa from Japan in Beijing 2008. Women's football was introduced in 1996

Over time more women's events were added, and in Beijing in 2008, boxing was the only sport not open to women. At the time there were concerns that the sport was not competitive enough in some countries, leading to possibly dangerous mismatches. However, women's boxing has become increasingly popular and in 2009 the IOC voted to lift the barrier to this last all-male summer sport, meaning that women will compete in boxing in 2012 in London.

Currently, two sports — synchronised swimming and rhythmic gymnastics — are for women only. Softball was another — it has been dropped but its fans still hope that it will be reinstated.

Facts

- Women first competed in swimming in 1912, but none came from America, which did not allow its female athletes to compete in events without long skirts.
- In 1928, women first competed in track and field events; however, so many collapsed at the end of the 800 m race that the event was banned until 1960.
- In only two Olympic sports do men and women compete against each other: sailing and equestrian.

In the Winter Olympics the only two sports that women do not compete in are Nordic combined and ski jumping. There was a push to include women's ski jumping at the 2010 Vancouver Games. Although this was unsuccessful, the event is now being considered for the 2014 Games.

P T Usha became the first Indian woman to reach the finals of an Olympic event in the 1984 Olympic Games

The Olympic Village

The Olympic Village, or Athletes' Village, is a place for competitors and coaches to interact with participants from other nationalities, practising different sports.
It is the perfect place to put into practice the Olympic values of friendship and respect.

An Olympic Village is built in the city that hosts the Games for the session. It is a miniature accommodation hub for the participants, located close to the venue of the Games so that athletes don't have to spend too much time travelling, and it aims to offer all the facilities that they need during their time there, both for training and relaxing.

Before 1924, athletes stayed in rented accommodation located around the host city. At the suggestion of Pierre de Coubertin, the organisers for the 1924 Olympics in Paris built cabins near the Stade Olympique de Colombes to allow the athletes to easily access the Games' sporting venues.

The first proper Olympic Village was constructed in the Baldwin Hills neighborhood of Los Angeles, for the 1932 Games. The Village consisted of several hundred buildings, including post and telegraph offices, an amphitheatre, a hospital, a fire department, and a bank. However, it was only for male competitors. Female athletes were housed at the Chapman Park Hotel on Wiltshire Boulevard. The Village was dismantled after the Games.

Nowadays, Olympic Villages are huge constructions, sometimes representing an entire new suburb, or redevelopment of a rundown area. Training and leisure facilities are included to ensure the comfort and wellbeing of the athletes, and, since the Games in 1972 Munich, when members of the Israeli Olympic team were taken hostage and eventually murdered by the terrorist group Black September, extensive security measures are also incorporated into the plans.

The cost of the Village is huge, but in theory the investment is put to good use once the Games finish, when the Village can be turned into a residential area which can be bought or rented by the residents of the country.

Sometimes secondary Villages are built to host athletes whose events take them a significant distance away from the main Village. For example, for the 1992 Barcelona Olympics, separate Villages were arranged for those involved in white-water canoeing and rowing. For London 2012, it is planned that those competing in rowing and flatwater canoe/kayak events which will take place near Windsor Castle, will be housed at the Royal Holloway College, 10 miles away, rather than being bussed from the Olympic Village on the other side of London.

VILLAGE OLYMPIQUE

1924 Olympic Village in Paris

The proposed Olympic Village for 2012 in East London

Facts

- Before the Los Angeles Games in 1932, participants had to stay in cheaper accommodation like hostels, schools and barracks.
- In Amsterdam in 1928, the American team were quartered on board the boat that they had travelled in, which was moored in a rather smelly canal! Some of them were still a bit seasick by the time they reached the stadium!

Some athletes choose not to stay at the Olympic Village, as they prefer greater privacy, while others embrace the Olympic experience. Speaking about Beijing 2008, Andy Murray, the British tennis player, stated:

"Quite a few of the tennis players are staying in hotels, but . . . I wouldn't want to be staying anywhere other than in the Athletes' Village. It will be a great experience to be around the best athletes in the world and to speak to some of them."

London's 2012 Olympic Village

The 2004 bid figure for the cost of the Olympic Village in East London was £600m, but it has since been estimated that it could cost up to £1 billion.

Around 17,000 athletes and team officials will be able to stay in the heart of the Olympic Park, with some rooms offering views of the main stadium. The Village will offer landscaped squares, fountains, hairdressers, an internet cafe, medical facilities, a disco and a main dining hall big enough for 5,500 people.

After the Games it is planned that the Village will be transformed into a lively residential community featuring an Education Academy, community and healthcare facilities, including swathes of parks and open spaces, and benefiting from new transport links, in part of the overall Stratford City regeneration scheme.

The Summer Sports

As of 2012, the Summer Olympics will include 26 sports with 38 disciplines and about 300 events. Both the sports and the individual events are continually reviewed.

Archery

Archery made its debut in the 1900s but was later dropped from the Olympic programme. It was reinstated at the 1972 Games in Munich. Today's bows are made from special aluminium alloy and laminated carbon materials. They are designed to shoot specially designed arrows at speeds of more than 150 miles per hour — a far cry from the sport's origins in medieval England when tournaments were held to encourage the military art of the archer in peacetime (and lower class men were required to practise archery by law!)

Athletics

Part of the original Olympic Games in ancient Greece, athletics is one of the most popular Olympic sports and embodies the Olympic motto — "*Faster, Higher, Stronger.*" Today, there are close to 50 different events held on the track or in the field, involving running (sprints and distance), walking, throwing or jumping.

Running and *walking* races are held over distances ranging from 100 metres to 50 kilometres. They are held in a stadium apart from the *marathon* and *race walk* events, which take place on the road. *Hurdles* and *steeplechase* races require athletes to jump over barriers.

There are four jumping disciplines: *high jump*, where athletes attempt to clear a bar that is continually raised; *pole vault*, which follows the same rules, but athletes use a long pole to help launch themselves into the air; *long jump*, where athletes sprint down a runway before jumping as far as they can into a sand pit; and *triple jump*, where athletes have to complete a hop and step before making their jump.

The throwing disciplines are *shot put, javelin, discus* and *hammer*. Each competitor has six attempts to throw the object as far as he or she can into a field.

In the two-day men's *decathlon* and ladies' *heptathlon* competitions, athletes take part in a range of running, jumping and throwing events — 10 for men, 7 for women. Points are awarded based on times run and distances thrown and jumped and the winner is the one with the most points at the end.

Badminton men's singles gold medalist Lin Dan of China at the Beijing 2008 Games

Badminton

Badminton, which is especially popular in Europe and Asia (which has traditionally dominated the sport) first appeared as a demonstration event at Munich in 1972. It became a full medal sport 20 years later, at the Barcelona 1992 Games.

Basketball

Basketball was invented by a Canadian physical education instructor who wanted to create a game that could be played indoors during the winter. Today, the sport is played worldwide, although Russia and the US have tended to dominate Olympic basketball. It first appeared in the Games as a full medal sport at Berlin 1936, and out of the next 17 Games, the USA won gold 13 times!

Beach Volleyball

Beach volleyball is one of two disciplines in the Olympic sport of volleyball. It made its Olympic debut at the 1996 Atlanta Games. Two teams, each with two players, separated by a high net, try to score points against the other by grounding a ball on the other team's court.

Boxing

Boxing featured in the ancient Olympic Games, when opponents would fight each other with strips of leather wrapped around their fists, but although it had been extremely popular, organisers of the first modern Games in Athens did not include it, believing that it was too dangerous a sport. It first appeared on the programme in 1904. At the London 2012 Games, boxing will feature women's events for the first time.

Canoeing

The Canoe Slalom is a timed run down a white water course (fast-moving, turbulent water featuring rapids and violent currents) with up to 25 gates to negotiate. The canoe sprint paddlers race across calm water over distances of 200 m, 500 m and 1,000 m.

Canoe refers to both kayak and canoe. The kayak '*paddler*' is in a sitting position with a double ended paddle and the canoe '*paddler*' kneels in the boat using a single bladed paddle.

Cycling

Cycling has been contested at every Summer Olympic Games since 1896. Today there are four disciplines: *BMX* (short for Bicycle Motocross) riders race around short outdoor tracks featuring jumps, banked corners and other obstacles; *mountain bike* takes place over rough and hilly countryside with races over 40-50 km for men and 30-40 km for women; *road* — within this category, the *road race* is approximately 240 km (150 miles) for men and 130 km (80 miles) for women, while the *time trial* is against the clock over a shorter distance; in the velodrome *track* riders race around a banked, 250 m indoor track, both individually and in teams, against the clock and head to head.

Diving

Diving was first contested at the St Louis 1904 Games. Its appearance on the Olympic programme in both springboard and platform events has been continuous since 1908. Competitors perform a series of dives from either a springboard or a fixed platform, at a height of either three or ten metres and they are judged on their elegance and skill.

Equestrian

Chariot racing was one of the most exciting and dangerous events at the ancient Olympic Games. Today, horses feature in the Olympics — but without the chariots! The three equestrian disciplines are unique among Olympic sports, in that men and women compete on the same terms, and horse and rider are both declared Olympic medal winners for they are considered a team.

Dressage has a long tradition, and was introduced by the Greeks over 2,000 years ago to help train their horses for war. In the Olympics the event is held in a sand-based arena, and horse and rider are marked on accuracy of movement, calmness, suppleness and flexibility.

Jumping or *show jumping* takes place in an arena around a course of approximately 15 fences.

Gold medal winners Eric Lamaze of Canada and Hickstead in action at the Hong Kong Olympic Equestrian Venue during the Beijing 2008 Games

The most complex of the Olympic equestrian disciplines, *eventing* combines dressage, jumping and cross country, where riders have to complete a course over natural terrain including obstacles.

Fencing

Fencing is one of just four sports to have featured at every modern Olympic Games. There are three types of weapon used — *foil, épée* and *sabre* — with a separate competition for each. Each bout lasts for three three-minute rounds with the fencers scoring points by touching their opponent's body with the tip of their sword or, in sabre, with the edge of the blade.

Football

Football is one of the most widely played and oldest games in existence. It was first contested as a full medal sport in London in 1908, but until 1992 only amateur players were allowed to take part. At the Barcelona Games the rules were changed, allowing professional players to enter, but making it an under-23 event, with three players over this age allowed in every team. Women's football has no age limits and appeared at the Games for the first time in Atlanta 1996.

Gymnastics

Gymnastics has featured in all of the modern Olympic Games, and is one of the most popular events. The word '*gymnastics*' comes from the Greek for '*naked*' — in ancient Greece, male athletes trained and competed in the nude. Because of this, women were excluded from the Games, not just as competitors but even as spectators to begin with!
Artistic gymnastics is the oldest and best known of the Olympic disciplines. It is performed using apparatus. For the men the events are *floor, pommel horse, rings, vault, parallel bars* and *high bar*, and for the women the events are *vault, uneven bars, balance beam* and *floor*. Scores are awarded for the difficulty and execution of each exercise, and there are competitions for the best team, all-around gymnast and individual apparatus specialists.
Rhythmic gymnastics is for women only, and is a combination of gymnastics and dance, performed to music using a small piece of hand apparatus — a rope, hoop, ball, clubs or ribbon.
Trampoline is the newest Olympic Gymnastics discipline, first appearing in Sydney 2000. Gymnasts perform a series of 10 judged elements each containing somersaults and twists.

Handball

Ancient Greek literature has references to a sport very similar to handball. Today, in handball, two teams of seven players pass and dribble a small synthetic or leather ball using only their hands. The aim is to score a goal by throwing the ball past the defending goalkeeper in the other team's goal.

Hockey

Hockey is the oldest known ball and stick game — records exist of it having been played in Persia in 2000 BC. It is a popular sport played on an outdoor pitch by two teams of 11 players, using hockey sticks to hit or control the ball, attempting to hit it into their opponents' goal. For a long time India completely dominated the sport — between

1928 and 1956 they won all six Olympic gold medals and 30 consecutive games! — but it has become more competitive since then. It is sometimes known as field hockey, to distinguish it from ice hockey played at the Winter Games.

Judo

Judo is a grappling sport, which developed from *jujitsu*. Competitors use recognised moves to force their opponent to the floor, using their opponent's strength against him and adapting quickly to changing circumstances. It was first seen as a demonstration sport in 1932 at Los Angeles, and became a full medal sport for men in 1964 and for women in 1992.

Beijing 2008 Judo -60 kg gold medalist Choi Minho (r) of South Korea and Ludwig Paischer (r) of Austria

Modern Pentathlon

The modern pentathlon was invented by Pierre de Coubertin, the founder of the modern Olympic Movement. He saw the event as the equivalent of the pentathlon at the ancient Games, which consisted of running the length of the stadium, jumping, throwing the spear, throwing the discus and wrestling. In those days, the pentathlon was considered to be the climax of the Games, with the winner ranked as '*Victor Ludorum*' ('Winner of Games'). The modern pentathlon has been a part of the Games since 1912 and consists of five elements: *fencing, swimming, riding, running* and *shooting* — designed to simulate the experience of a nineteenth century cavalry soldier behind enemy lines who must ride an unfamiliar horse, fight with pistol and sword, swim, and run!

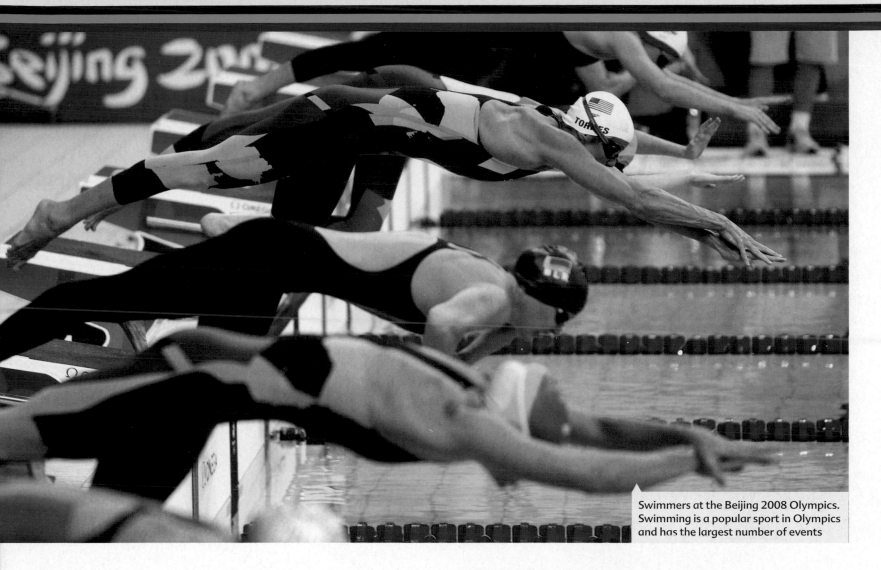

Swimmers at the Beijing 2008 Olympics. Swimming is a popular sport in Olympics and has the largest number of events

Rowing

There are two types of Rowing at the Olympic Games: *sweep rowing*, where rowers use a single oar and compete in crews of two, four or eight (the eight is steered by a cox who also gives directions); and *sculling*, where scullers have an oar in each hand, and compete alone, in doubles and quads (fours).

Sailing

Sailing was on the programme at the very first Olympiad in Athens, but had to be cancelled due to bad weather! The sport of sailing at the London 2012 Games will feature 10 different classes, including *windsurfing (sailboard), dinghy (Laser, Laser Radial, Finn, 49er* and *470)*, and *keelboat (Star* and *women's match racing - Elliot 6m)*. The boats used by all competitors in any event are identical, so the winner is determined by skill and strategy and not the equipment.

Shooting

Shooting has been around since the earliest days of the modern Olympic Games. At the London 2012 Olympic Games, it will feature three disciplines: *rifle* and *pistol* (where competitors fire bullets at a target from a set distance) and *shotgun* (where lead pellets are fired at moving clay targets.

Swimming

One of the most popular Olympic sports, swimming has featured in every edition of the modern Games. Early Olympic events were conducted in freestyle (crawl) or breaststroke. Backstroke was added in 1904 and butterfly in 1956. At the first three modern Olympic Games, swimming took place in open water. At the very first Olympiad, one of the American swimmers climbed straight back out because the icy water of the Bay of Zea was so cold! A pool was used for the first time at the London 1908 Games. Races take place over distances ranging from 50 m to 1,500 m, except for the newest swimming event — the outdoor 10 km *marathon*, which took place for the first time in Beijing in 2008. Unless it is a *freestyle* event (in which swimmers usually use *front crawl* as it is generally the fastest stroke), competitors have to use a particular stroke: *breaststroke, butterfly* or *backstroke*. There are also *Medley* events which combine all four strokes.

Synchronised Swimming

Synchronised swimming is sometimes called '*water ballet*,' as competitors perform short routines to music in the pool. Routines are judged on technical merit and artistic impression. The event is for women only.

Table Tennis

Based on the same idea as tennis, but using a table instead of a court, table tennis began as an after-dinner game, played by upper-class English families! It entered the Olympic programme at Seoul in 1988, and has featured in every Games since. The sport is especially popular in Asia, where most of the world's top players are based.

Ma Lin (r) of China, playing against Bojan Tokic, of Slovenia at the Beijing Olympics. Ma won gold in both the singles and team competitions in 2008

Taekwondo

'*Taekwondo,*' which has its roots in Korean martial art, translates into English as '*the way of foot and fist.*'
The aim is to land accurate kicks on the scoring area of your opponent. At the Olympic Games, events are held in four weight classes for both men and women. Competitors wear a white uniform called a '*Dobok,*' and protective equipment — one red and the other blue, to help the judges differentiate.

Tennis

The origins of tennis date back to the eleventh century from a game played in French monasteries and palaces, but it later developed in England, where croquet lawns were used to stage the first official lawn tennis matches. It was played at the first modern Games in Athens. Arguments over the '*amateur*' status of players saw it dropped from the programme in 1922, but it eventually returned at Seoul 1988.

Triathlon

The triathlon made its Games debut at Sydney 2000, where half a million spectators lined the streets to watch the event. Triathlon is thought to be the fastest-growing individual sport in the UK. It combines three different disciplines.

The Olympic triathlon starts with a *1,500 m swim* in open water. Competitors then have to complete a *40 km cycle ride* before finishing with a *10 km run*.

Volleyball

In Olympic volleyball, two teams of six play on an indoor court, and aim to hit a ball over a tall net to land in the other team's half of the court. Players normally use their hands, but the ball can be played by any part of the body. Each team is allowed three touches of the ball before it must cross back over the net.

Water Polo

In the late nineteenth century, several water sports developed, including water polo, in which players rode on floating barrels, painted to look like horses, and struck the ball with a stick. Water rugby became more popular, but the name water polo became attached to it (some theories state that it is because the rubber ball used in the game came from India where it was known as a 'pulu' pronounced as 'polo' by the English.) Today's water polo is a water-based version of handball. Players use their hands to score goals in a net that sits on top of the water. Each team only has 30 seconds to score before the ball is passed to the opposition and players may not touch the bottom or the side of the pool during a match. Top water polo players can swim five kilometres (three miles) in each match so they need plenty of strength and stamina!

Weightlifting

Early '*strongman*' contests developed into the modern sport of weightlifting during the nineteenth century. Weightlifters perform two types of lift: the '*snatch*' where the bar is lifted from the floor to above the head using one smooth movement; and the '*clean and jerk*' where the bar is first brought up to the shoulders and is then raised above the head. The weight has to be held for at least two seconds.

Wrestling

Wrestling, a body-to-body combat sport where the aim of the wrestler is to force the back of his opponent's shoulders on to the ground, formed part of the original Olympic Games. *Greco-Roman wrestling*, where use of the legs to make contact and use of the arms below the waist of the opponent are forbidden, was a feature of the first modern Games, and *freestyle wrestling*, where competitors can use all parts of their body, was introduced in Saint Louis in 1904 (when all 40 wrestlers who participated were American!) Women compete only in freestyle.

The Winter Sports

The list of sports in the Winter Olympics has expanded dramatically in recent years, with exciting events like snowboarding, ski cross, and short track speed skating introduced in response to the demands of ever growing television audiences.

Alpine Skiing

In alpine skiing, racers can reach speeds of more than 130 km an hour, travelling down a vertical drop that ranges from 180 m for men and 140 m for women in the *slalom*, to 1,100 m for men and 800 m for women in the *downhill*, passing through a series of gates on the way.

Biathlon

The Biathlon, part cross-country skiing and part rifle shooting, has its origins in the military training of troops in Scandinavian countries, where troops on skis were used from the mid sixteenth century. Today, skiers combine speed and accuracy to complete the course in the quickest time, hitting as many targets as possible to avoid time penalties.

Bobsled

The bobsled or bobsleigh is the best known of the Olympic sliding sports. It is fast and dangerous, as teams of two or four push off from the top of the run and then jump into the bobsled for a descent down narrow, twisting, banked, iced tracks, reaching speeds of 150 km an hour! Some people believe that the name comes from the way crews bob back and forth to increase their speed! The *four-man bobsleigh* was on the program of the first Olympic Winter Games in 1924, while the *two-man* event was added later. Women began competing in 2002 at the Salt Lake City Winter Games.

Cross-Country

Cross-country skiing has long been a part of survival in cold climates — paintings found in Russia believed to be at least 6,000 years old, show a hunter wearing wooden skis alongside some reindeer. Cross-country skiers competed at the first Olympic Winter Games. Today, racers use two basic techniques: *classic technique*, where the skis move parallel to each other through tracks in the snow; and *free technique*, where skiers propel themselves in a manner similar to speed skating, pushing off with the edge of their skis — skis which are lighter and narrower than those used in alpine skiing and have long curved tips.

The Men's Cross Country Skiing 50km at the 2010 Vancouver Winter Olympic Games

The Swiss bronze-medal winning curling team in action at the 2010 Vancouver Winter Olympics

Curling

Curling is an ancient sport (the earliest written records of it are found at Scotland's Paisley Abbey and date back to 1541), and although it was included on the programme of the first Winter Games, it wasn't until Nagano in 1998 that it became an official Olympic sport. The game is played on ice, and two teams take turns pushing stones weighing 17-20 kg towards a series of concentric rings or circles. The object is to get the stones as close to the centre of the rings as possible. There are tournaments for women and men. It is a game of strategy, and has sometimes been called 'chess on ice.'

Figure Skating

Figure skating, a combination of athleticism, speed and grace, has always been a popular sport at the Olympics. In fact figure skating was an Olympic sport before there was an Olympic Winter Games. Figure skating first appeared at the London 1908 Olympic Summer Games with events for pairs and singles. Ice dancing, similar to ballroom dancing in many ways, joined the Olympic Winter Games in 1976, when the Games were held in Innsbruck, Austria.

Freestyle Skiing

Freestyle was originally a mix of alpine skiing and acrobatics. There are three Olympic freestyle skiing

events for both men and women: *aerials* (skiers perform backflips, twists and turns off a jump and are judged on technique); *moguls* (contestants navigate a series of bumps and perform tricks); and *ski cross* (newly introduced in Vancouver in 2010, four skiers at a time race down a course packed with traverses, flats, rolls. banks, moguls, and jumps, all connected with turns). Tricks in freestyle skiing include the Twister, Spread-eagle, Eggroll, Daffy, Iron Cross, and the Helicopter — an upright 360-degree spin!

Ice Hockey

Ice hockey is one of the most popular sports at the Winter Olympics. Each ice hockey team must not have more than six players on the ice while play is in progress. The object is for one team to get the *puck* (a hard black rubber disc) past the other team's goaltender and into the net.

Luge

The Olympics luge is an exciting spectacle in which the athletes lie on their backs on open fibreglass sleds which hurtle down an icy track in a chute of concrete at breathtaking speeds. In luge (the French word for '*sled*'), racers keep their heads back to be as aerodynamic as possible, steer using their legs and shoulders, and brake by sitting up, putting their feet down and pulling up on the sled runners. Speeds now regularly reach 140 km an hour or more and the g-force can reach over 5 g on banked turns!

Nordic Combined

Throughout Norway in the 1800s, skiers gathered each winter for a series of ski festivals combining competitions and entertainment. Those who took part in the Nordic combined were considered the elite of all the athletes, specialising in both cross-country skiing, demanding endurance and strength, and ski jumping, requiring physical strength and technical control. Men have competed in Nordic combined events since the first Olympic Winter Games in Chamonix. Today, the ski jumping is held first, followed by a free technique cross-country race.

Short-Track Speed Skating

Short-track speed skating became an Olympic medal sport in 1992. It takes place on an oval track within a hockey rink, with skaters competing against each other, rather than the clock. It is an exciting spectator sport with high speeds, passing, bumping and crashing.

Skeleton

Skeleton is the newest Olympic sliding sport. Skiers descend the icy track face first on a small sled at speeds of up to 135 km per hour, steering by shifting their bodies very slightly. Skeleton got its name from the sled used — originally metal, now fiberglass and metal — as an observer commented that the earliest version resembled a human skeleton! Athletes train much like sprinters to develop powerful legs to get the best possible start — a tenth of a second lead at the start can become three-tenths of a second by the bottom of the run. They must also find the best line and steer smoothly through each turn to keep up speed.

Ski Jumping

The first known ski jumper was a Norwegian lieutenant named Olaf Rye, who, in 1809, launched himself 9.5 metres in the air before an audience of other soldiers. Today, ski jumpers can cover the length of two football fields, skiing down a long ramp, and launching themselves into the air at speeds of up to 95 km per hour. Technique is integral to ski jumping as athletes must perform a very precise and well-timed takeoff and a careful landing. Once in the air, jumpers assume the V-style (where a ski jumper holds his skis in a V-shaped position instead of parallel) and adjust their position to maximise lift and minimise drag. Marks are awarded not only for distance jumped but also for the style of the jump and of the landing.

Snowboard

Snowboard is one of the newest Winter Olympic sports, combining elements of surfing, skating and skiing.
In the *halfpipe*, a snowboarder performs a routine of acrobatic jumps, twists and tricks on the inside of a half-cylinder-shaped snow tube or ramp, and is judged on the height and style of his or her tricks.
In the *parallel giant slalom*, two snowboarders race head-to-head down a course, turning through a series of gates, with the winner progressing to the next round.
In *snowboard cross*, four snowboarders race against each other over rolling terrain and a series of jumps and ramps. The fastest two from each heat move on to the next round.

Sergio Berger of Switzerland competes in the men's halfpipe at the Vancouver 2010 Olympics

Speed Skating

Speed skating is believed to have started more than 1,000 years ago in Scandinavia and the Netherlands. The first organised race that we know about took place in 1793 in Edinburgh, Scotland. Long-track speed skating is one of the most watched sports at the Winter Olympics. It takes place on a 400 m oval ice rink and is the fastest human powered, non-mechanically aided sport in the world. Skaters can reach speeds of up to 70 km an hour!

Significant Events

776 BC
Olympic Games held in Olympia, Greece

393 CE
Olympic Games banned by Emperor Theodosius I

1894
International Olympic Committee (IOC) founded

1896
First modern Games held in Athens; about 245 men from 14 countries compete in 43 events

1900
Paris Games Women allowed to take part in golf and lawn tennis

1960
Rome Games The first Summer Games covered by television worldwide

1956
Melbourne Games During the Closing Ceremony athletes enter stadium in unity, rather than by nation

1940-44
Games not held due to WWII

1936
Berlin Games Olympic torch run is established

1968
Grenoble Winter Games IOC orders the first drug and gender testing of competitors

1968
Mexico City Games Two American athletes are suspended when they raise their fists in a Black Power salute while on the podium

1972
Munich Games Arab terrorists take hostage and assassinate 11 athletes and coaches from Israeli team

1980
Moscow Games First held in a communist country, but US leads more than 60 nations in a boycott to protest the Soviet invasion of Afghanistan

1984
Los Angeles Games Soviets lead boycott in retaliation

1906
First and only Intercalated Games held in Athens

1908
London Games
Athletes march into stadium behind their nations' flags

1912
Stockholm Games
First use of electronic timing devices and a public address system; women compete in swimming for the first time

1916
Games not held due to WWI

1920
Antwerp Games
Olympic flag unfurled for first time and Olympic Oath first taken

1928
Amsterdam Games
Slow-motion film techniques used to judge close finishes; women's track and field events first held; Olympic flame first lit

1924
The 'International Winter Sports Week' takes place in Chamonix — later named the first Olympic Winter Games

1932
Los Angeles Games
First proper Olympic Village built for athletes

1996
Atlanta Games
Terrorist bomb explosion in which two die (one indirectly of a heart attack) and 111 are injured

2004
Athens Games
Video coverage of the Olympics over the Internet

2008
Beijing Games
10,942 athletes from 204 NOCs compete in 28 sports and 302 events

1992
Barcelona Games
Professional athletes can take part; Germany sends a unified team, while the Soviet Union has been divided into 15 countries, 12 of which participate as the 'Unified Team'

2012
London Games
Women's boxing contested for the first time

Olympic Timeline

Athens 1896
First modern Games held in Greece; 241 men representing 14 countries compete in 43 events; no women are allowed to compete

London 1908
2,000 athletes participate; athletes march into the stadium behind their nations' flags; marathon is run for the first time at its current length

Paris 1924
The last Games to be organised under the presidency of Pierre de Coubertin; 44 nations send 3,000 competitors; Germany is still banned, but the other four nations banned in 1920 take part; cabins built near the stadium especially for athletes; Scotland's Eric Liddell wins 400 m race, England's Harold Abrahams wins 100 m — their story becomes the 1981 film 'Chariots of Fire'

The 'International Winter Sports Week' takes place in Chamonix — this is later named as the first Olympic Winter Games

St Louis 1904
Many Europeans won't travel to the Games — only 12 countries participate

1916
Games scheduled to be held in Berlin are not held due to WWI

1896 1900 1904 1906 1908 1912 1916 1920 1924 1928

Paris 1900
997 athletes from 24 countries compete, but the Games are incorporated into and overshadowed by the Paris Exposition; women allowed to take part in golf and lawn tennis

Athens 1906
First and only Intercalated Games held in Athens; medals won here are considered unofficial by the IOC

Stockholm 1912
First use of electronic timing devices and a public address system; women compete in swimming events for the first time, but America, which bars its female athletes from competing in events without long skirts, sends none; Jim Thorpe, an American Indian, wins both pentathlon and decathlon — a feat that remains unmatched

Antwerp 1920
Olympic flag unfurled for first time and Olympic Oath first taken; Austria, Bulgaria, Germany, Hungary and Turkey are not allowed to participate; figure-skating events are held for the second time, and ice hockey for the first

Amsterdam 1928
The first 'Summer' Olympic Games; slow-motion film techniques used to judge close finishes; Olympic flame is introduced; Germany is allowed back; women's track and field events first held (but so many collapse at the end of the 800 m race that it is banned until 1960)

St Moritz
Winter Games: Warm weather means the 10,000 m speed-skating race is cancelled and some other events are affected

Los Angeles 1932

105,000 attend Opening Ceremony; first proper Olympic Village built for athletes

Lake Placid

Canada continues to dominate ice hockey

London 1948

The first Games to be shown on home television; Germany and Japan aren't invited, but 59 other countries attend; Fanny Blankers-Koen of the Netherlands is the first woman to win four golds in one Games

St Moritz

Winter Games
Held in St Moritz as it has been unaffected by the War

1940

Games scheduled to be held in Tokyo (and then changed to Helsinki) are not held due to WWII

Melbourne 1956

The first in the southern hemisphere; several countries boycott for political reasons; East and West Germany are represented by one combined team; equestrian events are held in Stockholm due to Australian quarantine laws; in the Closing Ceremony athletes enter the stadium in unity, rather than by nation

Cortina d'Ampezzo

Winter Games
The Soviets win a gold in ice hockey, breaking Canada's monopoly

Tokyo 1964

Japan spends around $3 billion on the Games; South Africa are absent because of international opposition to the apartheid regime

Innsbruck

Winter Games
The Austrian army has to bring ice and snow from higher elevations to compensate for poor weather conditions; South Africa is barred (it is only allowed back in 1992)

| 1932 | 1936 | 1940 | 1944 | 1948 | 1952 | 1956 | 1960 | 1964 | 1968 |

Berlin 1936

Olympic torch run is established — more than 3,000 runners carry the flame between Olympia, Greece, and Berlin; the Games are the first to be televised

Garmisch-Partenkirchen

Winter Games
Alpine skiing events are held for the first time, but ski instructors are barred as being professionals, causing the Austrians and Swiss to boycott the Games

1944

Games scheduled to be held in London are not held due to WWII

Helsinki 1952

Soviet Union rejoins Games after 40 years

Oslo

Winter Games
The Olympic torch is lit in the fireplace of skiing pioneer Sondre Norheim, and relayed by 94 skiers to the Games in Oslo

Rome 1960

The first Summer Games covered by TV worldwide; Cassius Clay wins boxing title aged 18; Abebe Bikila from Ethiopia, running the marathon barefoot, becomes the first black African to win a gold medal

Squaw Valley

Winter Games
Russia dominates the Games, but the US ice hockey team wins its first gold

Mexico City 1968

The high altitude leads to world records in some events and difficulties for others; Richard Fosbury wins the high jump with 'Fosbury flop' technique; two US athletes are suspended when they raise their fists in a Black Power salute on the podium

Grenoble

Winter Games
East and West Germany compete on separate teams; gender and drug tests are introduced; the first unofficial Olympic mascot is introduced — Schuss, a styled skier

Munich 1972

Worldwide TV audience 1 billion but tragedy overshadows Games when Arab terrorists take hostage and assassinate 11 athletes and coaches from Israeli team; Mark Spitz wins 7 swimming gold medals and gymnast Olga Korbut is the darling of the Games; the first official mascot is introduced — Waldi, the dachshund

Sapporo
Winter Games
Controversy regarding amateur status leads to a boycott by Canada

Moscow 1980

Games held for the first time in a communist country, but US leads a massive boycott to protest Soviet invasion of Afghanistan

Lake Placid
Winter Games
Artificial snow is used for the first time

Seoul 1988

9,600 athletes take part; Ben Johnson of Canada and 10 other competitors disqualified for using performance-enhancing drugs; tennis is reintroduced into the Games with Steffi Graf completing her '*Golden Slam*' by claiming gold

Calgary →
Winter Games
Games are spread over 16 days; Christa Luding-Rothenburger of East Germany becomes the first and only athlete to win medals at Winter and Summer Olympics in the same year

Lillehammer 1994
Winter Games
The first Winter Games to take place in the third year of the Olympiad

Nagano 1998

Winter Games 2,177 athletes from 72 countries participate; snowboarding, curling, and women's ice hockey are held for the first time; cross-country skier Bjørn Dæhlie of Norway wins 3 gold medals in Nordic skiing to become the first winter Olympian to earn 8 career gold medals and 12 total medals

1972	1976	1980	1984	1988	1992	1994	1996	1998

Montreal 1976

28 nations boycott in an anti-apartheid protest; the Republic of China (Taiwan) team withdraw when not allowed to compete under the name 'the Republic of China'; 14 year old Nadia Comaneci becomes first Olympic gymnast to score a perfect 10 in competition — and goes on to score six more!

The 1976 Olympic medal

Innsbruck
Winter Games
Ice dancing features for the first time

Los Angeles 1984

Soviets boycott Games in retaliation for 1980 along with 13 other countries; these are the first privately-financed Olympics since the Games were opened up to corporate sponsorship the previous year

Sarajevo
Winter Games
Held for the first time in a socialist country; 49 nations send athletes

Barcelona 1992

More than 15,000 athletes, coaches and officials from 169 countries; US 'Dream Team,' dominates basketball now professional athletes can take part; for the first time since 1972, the Games are boycott-free — South Africa has abolished apartheid and sends a unified team, Germany sends a unified team, while the Soviet Union has been divided into 15 separate countries which participate as the 'Unified Team'

Albertville
Winter Games
East and West Germany are now unified, whilst the Soviet Union has broken up

Atlanta 1996

179 nations participate in the Centennial Games and Muhammad Ali lights the cauldron; Games marred by a terrorist bomb explosion

Salt Lake City 2002

Winter Games
The Games are overshadowed by scandals relating to bribery (of IOC members), doping and scoring

Sydney 2000 official mascots

Turin 2006

Winter Games
Turin (or Torino) is the largest city ever to host the Olympic Winter Games; live video coverage of the Games is available on mobile phones; Albania, Madagascar and Ethiopia are all represented for the first time; snowboard cross is introduced for the first time

Vancouver 2010

Winter Games
Canada celebrates their first home gold in Olympic history and goes on to break the record for the most gold medals won at a single Winter Olympics; there are 15 sports, including the new one of ski cross; Georgian luger Nodar Kumaritashvili tragically dies after a crash during a training run on the controversially fast luge track just hours before the Opening Ceremony

Sochi 2014

Winter Games
The first time that the Russian Federation will host the Winter Games

| 2000 | 2002 | 2004 | 2006 | 2008 | 2010 | 2012 | 2014 | 2016 |

Sydney 2000

199 nations send 10,651 athletes (4,069 women); the only nation excluded is Afghanistan; North and South Korea enter the stadium under one flag; Australian Aborigine Cathy Freeman lights the cauldron at the Opening Ceremony, and goes on to win the 400 m race; Steven Redgrave, a British rower, becomes the first athlete to win gold medals in five consecutive Olympics

Athens 2004

For the first time, the flame travels around the world in a relay to former Olympic and other large cities, before returning to Greece; major broadcasters are allowed to serve video coverage of the Olympics over the Internet

Beijing 2008

Despite protests by some about China's human rights record and worries about air pollution, the Games are declared 'truly exceptional by the IOC president; the Games are the first to be produced and broadcast entirely in high definition (HD) by the host broadcaster; Michael Phelps wins 8 gold medals in the pool; nine new events are held, including two from the new cycling discipline of BMX

London 2012

London will become the first city to officially host the modern Olympic Games three times; the successful bid was headed by former Olympic champion Sebastian Coe; there will be 302 events in 26 sports (the 2012 Paralympic Games programme has 20 sports and 21 disciplines); women's boxing will be contested for the first time

Rio de Janeiro 2016

Rio overcomes stiff competition from Chicago, Tokyo and Madrid in order to get the Games; Brazil will become the first South American country to host the Olympics and only the second in Latin America; golf and rugby sevens are added to the programme

THE
MODERN OLYMPIADS

1896 - 2012

A history of the modern Olympic Games from 1896 to 2012

1896 Athens Olympics

The 1896 Olympic Games were celebrated from April 6 to April 15 in Athens, Greece. They were officially titled the **Games of the I Olympiad** and recognised as the first Olympic Games of the modern era. Baron Pierre de Coubertin had been keen to hold the first Games in Paris in 1900, but, at the plea of the Greek delegation, and in the interests of tradition and history, it was agreed that Athens would be the inaugural seat of the Games. The Games began on the date of the 75th anniversary of Greece's independence from Turkey.

The Venue

When Athens was chosen in 1894 as the host city for the Games, the Greeks were left with only two years to prepare for the event. They used money raised from donations and commemorative stamps to restore the Panathinaiko Stadium. The 2,000 years old ruins were rebuilt in marble with a capacity of about 70,000 spectators. At the time, the stadium was the biggest in the modern world, and it witnessed the largest crowd collected ever to watch a sporting event.

Unfortunately, the long, thin design of the stadium led to very tight corners, and probably as a result of this, in addition to the poor track surface, times for races were rather disappointing. In fact, no world records were set at all at the 1896 Games.

In this image from the Games, Goddess Athena, with the olive branch, is reaching out to the victor from the modern day stadium. On the right is the horseshoe shaped Acropolis. The inscription (776-1896) seals this bond between the Games of antiquity and the first Games of the modern era

The 1896 Games had the largest international participation of any sporting event up until then

Stadium teeming with people at the 1896 Olympic Games in Athens

The Medals

At the very first Games, gold, silver and bronze medals were not awarded to the first three in an event. Instead, the winner received a silver medal and a crown of olive branches, and the runner up a bronze medal and a crown of laurel branches. Both received certificates to commemorate their achievement. The IOC has assigned gold, silver and bronze medals to the three best placed athletes in each event retroactively to tie in with modern tradition.

Quick Facts

- Host city: Athens, Greece
- Nations participated: 14
- Athletes participated: 241
- Events organised: 9 sports, 43 events
- Opened by: King George I

Winners were awarded a silver medal. The front side of the medal shows the supreme god Zeus, holding a globe with the winged Goddess of Victory on the top. The caption in Greek reads as "*Olympia.*" The reverse side (below) had the Acropolis site with the caption in Greek "*International Olympic Games in Athens in 1896*"

Demetrius Vikelas was a writer and the first president (1894-1896) of the IOC

Facts

- After the Games, the Greeks petitioned for all following Games to be held in Greece. However, except for the Intercalated Games of 1906, the Olympics did not return to Greece until 2004 — 108 years later.
- The Olympic Hymn was composed by Spyridon Samaras and words were written by poet Kostis Palamas — it was first played at the 1896 Games but wasn't declared the official hymn by the IOC until 1957.
- Some contestants were tourists who happened to be in the area during the Games — John Boland, on holiday in Athens, was entered in the tennis by a Greek friend and went on to win!
- Host Greece won the most medals (47) at the first Olympic Summer Games in 1896.

Most Memorable Winners

German athlete, Carl Schuhmann won four gold medals and was the most successful competitor at the Games. He was a member of the German gymnastics team that won the team events in the horizontal bar and parallel bars events and won the individual title in the horse vault event. He also took part in the long jump, triple jump, shot put and weightlifting although without success, and the wrestling competition, which he won, even though he was much lighter and smaller than most of the other contestants.

Carl Schuhmann performs in the horse vault event, in which he won the gold medal

The Sports

There were nine sports at the first Olympiad, contested in 43 events. A tenth sport, rowing, had to be cancelled due to bad weather.

Athletics

In athletics there were 12 events — nine of which were won by the Americans, who managed to triumph despite the disadvantage of having arrived just the day before the start of the Games, following a long boat journey, due to a misunderstanding about the starting date!

Times for races were not outstanding, possibly due to the shape of the track and the loose cinders underfoot. The Greeks were disappointed with their lack of success, especially when the discus was won by an American, Bob Garrett, who had never thrown a proper discus before, and yet managed to beat the stylish, classical throws of the Greek contingency by nearly a foot, even after completely messing up his first two attempts!

Redemption for the Greeks came in the form of the marathon. The idea for this race had been suggested by a French student who had studied the (widely debated) story of the legendary Greek hero who had run from the plains of Marathon after a battle all the way to Athens (a distance of nearly 25 miles) to tell the people in the city that the heavily outnumbered Athenian soldiers had managed to repel a Persian invasion. Thus the marathon race, to be run over the same route that the hero had supposedly covered, was both the final athletic event and the highlight of the Games. The Greeks pinned all their hopes on a handsome 25 year old called Spiridon Louis.

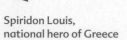

Spiridon Louis, national hero of Greece

For most of the race, he was well down the pack, yet the early leader ran too fast and dropped out after 32 km, and the second place runner collapsed at 36 km, leaving Louis to jog into the stadium a full seven minutes ahead of his nearest rival, to tumultuous applause. King George and Crown Prince Constantine of Greece ran round the track with him on his final lap. In the end, five of the first six finishers were Greeks, so Greek honour was restored. Louis became a national hero and enjoyed some unusual perks, such as free groceries and transport and free haircuts for life!

Cycling

Cycling consisted of six events: three short (all won by Paul Masson of France); and three long. The longest was a 50

Cyclists Paul Masson (left) and Léon Flameng pose with their cycles after the victory

Carl Schuhmann is carried in triumph by teammates, Alfred Flatow and Hermann Weingartner

mile marathon, from Athens to Marathon and back. The victor, Aristidis Konstantinidis of Greece, won despite breaking both his own bicycle and a borrowed one. He finished on a third, some 20 minutes ahead of his nearest rival.

Swimming

The swimming events were held in the freezing cold Bay of Zea, which caused problems for swimmers who had only trained in heated pools! Only three of the 29 entries for the 500 m race took part, and one American 100 m swimmer allegedly jumped straight back out of the icy water, refusing to finish the race! One of the more obscure events — never to be repeated — was the 100 m swim for 'Sailors of the Royal Navy!' The Greek sailor who won this (only three took part!) finished in a time nearly one minute slower than that of Alfred Hajos (born Arnold Guttmann) of Hungary, the winner of the standard 100 m swim.

Alfred Hajos from Hungary was the first Olympic swimming champion. In 1924, he won a silver medal for architecture!

Gymnastics

Gymnastics saw victories for Germany, Greece and Switzerland, in events which are still held today — except for the strangely named 'arm exercises with smooth cord,' otherwise known as rope-climbing!

Tennis

The tennis tournament was rather casually organised. John Pius Boland, on holiday at the time from Ireland, only entered on the urging of his Greek friend but went on to win the men's singles and then won the doubles title, too, together with a German player whose previous partner had sustained an injury.

Shooting

Shooting was dominated by America and Greece — the only other country to gain a position on the medal table was Denmark.

Fencing

Unlike other sports, professionals were allowed to compete in fencing, though in a separate event.

Weightlifting

Viggo Jensen from Denmark won the two handed (clean and jerk) lift and Launceston Elliot (whose good looks made him a favourite with the crowd) won the one handed (snatch) lift. Legend has it that after the contest, a servant ordered to remove the weights could not manage to do so. King George supposedly stepped in, picking up the heaviest weight easily and throwing it some distance!

Wrestling

No weight classes existed for the wrestling competition, leading to a single champion: Carl Schuhmann, who put out Launceston Elliot in the first round and went on to beat a Greek wrestler in a match that took place over two days.

Facts

- The day after the marathon race, a Greek woman, Stamata Revithi, ran the same course. Since women were not allowed to compete, she was forbidden to enter the stadium on completing the run.
- King George I and the Crown Prince Constantine performed the Opening Ceremony after a speech by the President of the Organising Committee.
- The Closing Ceremony was postponed by a day due to heavy rains. There was a banquet for officials and athletes, followed by the Greek National Anthem, after which King George awarded the prizes.

Launceston Elliot was Britain's first Olympic gold medalist. He won the medal in the single-handed lift category

1900 Paris Olympics

The Games of the II Olympiad took place in Paris, France. They were held to coincide with the Paris International Exhibition and ran from May to the end of October.

It is difficult to say exactly which of the many events were truly part of the Olympic programme, and, in fact, there were times when the athletes themselves didn't know! No opening or closing ceremonies were held for the Games.

Organisation

The second modern Olympic Games were a disappointment to their founder, Pierre de Coubertin. The IOC and Coubertin lost control of the Games to the French government and they became relegated to a sideshow of the World Exhibition, which was being held in Paris in the summer of 1900. They were poorly organised and promoted, with events conflicting with one another, running events held on grass (rather than a proper track) that was sometimes uneven and even wet, hurdles made out of broken telephone poles and swimming events held in the River Seine, despite its strong current. Indeed, because there were other sporting events held in connection with the exposition, some athletes didn't even know they had taken part in an Olympic competition. The sporting events rarely used the term '*Olympic*' — indeed the term '*Olympic Games*' was replaced by '*Concours Internationaux d'exercises physiques et de sport*' *(International Competition for Exercise and Sport)* in the official report of the sporting events of the 1900 World's Fair.

Even Pierre de Coubertin himself is quoted as declaring of the 1900 Paris Games, "*It's a miracle that the Olympic movement survived that celebration.*"

An official poster from the 1900 Paris Olympic Games on display at the IOC Olympic Museum in Lausanne, Switzerland

The Velodrome de Vincennes Stadium where many of the events were held

Sunday Competitions

American athletes protested when events were held on a Sunday. Myer Prinstein was leading in the long jump competition, but refused to take place in the final which was on a Sunday. His qualifying jump earned him second place, but he was so angry with the winner, fellow American Alvin Kraenzlein, for taking part in the final, that he allegedly punched him in the face!

Quick Facts

- Host city: France, Paris
- Nations participated: 24
- Athletes participated: 997 (975 men; 22 women)
- Events organised: 19 sports; 95 events

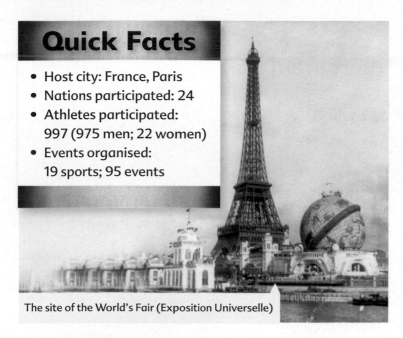

The site of the World's Fair (Exposition Universelle)

Unusual Events

Events like equestrian high and long jumps, a swimming obstacle race, two-day cricket and live pigeon shooting were held for the first — and last! — time during the 1900 Games.

The Sports

There were some changes to the programme from the previous Games: wrestling and weightlifting were dropped, while there was only one title in gymnastics — the all-around champion. Several team sports were added, including cricket, rugby, soccer, polo, water polo and croquet, and there were also equestrian events, archery, rowing and golf. Two other sports were *Basque pelota* (a court game which is a mix of squash and handball) and tug-of-war.

Events in unofficial and demonstration sports during the same period are not considered by the IOC to be official Olympic sports. They include such activities as angling, life saving, ballooning, boules, motor racing, water motorsports and even kite flying, pigeon racing and fire fighting!

Once a polio-afflicted child, Ray Ewry won three gold medals in standing jump competitions at the Paris Olympics in 1900

Polo was introduced in the 1900 Summer Olympic Games in Paris, but was removed from the official programme after the 1936 Games

A swimming race begins at the Paris Olympics

out for four, a final was run without them, but the officials subsequently decided to run another 'final' for the boycotting crews. The winning Dutch coxed pairs rowed to victory without their usual coxswain. Instead they 'borrowed' a young French boy — weighing much less! — to cox for them and so had a lighter boat. Nobody has ever managed to track down this boy, but he is probably the youngest Olympic medal winner ever!

Swimming and Rowing Peculiarities

• Swimming took place in the River Seine, despite fierce currents which helped to produce fast times. France's only gold medal in swimming came in the underwater swim, with Charles de Vendeville achieving a distance of 60 m and staying under for more than a minute. There was also an obstacle race which required racers to swim through the River Seine, climb up and down a pole, then go over and under several boats!

• Two finals were held in the coxed fours — when the original qualifiers boycotted the final in protest at the decision to run six boats on a course laid

Frantz Reichel was a member of the winning French rugby team

Memorable Winners

• The star of the athletics was Alvin Kraenzlein, an American who won four gold medals — the 60 m dash, the 110 m hurdles, the 200 m hurdles, and the long jump — although he may well have been lucky to win the long jump as his major competitor, Myer Prinstein, refused to compete in the final as it was held on a Sunday. (Prinstein did manage to get a gold in the triple jump.)

• American Ray Ewry won the three standing jumps — high, long and triple.

• The French winner of the marathon was accused by American runners of cheating and taking a short cut!

RÉPUBLIQUE FRANÇAISE
MINISTÈRE DU COMMERCE, DE L'INDUSTRIE, DES POSTES ET TÉLÉGRAPHES
EXPOSITION UNIVERSELLE DE 1900
Direction génle de l'Exploitation

Concours
d'Exercices physiques
et de Sports.

CONCOURS
INTERNATIONAUX
D'ESCRIME

FLEURET
du 14 Mai au 1er Juin
DANS LA SALLE DES FÊTES DE L'EXPOSITION

19.500 frs de Prix

ÉPÉE
du 1er au 15 Juin
SUR LA TERRASSE DU JEU DE PAUME AUX TUILERIES

16.000 frs de Prix

SABRE
du 18 au 27 Juin
DANS LA SALLE DES FÊTES DE L'EXPOSITION

9.000 frs de Prix

Pour tous Renseignements S'Adr. 10, RUE BLANCHE, PARIS

Imp. CHARDIN
17, Passage Daudin Paris

Specific sports posters were created for rowing, cycling and gymnastics. Even though women did not compete in fencing until 1924, here is a poster from the 1900 Games showing a female fencer. She is holding in her right hand the three traditional weapons of fencing — foil, épée and sabre

Medals or Cups

During the 1900 Paris Games, the winners were awarded cups and trophies instead of medals. In some of the team sports, like sailing, tennis, polo and some athletics events, medals were won by teams comprising athletes of different nationalities.

Top 10 Ranking Nations	Gold	Silver	Bronze	Total
France	26	41	34	101
USA	19	14	14	47
Great Britain	15	6	9	30
Mixed Team	6	3	3	12
Switzerland	6	2	1	9
Belgium	5	5	5	15
Germany	4	2	2	8
Italy	2	2	0	4
Australia	2	0	3	5
Denmark	1	3	2	6

A newspaper report shows the legendary American athlete, Alvin Kraenzlein, participating in the four events in which he won a gold medal — the first to ever achieve this

Women at the Games

For the very first time, three events — golf, tennis and croquet — were open to women. England's Charlotte Cooper became the first woman to win a gold medal at the Olympics. She won the tennis singles and mixed doubles with her partner, Reginald Doherty.

Margaret Abbott of the US won the women's nine-hole golf tournament, the first American woman ever to win a gold medal at the Olympics, but due to the confusion surrounding the Games (which events were '*Olympic*' and which were not) she died in 1955 without knowing it.

British tennis player Charlotte Cooper poses for a picture

Women golfers participating in the golf event at the Games

1904 St. Louis Olympics

The 1904 Olympic Games, officially known as the Games of the III Olympiad, were held from July to November in St. Louis, Missouri in the United States of America. The Games suffered from the same curse as the Paris Games in that they were subordinate to another event — in this case, the Louisiana Purchase Exposition.

The Organisation

The bid for the 1904 Games was originally won by the city of Chicago, Illinois. However, the Louisiana Purchase Exposition (also known as the World's Fair) was being held in St. Louis in the same year, and officials there

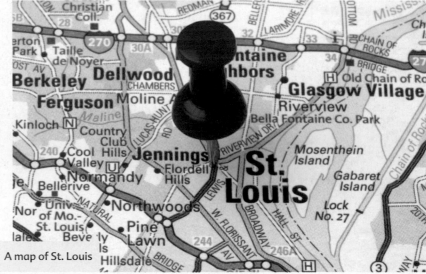

A map of St. Louis

Poster for the 1904 Summer Olympics

Quick Facts

- Host City: St. Louis, Missouri (USA)
- Nations participated: 12
- Athletes participated: 651 (645 men; 6 women) *(n.b. open to debate)*
- Events organised: 16 sports, 91 events
- Opened by: David Francis, President of the Louisiana Purchase Exposition

Venue

The 1904 Games were held at the Washington University campus at St. Louis. The campus area where the Games were held is now known as Francis Field.

Spectators at the Francis Field stadium. The stadium had a seating capacity of 19,000

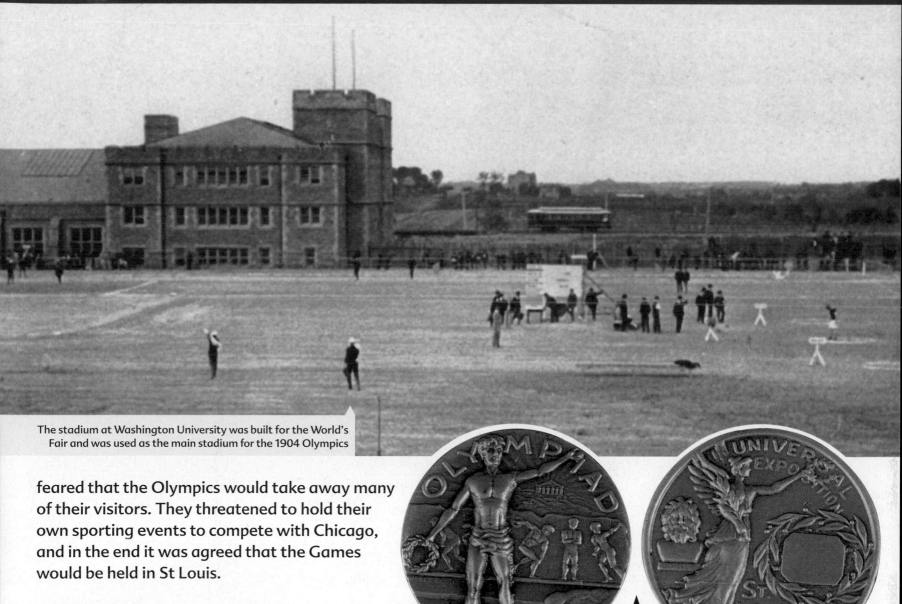

The stadium at Washington University was built for the World's Fair and was used as the main stadium for the 1904 Olympics

feared that the Olympics would take away many of their visitors. They threatened to hold their own sporting events to compete with Chicago, and in the end it was agreed that the Games would be held in St Louis.

The same mistakes were repeated as had been made at the 1900 Olympics in Paris. Competitions were overshadowed by the hustle and bustle of the World's Fair and its popular cultural exhibits, but whilst organisers in Paris had hardly used the term '*Olympic*' at all, in St Louis, almost everything was called '*Olympic*' — even interscholastic schoolboy events!

The president of the committee for the Fair insisted on opening the Games himself — a very low-key event. No official Closing Ceremony was held.

The Competitors

Less than half the events included athletes who were not from the US — many Europeans stayed away, partly because of the Russo-Japanese War and partly because of the expense of getting to St. Louis. Only 12 countries were represented. Even Pierre de Coubertin did not attend the Games!

The front face of the 1904 gold medal shows a man holding a laurel wreath crown, a symbol of victory. In the background is a Greek temple with disciples from various sports. The reverse shows Greek Goddess Nike who symbolises victory. In front of Nike is a crown, which has space in the middle to inscribe the discipline. Behind Nike is the bust of Zeus on a plinth

Facts

- The first Games at which gold, silver and bronze medals were awarded for first, second and third place.
- Only 42 of the events (less than half) included athletes who were not from the US.
- Boxing was added and wrestling was restored, but competitors in both sports were all from the US.
- The marathon included the first two black Africans to compete in the Olympics.

The Sports

Athletes competed in 16 sports in the 1904 Games (swimming, water polo and diving came under the banner of aquatics). Boxing and freestyle wrestling were held once again, while dumbbells, lacrosse and the decathlon were added to the programme. They were the first and only Games in which *roque* (an American variant of croquet) was contested. Basketball and baseball were conducted as demonstration sports.

Memorable Winners

• There were only two non-American gold medal winners in athletics: Canadian Étienne Desmarteau who won the 56 lb throw, and Irishman Tom Kiely who won the decathlon. There were four triple gold medal winners: Archie Hahn in the 60, 100 and 200 m; James Lightbody in the 800, 1,500 m and steeplechase; Harry Hillmann in the 400 m and 200 and 400 m hurdles; and Ray Ewry who repeated his 1900 hat-trick, winning the three standing jumps.
• One of the most remarkable athletes was US gymnast George Eyser, who won six medals even though his left leg was made of wood!

A Mad Marathon

The most bizarre event of the Olympics was, without doubt, the marathon. It was held on a hot

Participants in the 100 m hurdle race

and humid day — temperatures had already topped 90 degrees when the runners started the 40 km course. Automobiles and horses that were supposedly clearing the way kicked up clouds of dust and 18 of the 32 starters failed to finish. Fredrick Lorz was originally crowned champion, until it transpired that he had actually dropped out after 9 miles, but having had a lift in a car, had run the last 5 miles into the stadium! He claimed that he wouldn't have kept the medal, but nevertheless faced a ban. The true winner, British-born Thomas Hicks running for the US, also had a controversial victory, as he had been sustained

Myer Prinstein of America won both the long jump and triple jump events in the 1904 Olympics. He is the only athlete to win both the titles in the same Games

Étienne Desmarteau, a Canadian police officer from Montreal, won the weight throwing event in the 1904 Olympics

More Marathon Facts

- Two African runners that the organisers tried to pass off as uneducated tribesmen (they were actually there as part of the Boer War exhibit) were really students from Orange Free State in South Africa.
- One of the African runners, Len Taunyane, finished in ninth place — but he might have done better if he had not been chased nearly a mile off course by dogs!
- Cuban postman Felix Carbajal raced in trousers that he cut off to make into shorts. He stopped off en route to eat some apples that turned out to be rotten. This caused him some discomfort but, after resting, he resumed the race and still managed to finish fourth!
- Albert Coray, who gained the silver medal, was actually French, but did not have the right paperwork so was listed with the US team.

during the run with brandy, raw eggs and potentially deadly shots of strychnine. Not surprisingly, Hicks required medical assistance following the race!

Thomas J Hicks, winner of the Olympic marathon in 1904, with his trophy

An International Games?

Americans won almost all the gold medals at St Louis. The only sports in which there was truly international competition were fencing, where Cuba won five out of six contests, and swimming, where Hungary and Germany managed to take six events between them, but even then, only three countries other than the US took part in the swimming, and only two others in the fencing.

Athletes line up at the start of the marathon

The tug-of-war was contested in Olympics from 1900 to 1920 as one of the track and field events

Anthropology Day

'*Anthropology Day*' was held on the 12th and 13th of August. Various indigenous men from around the world, who were at the World's Fair as part of the exhibits, competed in sporting events so that anthropologists could compare their sports abilities with those of the white men.

Top 10 Ranking Nations	Gold	Silver	Bronze	Total
USA	78	82	79	239
Germany	4	4	5	13
Cuba	4	2	3	9
Canada	4	1	1	6
Hungary	2	1	1	4
Great Britain	1	1	0	2
Mixed Team	1	1	0	2
Greece	1	0	1	2
Switzerland	1	0	1	2
Austria	0	0	1	1

1908 London Olympics

The Games of the IV Olympiad, or the 1908 Games, were scheduled to be in Rome. But when Mount Vesuvius erupted in April, 1906, the Italian Government could no longer host the Games. London stepped into the breach, and despite the short notice, the Games were exceptionally well organised. They ran from April to October.

Bird's eye view of the Olympic stadium

Venue

The Games were held in White City alongside the Franco-British Exhibition and were the first Games for which a new stadium — the White City or Great Stadium — was specifically built. It could seat 68,000 and accommodated running, swimming, cycling, wrestling, gymnastics and soccer matches.

The Olympic Movement

The chaos of the Paris Games had seriously damaged the Olympic Movement, and the 1904 Games had almost killed it. Fortunately, the Intercalated Games* that were held in Athens in 1906, helped to bring the Olympics back on track, and the highly successful London Games in 1908 secured its future, attracting more international competitors and introducing better organisation and some of the traditions that are now an essential part of the Games.

The Medals

The front of the medal had two women crowning a winning athlete with a laurel wreath. On the reverse, there was an image of St. George, patron saint of England, slaying a dragon. The name of the champion and of his sport was incised upon the rim.

The Intercalated Games were an endeavour by the Greeks to hold intermediate Games every four years in Athens, although these turned out to be the only ones (due partly to problems in the Balkans, and also the fact that two years between Games proved to be not long enough). They were well organised and were the first Games to have all athlete registration go through the NOCs. They were at the time considered to be Olympic Games, but they are no longer recognised by the IOC as being official Games, nor are the medals considered Olympic medals.

THE GREAT
STADIUM
SHEPHERD'S BUSH LONDON

THE OLYMPIC GAMES 1908
PROGRAMME
6d

The programme cover for the 1908 Olympic Games. Official posters had not been introduced for the Games at that time. The practice started in 1912 with the Games in Stockholm. The programme cover took a departure from those of earlier Games. For the first time, one could see the image of a modern athlete, wearing spiked shoes (which would later cause some controversy during the Games). The athlete is attempting the standing jump

Aerial view of the Franco-British Exhibition at White City, London

Quick Facts

- Host city: London, England
- Nations participated: 22
- Athletes participated: 2,008 (1,971 men, 37 women)
- Events organised: 28 sports; 110 events
- Opened by: King Edward VII of England

Swedish diver, Arvid Spangberg won a bronze in the 10 m platform event

The Royal Marathon

At the previous Games the marathon had been 25 miles (40 km). However, this was changed so the marathon could start at Windsor Castle (indeed, at the request of Princess Mary, the start was beneath the windows of the Royal Nursery!) — and finish in front of the Royal Box at the stadium (it was either change the length of the course or move the Royal Box!) As a result of these changes, the marathon covered a distance of 26 miles 385 yards (42.195 km), which became the standard length starting with the 1924 Summer Olympics.

Melvin Sheppard of the USA won the 1,500 m final at the 1908 London Olympics

Facts

- The organisers claimed that the Games only cost around £20,000 (this would have been a lot higher had it included the cost of the stadium!) One third of the budget was for 'Entertainment Expenses'!
- It took only 10 months to build the stadium.
- Most of the money for the Games was raised through donations.
- The Games prompted the establishment of standard rules for sports, and selection of judges from different countries rather than just the host country.
- In an example of true sportsmanship, the middleweight Greco-Roman wrestling final between Frithiof Martensson and Mauritz Andersson was postponed by one day to allow Martensson to recover from an injury. He recovered and won!

The start of the 200 m race in the 1908 Olympics

New Traditions

• These were the first Games to hold a proper Opening Ceremony — King Edward VII was the guest of honour.

• For the first time, competitors marched behind their country's flag in sportswear. (Australia and New Zealand were represented by a single delegation, under the name of Australasia.)

• During a service for athletes and officials at St Paul's Cathedral, a bishop from Pennsylvania stated "*the Games themselves are better than the race and the prize.*" Pierre de Coubertin paraphrased his words and so created the Olympic creed — "*the most important thing ... is not to win but to take part.*"

John Hayes of the USA, winner of the marathon

The Sports

Similar sports to 1904 were contested, but rugby union was reintroduced, while jeu de paume, rackets and motorboat racing were official sports for the only time, and figure skating made its debut. Four events were contested in this and gold medals went to Sweden (men's singles), Russia (men's special figures), Great Britain (ladies' singles) and Germany (pairs).

Memorable Winners . . . and Losers

• The New York Times called it "*the most thrilling athletic event*" since the marathon in ancient Greece, where the winner raced to the finishing line but sadly, fell dead. Dorando Pietri's run to the finish line in the marathon was equally dramatic. He entered the stadium dazed and turned the wrong way. After being helped back onto the track, he only just staggered over the finish line with the aid of official — and so was disqualified. He needed medical assistance after the race, but the crowd fell in love with him for his determination, and Queen Alexandra later presented him with a gold cup. The race was won by John Joseph Hayes from the USA.

• The 400 m race has also gone down in history — British officials claimed that American, JC Carpenter, had edged British runner, Wyndham Halswelle, out of his way (at the time, British and US rules were different) and so the race was declared void. It was ordered to be rerun, but the American runners refused to take part in protest and so Halswelle ran the race all by himself to win gold, making it the only walkover win in the history of the Olympics.

• Also in athletics, Ray Ewry won two further medals in the standing jumps (long and high) giving him a total of 8 gold medals and making him undisputed champion of the (now discontinued)

Dorando Pietri staggers as he crosses the finish line

standing jump. Indeed, his world record in the standing long jump (3.48 m) was still standing when the event was discontinued internationally in the 1930s.

More Firsts

• For the first time a relay, the 1,600 m medley, was introduced in athletics. In teams of four, the first two runners ran 200 m, the next ran 400 m and the last ran 800 m. Runners did not carry a baton and transfer was by touch. The race was won by the Americans whose team included African-American John Taylor, the first black athlete to win a gold medal. The Italian team were seen as likely finalists, but withdrew at the last minute to lend their support to Dorando Pietri, who was approaching the stadium in the closing stages of the marathon.
• This was the first time that swimming events were not held in open water, but in a specially constructed 100 m pool. All six of the 1908 events have continued as part of the Olympic swimming programme. Diving also became more structured as a special diving platform and springboard were introduced — it was dominated by the Swedes.

Ray Ewry who won two gold medals for standing jumps in the 1908 Olympics

Controversy

New nation states were still emerging and rebellion was evident at the Games. Britain had recently refused Ireland its independence. As a result, Irish athletes boycotted the Games. Protest came from the Americans too. Quite a few were either Irish migrants or were of Irish lineage. At the time of the Opening Ceremony, the American contingent did not dip the US flag to the British royalty (a tradition the US continues to this day). Since Finland was part of the Russian Empire, the Finnish team were expected to march under the Russian rather than Finnish flag, so many chose to march without a flag at all.

Martin Sheridan of the USA won two gold medals in the discus throw and a bronze in the standing long jump

Top 10 Ranking Nations	Gold	Silver	Bronze	Total
Great Britain	56	51	39	146
USA	23	12	12	47
Sweden	8	6	11	25
France	5	5	9	19
Germany	3	5	5	13
Hungary	3	4	2	9
Canada	3	3	10	16
Norway	2	3	3	8
Italy	2	2	0	4
Belgium	1	5	2	8

1912 Stockholm Olympics

The Stockholm Games, officially known as the Games of the V Olympiad, were held in Stockholm, Sweden, and ran from May 5 to July 27. They were very successful — both well attended and well organised — and helped to establish the modern Olympic tradition.

The Opening Ceremony at the Stockholms Olympiastadion

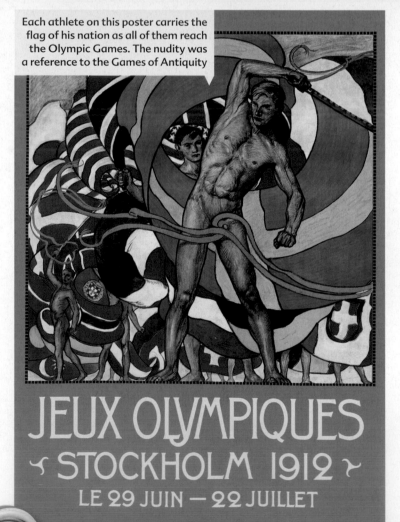

Each athlete on this poster carries the flag of his nation as all of them reach the Olympic Games. The nudity was a reference to the Games of Antiquity

JEUX OLYMPIQUES
STOCKHOLM 1912
LE 29 JUIN — 22 JUILLET

A. BÖRTZELLS TR. A. B. STOCKHOLM

A Model of Efficiency

With the 1912 Stockholm Games, the Olympics truly got into their stride. Not only were they a model of efficiency, with unofficial electronic timing devices introduced by the Swedish hosts for the track and swimming events, as well as a public address system and scoreboard, but for the first time, they truly met their international ambitions, with athletes coming from all five continents. They were also the first Games to be independent of any commercial exhibitions, were held within a reasonably short time span, and they generated far less controversy, so that the focus was truly on the sports.

On the front of the 1912 medal, two female figures place a laurel crown on the head of a winning athlete. On the back, a herald proclaims the opening of the Games with a statue of Ling, the founder of the Swedish gym system, in the background

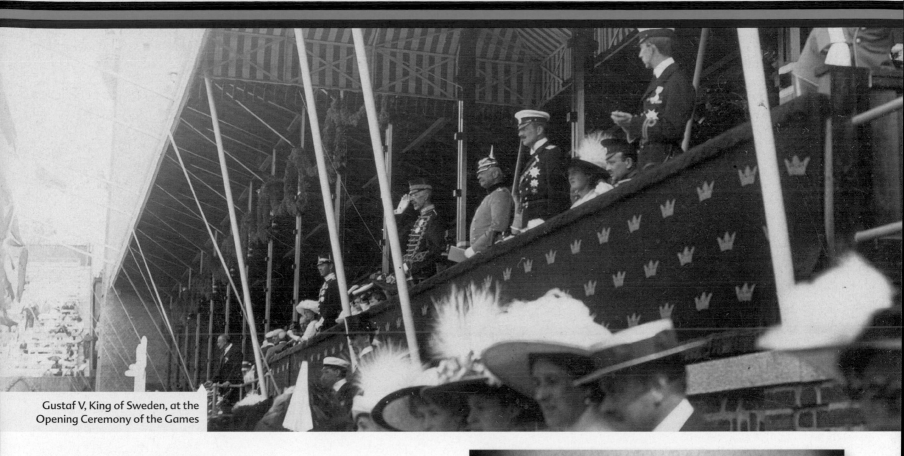

Gustaf V, King of Sweden, at the Opening Ceremony of the Games

Art Competitions

In 1912 art competitions were added to the Olympic programme, with medals awarded for works of art inspired by sport, divided into five categories: architecture, literature, music, painting, and sculpture. Baron de Coubertin, under a nom de plume, was awarded the first place for his literary work '*Ode to Sports.*' Walter Winans from America won a medal for a sculpture of a horse, and, in the same Games, won a medal for shooting, making him one of two individuals to win Olympic medals in both sports and arts. The other is Hungarian architect Alfred Hajos, who won a medal for swimming at the first Games in Athens, and then one for his plan of a stadium in the arts competition in Paris in 1924.

Facts

- For the first time, people from all the five continents took part in the Games.
- Japan participated in the Olympics for the first time.
- Solid gold medals were given for the last time (since then, medals have been gold plated and made of silver).
- Women's events in swimming and diving made their Olympic debut.

Ralph Rose of the USA preparing to throw during the shot put event. He won the silver medal

Walter Winans is the only American to have won medals both in the art category and the sports category (for shooting). He won both at the 1912 Games

The Opening Ceremony in the Stockholms Olympiastadion

The Sports

The modern pentathlon, the brain-child of Pierre de Coubertin, was added — a new sport designed to find the best all-round athlete in the world, testing fencing, shooting, swimming, show jumping and cross country running. This proved very popular, with the Swedes gaining the first four places and the gold medal going to Gustaf Lilliehook.

In a break-through for women, women's events in swimming and diving were introduced. Boxing, however, was off the agenda, as Sweden would not allow boxing contests to be held in their country. After the Games, the IOC decided to limit the power of host nations in deciding the Olympic programme.

Memorable Winners

• The most popular hero of the Games was Jim Thorpe of the US, of Native American and European descent. Thorpe won the classic pentathlon and

shattered the world record in the decathlon. At the award ceremony, the king of Sweden said he was "*the greatest athlete in the world.*" However, the following year he had his medals taken away when he was found to have taken a (small) sum of money for playing baseball, violating Olympic principles. In 1982, the IOC reinstated him and gave his medals back to his daughter. His story was told in the film '*The Bronze Man*,' in which he was played by Burt Lancaster!

Jim Thorpe of the USA. While presenting the gold medals, King Gustaf V said, "*You, Sir, are the greatest athlete in the world!*"

• Other stars of the track were America's Ralph Craig, winner of the 100 m and 200 m, and Finland's Hannes Kolehmainen, who won three gold medals in long-distance running (at these Games the Finns began to emerge as truly great runners).
• Star of the pool was Duke Paoa Kahanamoku from Hawaii. Competing in the 100 m freestyle, he equalled

Alfred Asikainen (l) and Martin Klein in the epic Greco-Roman wrestling middleweight semifinal

the world record in a qualifying heat, and in the final was so far ahead that he was able to look back to check on his rivals and still win by two metres! He went on to play a major role in introducing the sport of surfing around the world.

• In Greco-Roman wrestling, the middleweight semifinal match between Russian Martin Klein and Finland's Alfred Asikainen lasted 11 hours and 40 minutes — the world's longest wrestling match. Sadly, Klein, the winner, was so exhausted by this marathon that he couldn't compete in the final and had to settle for silver — the gold medal went to Claes Johansson.

Tragedy

The 1912 Games sadly saw the Games' first tragedy. As in previous Games, the marathon was run in sweltering conditions. Of the 68 runners, half dropped out. During the race, Francisco Lázaro, a young Portuguese runner, collapsed from the heat. He was taken to hospital but later died — the first athlete in the history of the modern Olympics to die during competition.

George S Patton (USA) took part in the first modern pentathlon, coming fifth. He later became a general during World War II

Alfred Swahn, Ake Lundberg, Oscar Swahn and Per Olof Arvidsson of Sweden were champions in the team running deer shooting event

Arnold Jackson (left) of Great Britain finishing the 1,500 m event to win the gold

Gruelling

The course for the cycling time trial road race (the only cycling event) was 320 km (199 miles) — the longest race of any kind in Olympic history. The first riders had to set off at two o'clock in the morning in order to get everyone round the course!

Top 10 Ranking Nations	Gold	Silver	Bronze	Total
USA	25	19	19	63
Sweden	4	24	17	65
Great Britain	10	15	16	41
Finland	9	8	9	26
France	7	4	3	14
Germany	5	13	7	25
South Africa	4	2	0	6
Norway	4	1	4	9
Canada	3	2	3	8
Hungary	3	2	3	8

1920 Antwerp Olympics

After an eight year gap, the 1920 Antwerp Games, or the Games of the VII Olympiad, were conducted in Antwerp, Belgium. The 1916 Games, which were to have taken place in Berlin in Germany, were cancelled due to the First World War. They ran from April 20th to September 12th.

The delegations gather in the Olympic Stadium during the Opening Ceremony

The Host City

Budapest in Hungary had initially been selected to host the Olympic Games, but as the Austro-Hungarian Empire had been a German ally in World War I, the 1920 Games were awarded to Antwerp in Belgium — which had been heavily bombed during the war — out of respect for the suffering that had been inflicted on the Belgian people during the First World War. Germany, Hungary, Austria, Bulgaria and Turkey were banned from competing in the Games.

Venue

The 1920 Games were held in the Olympisch Stadion. It is currently used by the Belgian Football Club. Scottish architect Archibald Leitch is said to have possibly helped to design the stadium as he visited the place several times prior to the Games.

Some Important Firsts

At the Opening Ceremony the Olympic flag was flown for the first time. It was the first time that the Olympic oath was taken by a competitor and doves were released as a symbol of peace. These were also the first Games where only the National Olympic Committees could enrol participants.

The medal shows an athlete holding a palm leaf and a laurel wreath — the symbols of victory. On the reverse is a monument symbolising the legend of Brabo, a legendary hero of Antwerp who killed a giant

Quick Facts

- Host city: Antwerp, Belgium
- Nations participated: 29
- Athletes participated: 2,626 (2,561 men; 65 women)
- Events organised: 24 sports; 154 events
- Opened by: King Albert I of Belgium

The 1920 Summer Olympics saw the Olympic flag raised for the first time

The Sports

Events were held in a wide variety of sports, and for the first time the Games also featured a week of winter sports, with ice hockey making its Olympic debut. Tug-of-war made its last Olympic appearance.

An interesting demonstration sport was *korfball* — a mixed gender team sport, with similarities to netball and basketball, that is very popular in the Netherlands.

Victor Boin of Belgium took the first Olympic Oath in the 1920 Summer Olympics

Albert I was the King of Belgium from 1909 to 1934

Facts

- 90,000 copies were made of the 1920 Games poster in 17 languages.
- These were the first Games when an Olympic oath was taken.
- The Olympic Flag was flown for the first time.

Laying of the first stone of the Olympic Stadium

Memorable Winners

• The Games saw the debut of Paavo Nurmi of Finland, probably the greatest distance runner ever. The 23 year old won the 10,000 m and 8,000 m cross country, took another gold in team cross country, and a silver in the 5,000 m run. He helped to break America's dominance in track and field.

Egyptian delegates parade during the Opening Ceremony of the Olympic Games

• Hawaii's Duke Kahanamoku held on to his 100 m freestyle title, winning his second consecutive gold. He matched his own world record in the semi-finals and then broke it in the final, and won another gold in the team relay.

ES ÉLIMINATOIRES DE WATER-POLO: L'ESPAGNE MARQUE UN BUT CONTRE L'ITALI

• Suzanne Lenglen of France, one of the greatest women tennis players of all time, dominated the tennis. She won the women's singles title, losing only four games in the process, and went on to win another gold in the mixed doubles and a bronze in the women's doubles.

• American swimmer, Ethelda Bleibtrey of the US, won gold medals in all three women's swimming contests. Including preliminary heats, she swam in five races and broke the world record in every single one.

• The Nadi brothers from Italy took the fencing world by storm. Nedo Nadi had an outstanding Games, winning five fencing golds — individual foil and sabre and three team events. His brother Aldo didn't do too badly either, as he took home four medals — the three team titles and a silver for the individual sabre.

Nedo Nadi was an Italian fencer who won 5 of 6 fencing events in the 1920 Olympics. He surprised the world with his exceptional performance

Top and bottom right: A waterpolo match between Spain and Italy *Bottom left:* Duke Kahanamoku won the 100 m and 4 x 200 m freestyle in Antwerp

- At the age of 72, Oscar Swahn from Sweden won a silver medal in the 100 m team running deer double shots event, making him not only the oldest Olympic contestant, but the oldest Olympic medalist ever. He competed in three Olympics (1908-1920), winning medals in each, as did his son Alfred (who went on to add two more bronze medals to the collection in 1924 — by then they had 15 medals between them, six of them gold!)
- Brazil's sharp shooter, Guilherme Paraense, won the first gold medal for his country.

Facts

- Germans were banned till 1925. Instead, they organised games called the *Deutsche Kampfspiele*.
- The youngest competitors were Aileen Riggin of the US, gold medallist in the 3 m springboard, and Nils Skoglund of Sweden, silver medallist in the plain high diving. They were both 14.
- Making Olympic history, the 12 foot dinghy event in sailing was held in two different countries. The first race was staged in Belgium, but the final two races were held in the Netherlands as the only two competitors in the event were Dutch.

France and USA in a rugby match — the only match at the 1920 Games as they were the only two countries who took part! The USA won the gold

The 42.75 km marathon course in Antwerp Games was the longest in history. Hannes Kolehmainen finished first, followed by Jüri Lossman

Top 10 Ranking Nations	Gold	Silver	Bronze	Total
USA	41	27	27	95
Sweden	19	20	25	64
Great Britain	15	15	13	43
Finland	15	10	9	34
Belgium	14	11	11	36
Norway	13	9	9	31
Italy	13	5	5	23
France	9	19	13	41
The Netherlands	4	2	5	11
Denmark	3	9	1	13

An athlete crosses an obstacle in the steeplechase

1924 Paris Olympics

The 1924 Summer Games, or the Games of the VIII Olympiad, were held in Paris, as the homeland of Pierre de Coubertin hosted the Olympics for the second time. The Opening and the Closing Ceremonies were held on May 4 and July 27, 1924, respectively.

Venue

The main venue for the Games was the Stade Olympique Yves-du-Manoir (also known as the Stade Olympique de Colombes), which at the time had a capacity of 45,000.

The emblem for the Paris Olympics, 1924. The Olympic motto was used for the first time

The poster shows athletes making the Olympic salute. Palm leaves in the foreground symbolise victory and the French flag flies in the background

The Olympic Stadium in Colombes, Paris. It could accommodate 45,000 people

The Host City

The 1924 Olympic Games had initially been scheduled for Amsterdam, Netherlands, but they were moved to Paris at the urging of Baron de Coubertin. These were his last Games before he retired from the IOC. He wanted to see them in his homeland one last time and give France a chance to do better than it had done in 1900. This time a great deal of effort was taken to ensure that the Games ran smoothly and were properly respected. Not only was there the Olympic Stadium, but swimming was held in the first purpose-built Olympic pool in Tourelles, and athletes were housed in wooden cabins in what was the first Olympic Village.

Quick Facts

- Host city: Paris, France
- Nations participated: 44
- Athletes participated: 3,089 (2,954 men; 135 women)
- Events organised: 17 sports; 126 events
- Opened by: President of France, Gaston Doumergue

Ceremony and Tradition

The Olympic motto, 'Citius, Altius, Fortius' (Faster, Higher, Stronger), was used for the first time during the 1924 Games, and, in what is now an integral part of the tradition of the Games, for the first time in the Closing Ceremony three flags were raised — the flag of the IOC, the flag of the host nation and the flag of the next host nation.

International and Popular Appeal

The Paris Games signalled the acceptance of the Games as a major event with widespread appeal. The number of participating nations soared from 29 to 44 (with over 3,000 athletes), there were some 625,000 spectators, and the Games were attended by over 1,000 journalists. The first live radio broadcast of the Olympics was also made.

Winter Sports Week

1924 was also a landmark year as the IOC decided to host what they called an 'International Winter Sports Week' (this was retroactively named the 'First Winter Games'). It was held from 25th January to 5th February 1924 in Chamonix in France. There were 16 events over seven sports: bobsleigh, curling, figure skating, ice hockey, military patrol, Nordic skiing (which included cross-country skiing, Nordic combined and ski jumping), and speed skating (although some of these might have been demonstration sports). 258 athletes from 16 nations attended, including 11 women (some sources state 13), all figure skaters, and the most successful nations were Norway and Finland. The event was a resounding success and paved the way for future Winter Games.

The Prince of Wales (second from left, front) at the Olympic Stadium with Baron Pierre de Coubertin (far left, front), and other IOC members

A view of the stadium at Chamonix, where the first Winter Games were held. One of the competitors was a young Norwegian figure skater. Sonja Henie was 11 years old at the time and came last, even checking with her coach at the rink side for advice during the competition! She needed no help the following Games and went on to become a 3-time Olympic champion!

Swimming Success

Swimming events were held, for the first time, in a 50 metre pool with marked lanes — this was the purpose built Olympic swimming pool in Tourelles. The star of the pool was Austro-Hungarian-born American Johnny Weismuller, who went on to become famous in Hollywood, starring as Tarzan in many films. At the time, however, he was more famous for his prowess in the water, winning three golds in the pool (for 100 m freestyle, where he beat Duke Kahanamoku to clinch gold; for the 400 m freestyle; and for the 4 x 200 m freestyle team relay) and a bronze for water polo. He was the first man to break the one-minute barrier for the 100 m freestyle.

Paavo Nurmi was the best middle and long distance runner during the 1920's

Gertrude Ederle, another US swimmer, won a gold medal as part of the 400 m freestyle relay team, and bronze medals for the 100 m and 400 m freestyle, but was disappointed, having hoped to win three golds. However, two years later she made history by becoming the first woman to swim across the English Channel. Even more astounding was her time — almost two hours faster than any man's!

The Flying Finns

If the British and Americans proved outstanding over middle and shorter distances, it cannot be denied that the long distance running events were dominated by the Finns. Paavo Nurmi was the star of the athletics, building on his success in 1920 by winning both the 1,500 m and 5,000 m — even though they were held with less than an hour between them — and also the cross country run, in addition to two team golds. Fellow Finns, Ville Ritola (winner of the 10,000 m and the 3,000 m steeplechase) and Albin Stenroos (winner of the marathon), helped to dominate the other long distance running events.

Johnny Weissmuller was one of the top swimmers at the Games. He set 28 world records during his swimming career

Harold Abrahams was the first British athlete to hire a personal trainer for the Olympics

long jump record with a leap of 25 feet, four inches, but only won a bronze medal . . . because he was competing in the pentathlon! The long jump was won with a jump of 24 feet, five inches.
• Women's fencing debuted and Denmark's Ellen Osiier won gold without losing a single bout.

Eric Liddell was a Scottish athlete who became a missionary at the end of his running career. The award-winning British movie, 'Chariots of Fire' tells the story of Liddell and Abrahams in the 1924 Olympics

Chariots of Fire

Harold Abrahams, a Jewish British athlete, won the 100 m and Eric Liddell from Scotland took the 400 m. Their stories were immortalised in the 1981 Oscar-winning film 'Chariots of Fire,' which examines their motives for running: Eric Liddell, who was a devout Christian ran for the glory of God, while Harold Abrahams hoped to overcome the prejudices that existed against Jews.

Other Memorable Winners

• Fencer Roger Ducret won five medals for France of which three were gold.
• In gymnastics, Albert Seguin scored a perfect 10 in rope climbing and side-vault (in fact, 23 men scored a 10 in rope climbing — an event that is now discontinued, and was only held one more time after this Games, in 1932).
• American Robert LeGendre shattered the world

Competitors in the 100 m sprint approach the finish line

Top 10 Ranking Nations	Gold	Silver	Bronze	Total
USA	45	27	27	99
Finland	14	13	10	37
France	13	15	10	38
Great Britain	9	13	12	34
Italy	8	3	5	16
Switzerland	7	8	10	25
Norway	5	2	3	10
Sweden	4	13	12	29
The Netherlands	4	1	5	10
Belgium	3	7	3	13

1928 Amsterdam Olympics

The 1928 Games, officially known as the Games of the IX Olympiad, were held in the Netherlands, when Amsterdam, who had bid for both the 1920 and 1924 Olympics, finally got their chance to host the Games. The Games commenced on May 17, although the Opening Ceremony was held on July 28, and they closed on August 12. The total cost was estimated to be US$ 1.183 million.

Venue

The 1928 Olympic Games were held at the Olympisch Stadion in Amsterdam. The stadium was constructed to host the 1928 Games and could seat 31,600 spectators at that time.

The Opening Ceremony

The Games were officially opened by Prince Hendrik, consort of Queen Wilhelmina. This was the first time a head of state had not personally officiated at an Olympic Opening Ceremony — apparently she did not approve of the Games, considering them to be a pagan festival!

Stamps showing different sports of the 1928 Olympics

The original poster of an athlete running in an Olympic stadium was designed by Jos Rovers. Only 10,000 copies of the poster were made. The IOC used a different poster as they could not get the copyright for the image

The Olympic Stadium in Amsterdam could accommodate 31,600 people

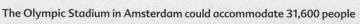

Quick Facts

- Host city: Amsterdam, Netherlands
- Nations participated: 46
- Athletes participated: 2,883 (2,606 men; 277 women)
- Events organised: 15 sports; 109 disciplines
- Opened by: Prince Hendrik

New Traditions

At the Opening Ceremony a flame was lit in a cauldron placed at the top of a tower in the stadium, designed by well-known Dutch architect Jan Wils. It remained lit throughout the Games. There was no torch relay, but this was the first lighting of a symbolic flame which has become synonymous with Olympic tradition.

In another first at the Opening Ceremony, the team from Greece led the Parade of Nations while the Dutch host team marched in last. This became part of Olympic protocol, and ever since, Greece have entered the stadium first, and the hosts have entered last.

Prince Hendrik (centre) of the Netherlands watching the Winter Olympic Games held in 1928 in St Moritz

The front of the Olympic medal shows Nike, the Goddess of Victory, holding a palm leaf (a symbol of triumph and victory in ancient times) in one hand, and a crown of laurel wreath (also a symbol of victory) in the other. The medal also shows the Colosseum of ancient Athens, a Greek vase known as an *amphora*, and the number of the Olympiad, the host city and the year. The reverse has athletes carrying the triumphant winner, holding a palm leaf, on their shoulders, with the Olympic stadium in the background. The design was created by Florentine artist Giuseppe Cassioli and was chosen after a competition organised by the IOC. The same design was used from 1928 until 1968

Facts

- The Olympic flame was lit for the first time.
- Creating a new tradition, Greece led Parade of Nations, and the host team marched last.
- These were the first Games to bear the name 'Summer Olympic Games.'

An International Games

While America still dominated the medals tables, the Games felt more international — gold medals were won by athletes from 28 different nations, a record that would last for 40 years. Germany, who had been excluded since the First World War, sent athletes once again (coming second in the medal count), and the Games were held in an atmosphere of peace and harmony.

Emancipation

In a breakthrough, two mainstream events were opened up to women — the number of female athletes more than doubled as women were finally allowed to compete in gymnastics and athletics. The women ran two individual races and a relay, and also competed in high jump and discus. Canada won the relay and Betty Robinson of the US took the gold for the 100 m. The winner of the 800 m was Lina Radke-Batschauer of Germany, but the event was marred when officials took offence at the number of competitors who finished in a state of exhaustion, some lying on the track (not unlike after the men's race) and it was decided that women should not run such long distances. Indeed, no women's event longer than 200 m was held in an Olympics until 1960. Dutch gymnast Helena Nordheim won a gold medal. She later died in a Polish concentration camp in 1943, during the Holocaust.

Memorable Winners

- Johnny Weissmuller of the US won two more gold medals in swimming to add to the collection that he had started in 1924.
- Paavo Nurmi of Finland won three more medals at these Games, including his ninth and final gold medal which he won for the 10,000 m. In fact, the Finns won all the men's track events from the 1,500 m upwards.
- Canada's Percy Williams surprised everyone by winning both the 100 m and 200 m sprint events.
- Silvio Cator was the only athlete from Haiti, but distinguished himself by winning a silver medal in the long jump.
- Mikio Oda of Japan won his country's first gold when he came first in the triple jump, while his teammate, Yoshiyuki Tsuruta, won the 200 m breaststroke.

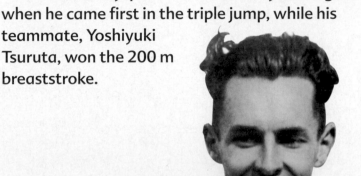

Canadian runner, Percy Williams, won the 100 m and 200 m

(l-r) Ville Ritola and Paavo Nurmi from Finland and Edvin Wide of Sweden in the 10,000 m

Facts

- Asia won its first gold medal.
- The American team were quartered on board the boat they had arrived in, which was moored in a smelly canal. Some of them still felt seasick when they turned up at the athletics track!
- Coca-Cola became the first company to sponsor the Olympic Games. The freighter that delivered the US team also delivered 1,000 cases of Coca-Cola which were sold from kiosks.
- The athletics track length of 400 m became the standard for future Games.
- The Indian field hockey team won a gold medal six times consecutively, from 1928 to 1956.

The Rower and the Ducks

The actions of Australian rower Henry Pearce at Amsterdam have passed into history. When he was midway through his quarterfinal, a family of ducks appeared before him on the water. Proving himself a true gentleman, he stopped and let them cross in front of him — and still went on to win the race and eventually the gold medal!

Henry Pearce's gesture made him a favourite with many children. He won his second Olympic gold in 1932

Coca-Cola

Coca Cola appeared as a sponsor for the first time at the 1928 Olympic Games

Japanese swimmer Yoshiyuki Tsuruta (l), gold medal winner in the 200 m breaststroke, shakes hands with Erich Rademacher of the German winning water polo team

Top 10 Ranking Nations	Gold	Silver	Bronze	Total
USA	22	18	16	56
Germany	10	7	14	31
Cuba	8	8	9	25
Canada	7	6	12	25
Hungary	7	5	7	19
Great Britain	7	4	4	15
Mixed Team	6	10	5	21
Greece	6	9	4	19
Switzerland	4	5	0	9
Austria	4	4	7	15

1932 Los Angeles Olympics

The 1932 Olympics were officially known as the Games of the X Olympiad and were held in California, USA. The Games commenced on July 30, and closed on August 14, with events staged over 16 days — this became the standard for all future Games.

The Parade of Nations at the Coliseum Olympic Stadium in Los Angeles

The Games

Los Angeles was the only city to bid for this Olympiad. The 1932 Games were held in the middle of the Great Depression, in the comparatively remote city of Los Angeles in California. Because of this, numbers were well down — only half as many athletes took part as had in 1928. However, despite the drop in numbers, the standard of competition was excellent (18 world records were either broken or equalled), the quality of the facilities was high, and the Games were a success. They were well supported — 100,000 people attended the Opening Ceremony and many of the era's big movie stars attended the Games, including such names as Charlie Chaplin, Gary Cooper, and Douglas Fairbanks.

The Coliseum Olympic stadium — now known as the Los Angeles Memorial Coliseum — had a capacity of more than 100,000, and offered scale and quality far beyond previous stadiums

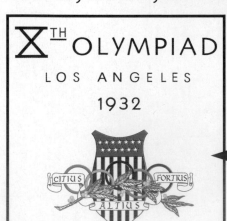

The Olympic emblem, with the American flag, the Olympic rings, a laurel branch and the Olympic motto "*Citius, Altius, Fortius*"

Quick Facts

- Host city: Los Angeles, California, USA
- Nations participated: 37
- Athletes participated: 1,332 (1,206 men; 126 women)
- Events organised: 14 sports; 117 events
- Opened by: Vice President Charles Curtis

Charles Curtis, Vice President of the United States of America 1929-1933

Innovations

During these Games, winners stood on a three-tiered podium to be awarded their medals after the event (previously medals had often been given for all events on the closing day), and the medal-giving ceremonies were accompanied by the playing of national anthems and the raising of flags which we are so familiar with today. These Games witnessed the introduction of electronic timing to one hundredth of a second and photo-finishes — when officials could not determine the winner of the 100 m race, newsreel film was carefully analysed to determine that Eddie Tolan of the US was the gold medal winner.

This was now the standard design for Olympic medals, with the Goddess Nike on the front, holding a palm leaf and winner's laurel crown, and on the back, athletes carry the winner on their shoulders. The winner is carrying a palm leaf

The Olympic Village

Male athletes were housed for the first time in a specially built Olympic Village, whilst females stayed at the Chapman Park Hotel on Wiltshire Boulevard.

Facts

- The world-wide depression and location of the Games prevented many athletes from coming — when the Brazilian contingent arrived in the US, they only had enough money to pay the entry head tax of $1 for 24 of their 60-odd strong team. The rest stayed on board their boat.
- Herbert Hoover, the US President, did not attend the Games, being too busy campaigning. Vice President Curtis took his place.
- The 1932 Games were attended by a record-breaking crowd of 100,000 during the Opening Ceremony.
- The 1932 Olympics were the first to last 16 days. The duration of the Olympics has remained between 15 and 18 days ever since.

Herbert Hoover, President, United States of America (1929-1933)

The Parade of Nations during the Opening Ceremony

Some Restrictions
• Participation was restricted to three athletes per country in each discipline.
• Finland's Paavo Nurmi, a star of earlier Games, was accused of professionalism and was banned from the Games. So was Frenchman Jules Ladoumègue.

Fair Play
The women's fencing final saw an act of true sportsmanship and gallantry. British fencer Judy Guinness came forward to inform the judges of two touches which her opponent, Ellen Preis of Austria, had scored against her that they had not recorded, thereby giving up her hopes for a gold medal.

Memorable Winners
• 21 year old American Mildred Ella (known as 'Babe') Didrikson won the javelin throw and the 80 m hurdles, and finished second in the high jump. In fact, she qualified for all five women's track and field events, but was only allowed to compete in three.
• The 100 m and 200 m sprint events were both won by American runner Eddie Tolan.

Gold medal winner Babe Didrikson throwing a javelin. She was named the most versatile female competitor by the Guinness Book of Records for her exceptional performances in golf, basketball, and track and field

Takeichi Nishi of Japan with his horse *Uranus*

Stanislawa Walasiewicz crosses the finish line

• Japan's Takeichi Nishi won gold for individual show jumping with his horse, *Uranus*. In 1945, Nishi, a Japanese officer, died while defending the island of Iwo Jima, as told in the film, '*Letters from Iwo Jima*.'

• Poland's Stanislawa Walasiewicz won the gold medal in the women's 100 m, becoming the first woman to break the 12 second barrier. When she was killed in 1980, a victim in a robbery attempt, an autopsy declared her to be a male. There is still controversy over her biological sex.

• Japan dominated the pool, winning five of the six men's swimming titles — in fact, they got all three of their permitted competitors through to the last six of every men's race, but America's pride was salvaged in the diving, where they took all 12 medals.

Not the 3,000 m Steeplechase
• The 3,000 m steeplechase was a bit of a misnomer — when winner, Finland's Volmari Iso-Hollo recorded a time of 10 min 33.4 seconds, yet had managed a world record time of 9 min 14.6 seconds in his qualifier, it emerged that the official responsible for counting the laps had been taken ill, and his stand in had failed to record one of the laps! The distance run was actually 3,460 m!

Facts

• China participated in the Games for the first time.
• French and Italian athletes bent the rules — despite '*Prohibition*' regulations banning alcohol, they were allowed wine with their meals as they said it was part of their training diet!
• Football was dropped from the Games, but shooting was brought back.

Top 10 Ranking Nations	Gold	Silver	Bronze	Total
USA	41	32	30	103
Italy	12	12	12	36
France	10	5	4	19
Sweden	9	5	9	23
Japan	7	7	4	18
Hungary	6	4	5	15
Finland	5	8	12	25
Great Britain	4	7	15	16
Germany	3	12	5	20
Australia	3	1	1	5

Japan's Chuhei Nambu set a world record of 15.72 m in the triple jump

1936 Berlin Olympics

The 1936 Summer Olympics or the Games of the XI Olympiad were held in Berlin, Germany. They commenced on August 1, and ended on August 16, 1936. A great deal of controversy surrounded the Games, as they were used as a political tool by the Nazi government, but nevertheless a record number of athletes and countries competed.

The Nazi Influence

Berlin won the bid to host the Games over Barcelona. The bid was won before the National Socialist German Workers Party (the Nazi party) gained power in Germany, but they subsequently used the Games as an opportunity to promote their beliefs, particularly the promotion of the superiority of the '*Aryan Race.*' Only members of the Aryan race were allowed to compete for Germany. However, although Germany won most of the medals, the star of the Olympics was black African-American athlete Jesse Owens, who won four gold medals.

Adolf Hitler with the sports minister Hans von Tschammer Und Osten

The official stand in the Olympic Stadium

Quick Facts

- Host city: Berlin Germany
- Nations participated: 49
- Athletes participated: 3,963 (3,632 men; 331 women)
- Events organised: 19 sports; 129 events
- Opened by: Chancellor Adolf Hitler

A German postage stamp from the 1936 Olympics. Eight different stamps showing different sports were issued for the Games

Controversy

There was much debate before the Games as to whether or not they should go ahead, for there was a lot of worry about Nazi anti-Semitism. When Avery Brundage, president of the US Amateur Athletic Union, paid a visit, Hitler removed signs stating '*Jews not wanted*' and similar slogans, and Brundage concluded that America should not boycott the Games. President Roosevelt took the same view, believing that America should be seen to remain politically neutral. However, for those countries or individuals who did approve a boycott, Spain was planning on staging an alternative — the '*People's Olympics*' — but they had to be cancelled when the Spanish Civil War broke out the day before they were due to start!

The Torch Relay

1936 saw the introduction of the torch relay based on an idea by Dr Carl Diem. A lighted torch was carried from Olympia to Berlin through 7 countries (Greece, Bulgaria, Yugoslavia, Hungary, Czechoslovakia, Austria and Germany) on a journey of more than 3,000 km, carried by more than 3,000 relay runners.

As part of the spectacle, there was a torchbearers' ceremony held in Delphi's ancient stadium where Diem had organised there to be a three foot tall stone altar with the modern ring design chiseled into its sides. The stone was never removed from the stadium, and two decades later, some British researchers visiting Delphi mistook it for an ancient altar, believing the ring design had been used in ancient Greece! In the end, the real story came out and '*Carl Diem's Stone*' was moved from the stadium and placed near the entrance to the historic site.

The five Olympic rings. The symbol's popularity and widespread use began during the lead-up to the 1936 Olympics.

THE
XITH OLYMPIC GAMES
BERLIN, 1936

The Olympic bell. The emblem was created by chance — artist, Johannes Boehland, designed an emblem containing the five Olympic rings, with an eagle and the Brandenburg Gate over it, but the President of the Organising Committee did not like the design. He opened the bottom part of it, which turned the design into a bell. On the side of the bell is the inscription *"Ich rufe die Jugend der Welt!"* (*"I call the youth of the world!"*)

Facts

- The German leaders were determined to make these Games a resounding success and in the end welcomed more athletes from more countries than any previous Olympics, and more than four million tickets were sold.
- With the aim of 'cleaning up' Berlin, the Berlin Police were authorised to arrest all gypsies and keep them in a special camp.
- The 1936 Olympics were the first to be broadcast on a form of television. Twenty-five large screens were set up throughout Berlin, allowing the local people to see the Games for free.

The Olympic Games were held in the Reichssportfeld which was constructed between 1934 and 1936 for the Olympic Games. The total area of the Reichssportfeld was 1.32 square km. It included the Olympic stadium and several other buildings

The Sports

For the first time, the programme included canoeing and men's handball, but polo was contested for the last time. Basketball also made its Olympic debut, and nobody was surprised when America won the gold. However, things did not look so good for them when, just before the competition, the International Basketball Federation decided to ban any players 6 ft 3 in (1.91 m) or taller. Fortunately for the US team, the ban, which would have applied to only three players, all Americans, was quickly rescinded!

Men's swimming was once again dominated by the Japanese, who won three of the six events, while the Netherlands won four of the five women's events — of those, three were won by Hendrika 'Rie' Mastenbroek, who also came away with a silver.

In cycling it was France who triumphed. Robert Charpentier and Guy Lapebie won five gold medals and one silver between them.

African-American sprinter, Jesse Owens won four gold medals in the 1936 Games, thwarting Hitler's attempt to prove Aryan racial superiority

German gymnast Alfred Schwarzmann won three gold and two bronze medals in the Berlin Games

Memorable Winners

• The star of the Games was African-American Jesse Owens, who became a sporting hero after winning four gold medals (100 m, 200 m, 4 x 100 m relay and long jump).
• Thirteen year old Marjorie Gestring of US won a gold medal in springboard diving. She is still the youngest gold medallist in Olympic history.
• Twelve year old Inge Sorensen of Denmark earned a bronze medal in the 200 m breaststroke, making her the youngest medallist ever in an individual event.
• Hungarian water polo player Olivier Halassy won his third medal despite the fact that one of his legs had been amputated below the knee following a streetcar accident.
• Two German gymnasts, Konrad Frey and Alfred Schwarzmann, dominated the men's gymnastics, with Frey collecting three golds, a silver and a bronze, and his teammate Schwarzmann coming away with three gold and two bronze medals.

Facts

- The 1936 Olympics poster featured the *Quadriga* (the statue of the winged Goddess of Peace driving a four-horse chariot) from Berlin's Brandenburg Gate, and a figure of a wreathed victor, his arm raised in the Olympic salute.
- During the long jump competition, Jesse Owens' German rival, Luz Long, publicly befriended him in front of the Nazis. It would become a lifelong friendship.
- Director Leni Riefenstahl was given the task of making a film about the Games. '*Olympia*' is very different from all previous sports-based movies. The director highlighted the beauty of the body by filming the movement of the body from every angle. This film brought about new perspectives in movie-making.
- Apart from medals, the athletes received a winner's crown and an oak tree in a pot.
- The Olympic salute, where the right arm is held out at a slight angle to the right sideways from the shoulder, was similar to the Hitler stiff-arm salute, which caused a little confusion and controversy!

• Rower Jack Beresford of Great Britain won a gold medal in the double sculls event, marking the fifth Olympics at which he earned a medal. He had previously won gold medals in the single sculls in 1924, coxless fours in 1932, silver in the single sculls in 1920 and the eights in 1928.

Naoto Tajima of Japan won a gold medal in the men's triple jump event

Hitler poses with javelin throw medalists

• The Egyptian weightlifter Khadr El Touni set a record that lasted for 60 years! Winning gold in the middleweight class, El Touni lifted 35 kg more than the silver medalist — and 15 kg more than the heavyweight gold medalist! Hitler was so impressed by El Touni that he ordered a street named after him in Berlin.

Top 10 Ranking Nations	Gold	Silver	Bronze	Total
Germany	33	26	30	89
USA	24	20	12	56
Hungary	10	1	5	16
Italy	8	9	5	22
Finland	7	6	6	19
France	7	6	6	19
Sweden	6	5	9	20
Japan	6	4	8	18
The Netherlands	6	4	7	17
Great Britain	4	7	3	14

1948 London Olympics

The 1948 Summer Olympics, officially known as the Games of the XIV Olympiad, were held after a break of 12 years due to World War II. Held in London, they began on July 29 and ended on August 14, 1948. They were nicknamed the Austerity Games as the time was one of shortages and making do, but still proved successful.

The World War and the Olympics

For six years, a large part of the world had been locked in the hostilities of World War II. When the Games came to London in 1948, it was after a 12 year gap. The 1940 Games had been scheduled for Tokyo, moved to Helsinki as WWII started, and finally cancelled, while the 1944 Games, which had been provisionally planned for London, were also cancelled. Some politicians and members of the press believed that London should not stage the Games, but should concentrate on rebuilding after the War. Nevertheless, despite the short time given to organising the event (just two years) and the pared-down budget (£730,000), the Games were very successful, and brought together record numbers of athletes and countries in a spirit of sportsmanship and friendly competition designed to put the aggressions of the War behind them.

HRH King George VI officially opened the London Games

An aerial view of Wembley Stadium, London

Quick Facts

- Host city: London, England
- Nations participated: 59
- Athletes participated: 4,104 (3,714 men; 390 women)
- Events organised: 17 sports; 136 events
- Opened by: King George VI

The Austerity Games

The Games were held in a time of shortage and austerity. Rationing was in force, with food, clothing, construction materials and petrol all rationed (money was so tight that leftover food went to local hospitals) and there was no money to build new facilities. Wembley Football Stadium was fitted with temporary athletic tracks for the Games and no Olympic Village was built. Instead, male athletes were housed at an army camp in Uxbridge and the women at Southlands College. However, the Empire Pool which was used for the swimming events, was the first covered Olympic pool to be used at the Games — although the black-out paint left over from the War (to stop light spilling out during air raids) had to be scraped off the windows before it could be used! The pool was longer than 50 m, so a wooden platform was constructed to shorten it and to house the judges and officials. In the spirit of economy and making do, boxers shared the venue, with a ring erected over the water. To cut costs, local athletes stayed at home, and competing countries contributed food for the athletes.

The official British emblem for the Games features 'Big Ben.' The hands of the clock point to 4 o'clock, the time at which the opening of the Games was planned. In the foreground are the Olympic rings

Olympic pictograms were first introduced at the 1948 Games. There were 20 of them — one for each Olympic sport and three for the arts competition, and the Opening and Closing Ceremonies. They were called 'Olympic symbols' and intended for use on tickets

Facts

- The Opening Ceremony and the Games were broadcast live on BBC television. The BBC paid 1,000 guineas (£1,050) for the broadcasting rights. These were the first Games to be shown on home television, although few people in Great Britain at that time owned television sets.
- Pictograms were first introduced at the 1948 Games, but only became an integral part of the Olympics after the 1964 Games.

Big Ben is one of London's best-known tourist landmarks. It is the popular name for the great clock at the north end of the Palace of Westminster in London (it was originally the nickname for the bell inside the tower). It is the largest four-faced chiming clock and the third-tallest free-standing clock tower in the world

Participating nations

A total of 59 countries sent in 4,104 athletes for the Games. 14 NOCs made their first official appearance: British Guiana (now Guyana), Burma (now Myanmar), Ceylon (now Sri Lanka), Iran, Iraq, Jamaica, Korea, Lebanon, Pakistan, Puerto Rico, Singapore, Syria, Trinidad and Tobago and Venezuela. It was also the first time that India and Pakistan competed as independent countries. However, Japan and Germany were not welcome in the aftermath of the War, although Italy, having defected to the Allies in 1943, was invited to send athletes to the Games.

Highlights of the Game

• Duncan White won the first Olympic medal for Sri Lanka (then Ceylon), when he came second in the 400 m hurdles, and Arthur Wint was the first Jamaican to win an Olympic medal — a gold in the men's 400 m, and a silver in the men's 800 m.

• 13 countries took part in the field hockey tournament, which was won by India, who defeated Great Britain to claim their first gold medal as an independent nation.

• The marathon had an exciting finish. The first man to enter the stadium was Etienne Gailly of Belgium, but he was totally exhausted and fell twice during the final lap. While he was struggling, Delfo Cabrera of Argentina and Thomas Richards of Britain passed him, with Cabrera taking gold. Gailly bravely managed to cross the finish line to take the bronze.

• With the absence of Japan, America took all the gold medals in the men's swimming.

• A women's canoeing event was held for the first time — it was won by Karen Hoff of Denmark.

• The Games were the first to see a political defection — Marie Provaznikova, the Head of the Czechoslovakian gymnastics team, became the first to take the opportunity of the Olympic Games to defect to the West.

The hockey match between India and Great Britain at Wembley Stadium

Memorable Winners

• This time the star of the Games was a woman — Fanny Blankers-Koen of the Netherlands. The 30 year old mother of two, nicknamed the '*Flying Housewife*,' won every event she entered, collecting golds for the 100 m, 200 m, 4 x 100 m relay and 80 m hurdles. She was also the world record holder in the high jump and long jump and might reasonably have been expected to win more medals, but at the time a ruling limited women to three individual events.

• Seventeen year old American, Bob Mathias, won the decathlon only 4 months after learning the sport. He is the youngest athlete in Olympic history to win a men's athletic event.

• Karoly Takacs, a member of the Hungarian world champion pistol shooting team in 1938, lost his right

Malvin Whitfield (USA) finishes first in the 800 m running event, followed by Arthur Wint from Jamaica

hand when a grenade shattered it. Takacs taught himself to shoot with his left hand and 10 years later in 1948, stunned his fellow competitors and the world when he won an Olympic gold medal in the rapid-fire pistol event.

• France's Micheline Ostermeyer, who took gold in the discus and shot, was also a talented concert pianist!

• The most individual medals were won by Veikko Huhtanen of Finland who took three golds, a silver and a bronze in men's gymnastics.

• Czechoslovakian Emil Zátopek burst onto the long-distance running scene, winning the 10,000 m and coming second in the 5,000 m.

American weightlifter Stanley Anthony Stanczyk won a gold medal at the 1948 Olympics

Facts

• It was the first Games after the death of Baron Pierre de Coubertin, the founder of the modern Olympic movement, in 1937.
• Starting blocks for athletes in sprint races were introduced for the first time.

Top 10 Ranking Nations	Gold	Silver	Bronze	Total
USA	38	27	19	84
Sweden	16	11	17	44
France	10	6	13	29
Hungary	10	5	12	27
Italy	8	11	8	27
Finland	8	7	5	20
Turkey	6	4	2	12
Czechoslovakia	6	2	3	11
Switzerland	5	10	5	20
Denmark	5	7	8	20

1952 Helsinki Olympics

The 1952 Summer Olympics, or the Games of the XV Olympiad, were held in Helsinki, Finland. Helsinki had been due to host the Olympics in 1940 but the Games had been cancelled because of World War II. The 1952 Games commenced on July 19 and closed on August 3, and were the stage for world record breaking competition.

Record-Breaking Games

The Helsinki Games were well organised and were the stage for a very high standard of competition with many Olympic and world records being broken. Indeed, in 19 out of the 24 events in men's athletics the Olympic record was beaten,

As for previous Games, the Helsinki Olympics had an official emblem. The emblem had the picture of the tower of the Olympic stadium in Helsinki along with the five rings of the Olympic flag. The emblem was worn as a badge by dignitaries and VIP guests at the Games

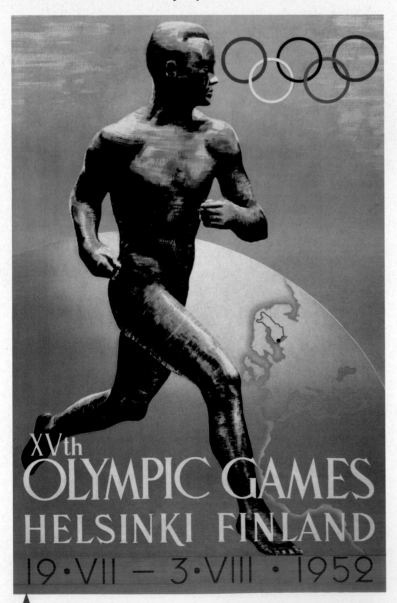

The poster with the figure of Paavo Nurmi was actually designed for the 1940 Games which did not take place because of the Second World War, but, with the dates updated, it was now used in 1952

and it was equalled in two others, while in the nine women's events seven new Olympic records were set. Six world records were also set, three in men's and three in women's athletics.

United Through Sport

The Soviet Union entered the Olympics, Russia having been absent since 1912. The Cold War provided a backdrop for the Games, with athletes from the Soviet Union and other Eastern bloc countries kept separate from Western athletes in their own Olympic Village, and chaperoned by Soviet officials to try to prevent contact with their Western rivals. Nevertheless, sport was the order of the day, and competition ran smoothly.

Germany and Japan were also present, having been invited again after being barred in 1948. Following the War, three German states had been established.

Teams from the Federal Republic of Germany (FRG), also known as West Germany, and the Saarland (which joined the FRG after 1955) sent athletes; but East Germany, or the German Democratic Republic (GDR), was absent.

A total of 69 nations participated in these Games, up from 59 in the 1948 Games. Twelve nations made their first Olympic appearance, including China, Hong Kong, Indonesia, Israel, Nigeria, Thailand, and Vietnam.

The Opening Ceremony

The 1952 Olympic Games in Helsinki started in spectacular fashion with Finnish legend, Paavo Nurmi, then aged 55, entering the stadium with the Olympic flame and lighting the cauldron on the ground. The torch was then carried to the top of the stadium tower, where the cauldron was lit by another Olympic hero, 62 year old Hannes Kolehmainen, considered to be the first of the 'Flying Finns.' Mid-way during the Opening Ceremony, in an unscheduled diversion, Barbara Rotbraut-Pleyer, a German peace activist, ran across the tracks to the speaker's podium to deliver a message of peace! She was nicknamed the 'Peace Angel' by the media.

Venue

The Helsinki Olympic Stadium, located 2 km from the centre of the Finnish capital Helsinki, is the largest stadium in the country. It was originally built for the 1940 Summer Olympics, which were cancelled due

Paavo Nurmi lights the Olympic flame in his home country

to World War II. The stadium capacity was at its maximum during the 1952 Summer Olympics with more than 70,000 spectators watching. Nowadays, the stadium is all-seated and has room for 40,000 spectators only.

Quick Facts

- Host city: Helsinki, Finland
- Nations participated: 69
- Athletes participated: 4,955 (4,436 men; 519 women)
- Events organised: 17 sports; 149 events
- Opened by: President Juho Paasikivi

The Olympic Stadium at Helsinki during the Opening Ceremony. The stadium was built for the 1940 Games that were cancelled due to World War II

A 500 markka coin was issued to commemorate the Olympic Games held in Helsinki. This was the first time a coin had been issued for the Olympic Games

Unforgettable Summer

The Helsinki Olympic Games of 1952 have been referred to as "*the last real Olympic Games,*" due to their sportsmanlike, non-commercial spirit. They have also been described as "*the whole people's Games.*" Thousands of volunteers helped out at the Games.

They were also a wonderful opportunity for Finland to market itself to the world. At the time it was still recovering from the Second World War. This was a chance for it to reinvent itself. Among other things, a new airport and quay were built, Helsinki's very first traffic lights were installed and the organisers tried to ensure that everything was in first class condition and order. Through the Games, Finland was able to promote itself as a distinctive but still Western country.

Memorable Winners

• The star of the track-and-field competition was Emil Zátopek, a long-distance runner from Czechoslovakia, who became the only person in Olympic history to win the 5,000, 10,000 and marathon at the same Olympics. It was the first time he had competed in a marathon! On the day he won the 5,000 m, his wife Dana won the gold medal in the javelin event.

• Equestrian Lis Hartel from Denmark was paralysed below the knees due to polio and had to be helped on and off her horse. Despite this handicap, she claimed the silver medal in the equestrian dressage.

• American Frank Havens won a gold in the Canadian singles 10,000 m canoeing event. Some 28 years earlier, his father, Bill Havens Sr., had been due to represent the USA in the coxed eights rowing in the 1924 Olympics (at the time he was national champion), but had stayed at home instead to await Frank's birth!

• The Indian national field hockey team won its fifth consecutive gold.

• The first gold medal for the USSR (Soviet Union) was won by Nina Romashkova in the women's discus throw event, and in gymnastics the Soviet women's team easily won the first of its eight

Emil Zátopek was a long distance runner from Czechoslovakia. He won the 5,000 m, 10,000 m and the marathon in the 1952 Games

Lis Hartel of Denmark competed alongside men in the equestrian competition. Hartel was paralysed below the knees

consecutive gold medals. From 1952 until the break up of the Soviet Union in 1991, the Soviet team dominated women's gymnastics, winning every Olympic team title (except in 1984, when the Soviet Union boycotted the Olympics).

• Lars Hall, a carpenter from Sweden, became the first nonmilitary winner of the modern pentathlon.

• American athlete Bob Mathias became the first person to win two successive Olympic decathlon titles. After a first gold medal in 1948 as the youngest-ever winner of an Olympic track and field event, in the Helsinki Games he set the world record defending his title.

• Josy Barthel won a surprise gold for Luxembourg, a tiny country, in the 1,500 m.

• Harrison Dillard won gold medals in both the 110 m hurdles and the men's 4 x 100 relay. In 1948 he had also won a gold medal in the men's relay and a gold for the 100 m sprint. The best hurdler of his time, Dillard became the only athlete ever to win Olympic gold medals in a sprint and a hurdle event.

Harrison Dillard from Cleveland, Ohio in the US, won the 110 m hurdle event in the 1952 Olympic Games

The Olympic Stadium at Helsinki

Facts

• Helsinki won the bid to host the Games over five American cities and Amsterdam.
• The first commemorative coin of the modern Olympic Games was made for the 1952 Games.
• The art competition was replaced by exhibitions.
• The procedure for choosing the host city became more formalised at this time, including each candidate city making a 30 minute presentation and changes in the voting system.
• The Olympic Stadium and runner Paavo Nurmi appeared on the former Finnish 10 markka banknote designed by Erick Bruun.
• The rules of the equestrian competitions changed allowing women to enter and to compete alongside men in the mixed events.

Top 10 Ranking Nations	Gold	Silver	Bronze	Total
USA	40	19	17	76
Soviet Union	22	30	19	71
Hungary	16	10	16	42
Sweden	12	13	10	35
Italy	8	9	4	21
Czechoslovakia	7	3	3	13
France	6	6	6	18
Finland	6	3	13	22
Australia	6	2	3	11
Norway	3	2	0	5

1956 Melbourne Olympics

The 1956 Summer Olympics, officially known as the Games of the XVI Olympiad, were held in Melbourne, Australia, with equestrian events taking place in Stockholm, Sweden. It was the first time that the Southern Hemisphere hosted the Games, and was, in fact, the first time that the Games were held outside Europe or North America. The Games commenced on November 22 and were closed on December 8.

The Olympic flame at the Olympic Stadium, Melbourne

The Olympic emblem with the map of Australia, the Olympic torch and the laurel wreath

Australian athlete Ron Clarke carries the Olympic torch in the stadium during the Opening Ceremony

Issues

The 1956 Olympics were the first Olympics to be suffer a major boycott. Less than three weeks before the beginning of the Games the USSR invaded Hungary to quash a revolution there against the Communist regime, and the Soviet presence at the Games led to the withdrawal of the Netherlands, Spain, and Switzerland. Meanwhile, Egypt, Lebanon and Iraq also boycotted the Games due to the Suez Crisis, during which Egypt was invaded by Israel, the United Kingdom and France after Egypt nationalised the Suez Canal. In addition, the People's Republic of China boycotted the Games to retaliate against Taiwan's participation under the name '*Formosa.*'

The 1956 Games were the first to be held in the Southern Hemisphere, and this raised concerns amongst many, for it meant that — due to the reversal of the seasons — the Games would have to be held during November and December — the northern winter months, when athletes would normally be resting in preparation for the next season. Also, due to the strict Australian quarantine regulations, the equestrian events were held five months earlier in Stockholm, Sweden. Additionally, there were problems with financing and disagreements among Australian politicians.

However, despite all these issues, once the Games opened, they ran smoothly, with the Australians proving to be both efficient and friendly, and they came to be known as the '*Friendly Games.*'

The poster for the Melbourne Olympic Games, with the Olympic rings in the foreground and the coat of arms of Melbourne in the background

Quick Facts

- Host city: Melbourne, Australia
- Nations participated: 72
- Athletes participated: 3,314 (2,938 men; 376 women)
- Events organised: 17 sports; 145 events
- Opened by: HRH Philip, Duke of Edinburgh

Aerial view of the Olympic stadium during the Opening Ceremony

The Friendly Games

A total of 72 nations competed in Melbourne. Ethiopia, Fiji, Kenya, Liberia, Federation of Malaya, North Borneo (modern-day Sabah of Malaysia), and Uganda participated for the first time in the Olympics. Athletes from East Germany and West Germany and the Saarland competed together as the United Team of Germany (EUA), under a black, red and yellow flag with the Olympic rings and with Beethoven's 'Ode to Joy' as their anthem. This arrangement lasted up until 1968 when East and West Germany competed as separate teams. Not so friendly was the rivalry between Hungary and the Soviet Union. In fact, the water polo match between the two countries became known as the 'Blood in the Water' match. The game became rough and when a Hungarian was forced to leave the pool with a cut over his eye, a riot almost broke out. Police restored order and the game ended early, with Hungary leading 4-0. The Hungarians went on to win the gold medal.

Memorable Winners

• Track and field were dominated by the American men, who won 15 of 24 events.

• Only two world records were set in track and field: American athlete Mildred McDaniel, set a high jump record; and Egil Danielsen of Norway set one with his javelin throw of 85.71 metres.

• 18 year old Australian athlete Betty Cuthbert was nicknamed the 'Golden Girl' by a delighted home crowd, when she won three track gold medals (100 and 200 m and the 4 x 100 m relay).

• The US basketball team put on the most powerful performance in Olympic history, winning each of their games by at least 30 points.

• French long-distance runner Alain Mimoun had been defeated on the track three times at the hands of Czech Emil Zátopek. However, in the marathon in 1956 it was Mimoun who proved victorious. He waited at the finish line for Zátopek, his old friend and great rival, who finished in sixth position.

• The pool was a scene of triumph for the Australians who won all of the freestyle races, men's and women's, and collected a total of eight gold, four silver and two bronze medals. 17 year old Murray Rose won three gold medals for Australia, while 18 year old Dawn Fraser, set to become one of the country's greatest Olympians, won gold medals for the 100 m and 400 m

Walkers on the track at the start of the 50 km walk

Participants of the 2,000 m tandem race

freestyle — both in world record times — and a silver medal with the 4 x 100 m women's relay team.

• Hungarian boxer Laszlo Papp defended his light-middleweight boxing title, gaining a third gold medal.

• Gymnastics was dominated by two athletes: Viktor Chukarin of the Ukraine earned five medals, including three gold; and Agnes Keleti of Hungary brought her career total to ten medals by winning four gold medals and two silver.

Top 10 Ranking Nations	Gold	Silver	Bronze	Total
Soviet Union	37	29	32	98
USA	32	25	17	74
Australia	13	8	14	35
Hungary	9	10	7	26
Italy	8	8	9	25
Sweden	8	5	6	19
Germany	6	13	7	26
Great Britain	6	7	11	24
Romania	5	3	5	13
Japan	4	10	5	19

Leon Rotman, a Romanian sprint canoer, won the 1,000 m and 10,000 m canoeing events, despite competing with a sprained ankle!

A Tradition is Born

A young Chinese student living in Australia named John Ian Wing, came up with a new idea for the Closing Ceremony. Instead of marching as teams, behind their national flags, the athletes mixed with one another, entering the stadium together in a symbol of global unity, beginning an Olympic tradition that has been followed ever since.

The Olympic flag being carried out of the stadium during the Closing Ceremony of the 1956 Summer Olympic Games

1960 Rome Olympics

The 1960 Olympics, officially known as the Games of the XVII Olympiad, were held in Rome, Italy. Fifty four years after Italy had to give up hosting the 1908 Games due to the eruption of Mount Vesuvius, the 'Eternal City' finally got its chance to stage the Games. They were celebrated from August 25 to September 11.

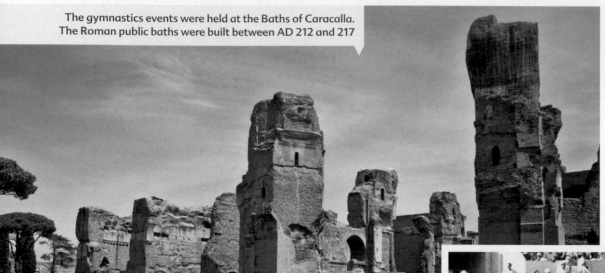
The gymnastics events were held at the Baths of Caracalla. The Roman public baths were built between AD 212 and 217

The Eternal City

Italy built a new Olympic stadium and a Sports Palace for the Games, but also restored several of their ancient historical sites, such as the Basilica of Maxentius and the Baths of Caracalla, to make the most of their cultural heritage.

Basilica of Maxentius and Constantine. The wrestling events were held here during the 1960 Olympic Games

The delegation of Czechoslovakia during the Opening Ceremony

CECOSLOVACCHIA

A Time of Change

In many ways, the 1960 Olympics, with the advent of widespread television, the success of black athletes, improved rights for women (including the return of the ditched 800 m!), challenges to the old concept of amateurism (especially with the financially supported Soviet athletes), and even issues of doping, marked the passing of the Olympics into a new era.

Eighty three NOCs sent over 5,000 athletes to compete in 150 events, and the Games were known for the number of records which were broken and set — 28 new Olympic records and 4 new world records were set in the athletics events.

The Olympic Anthem

In 1958, the anthem originally composed for the very first modern Games was adopted as the official Olympic anthem by the IOC and it was played at the 1960 Games for the first time in this capacity. It was composed by Spyros Samaras, with words by Kostis Palamas.

Facts

- The 1960 Games were the first to be fully covered by television and were broadcast live in 18 European countries and, with only a few hours time-lag, in the United States, Canada and Japan. This made it the most watched sporting event of that time.
- The US television network CBS paid $394,000 for the right to broadcast the Games in the United States.
- Due to its political differences with the Taiwan-based China Formosa, China refused to send any athletes.
- Singapore competed as an independent nation under its own flag for the first time.
- Nations which participated for the first time were Morocco, San Marino, Sudan and Tunisia.
- This was the last Olympic Games until 1992 in which South Africa participated, as it was subsequently excluded due to its policies of apartheid.
- The West and the East German teams participated once again as a united German team.
- Participants from Barbados, Jamaica, and Trinidad and Tobago represented the British colonised West Indies under the name Antilles for the first and only time, as Jamaica and Trinidad and Tobago competed independently again in 1964, and Barbados in 1968.

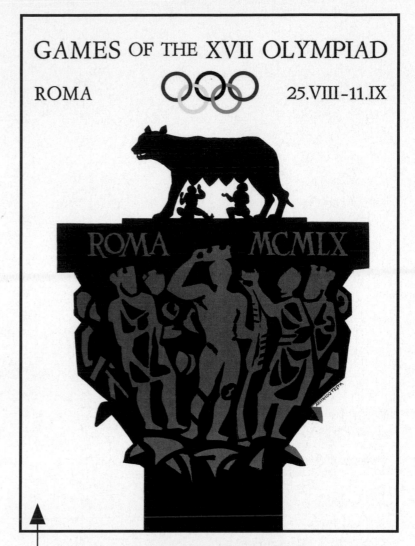

The poster was printed in 11 languages and 29,000 copies were made. It shows a pillar on which stands a she-wolf, suckling the twins Remus and Romulus, who were regarded as the founders of the city of Rome. The date, 1960, is written in Roman numerals. Below stands a crowned victorious athlete surrounded by people in togas

The medals for Rome followed the 1928 design, but were set in a circle of bronze featuring a laurel wreath and were matched with a chain also designed like a sequence of bronze laurel leaves

Highlights . . .

• The US dominated the pool, claiming 15 medals, nine of which were gold. American swimmer Jeff Farrell, despite undergoing an emergency appendectomy six days before the US trials, won two of those gold medals on the relay teams.
• Queen Sofia of Spain represented Greece in the sailing events, while the future king of Greece, Constantine II, won a gold medal for his country in the Dragon Class sailing event.
• In football, Yugoslavia qualified for the final by winning a coin toss after tying with Italy — the schedule was too busy for a replay and the present-day tie-breaker of taking penalties was not in use. They went on to win the tournament after losing in the final three times in a row.
• In field hockey, Pakistan not only broke India's dominance since 1928, but also won its first ever Olympic gold medal in the process.
• In gymnastics, the Soviet women's team won 15 of 16 possible medals, while in the men's competition, the Japanese team won the first of what would be five successive golds.

. . . and Lowlights

• For the first time since the 1912 marathon, the Games saw the death of an athlete — Danish cyclist, Knut Enemark Jensen collapsed during his event and later died. He was found to have taken amphetamines, although doctors claimed he had died of heat stroke. His death was partially responsible for the start of drug testing.
• In a controversial ruling in the pool, judges declared that the winner of the 100 m freestyle was John Devitt of Australia. Official times showed a faster time for silver medalist Lance Larson of the US and most of the audience and even the swimmers themselves believed that the American had won. Nevertheless, the ruling held.

Queen Sofia of Spain, who was, at the time, Princess Sophia of Greece and Denmark, represented Greece in sailing during the 1960 Summer Olympic Games

The future King Constantine of Greece (right) hands over the Olympic flame, which was transported from Greece to Italy for the Rome Olympics

Memorable Winners

• One of the true stars of the Games was Ethiopian runner Abebe Bikila who set a new world record while racing barefoot in the marathon. He went on to defend his title in 1964 (with running shoes on then!) He became the first black African Olympic champion.

• In the single-handed dinghy class, Paul Elvstrom of Denmark won his fourth consecutive gold medal, and in canoeing Sweden's Gert Fredriksson won his sixth.

• Hungarian Aladar Gerevich won his seventh gold medal in fencing as the Hungarian sabre team took their sixth consecutive gold. In the next three Olympiads, Hungary would win three more team golds — but in épée.

Wilma Rudolph, an American athlete, won three gold medals. She was the first American woman to do so

• American athlete Wilma Rudolph, the '*black gazelle*,' won three gold medals (100 m, 200 m and 4 x 100 m), despite falling victim to polio, pneumonia and scarlet fever during childhood.

• New Zealand's Peter Snell recorded an historic victory in the 800 m and Herb Elliott from Australia set a new world record in the 1,500 m.

• Cassius Marcellus Clay Jr., a boxer from the US, won the light-heavyweight gold medal. Shortly after the 1960 Olympics he turned professional and became hugely successful. He later changed his name when he joined the Nation of Islam, becoming known as Muhammad Ali, or, by his fans, as '*the Greatest*.'

American boxers (l to r):
Cassius Clay (later known as Muhammad Ali), Eddie Crook, and Wilbert (Skeeter) McClure

Sad But True

Suriname made its first Olympic appearance, but its lone athlete, Siegfried Esajas, failed to turn up for the 800 m in which he was due to compete, and the story circulated that it was because he had overslept. For years he was the laughing stock of the sporting world, and it wasn't until two weeks before his death in 2005 that his name was cleared when the Suriname Olympic Committee admitted that he had been mistakenly told by the Suriname OC Secretary General at the time that his event had been rescheduled for the afternoon. He was then properly honoured as Suriname's first Olympian athlete.

Top 10 Ranking Nations	Gold	Silver	Bronze	Total
Soviet Union	43	29	31	103
USA	34	21	16	71
Italy	13	10	13	36
Germany	12	19	11	42
Australia	8	8	6	22
Turkey	7	2	0	9
Hungary	6	8	7	21
Japan	4	7	7	18
Poland	4	6	11	21
Czechoslovakia	3	2	3	8

1964 Tokyo Olympics

The 1964 Summer Olympics were officially known as the Games of the XVIII Olympiad and were held in Tokyo, Japan. These were the first Olympics to be held in Asia and ran from October 10 to October 24. Television pictures were broadcast via satellite for the first time and the Games were watched in 40 countries around the world.

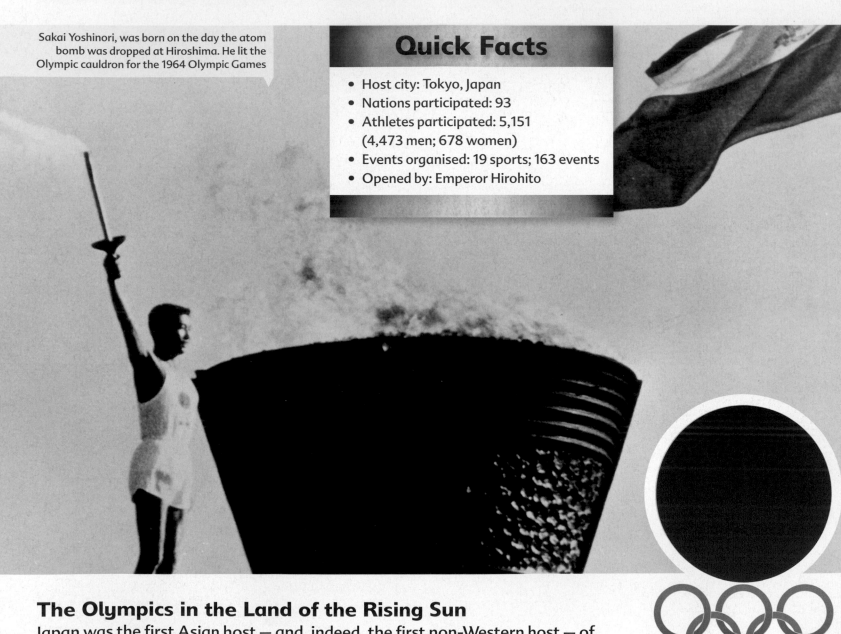

Sakai Yoshinori, was born on the day the atom bomb was dropped at Hiroshima. He lit the Olympic cauldron for the 1964 Olympic Games

Quick Facts

- Host city: Tokyo, Japan
- Nations participated: 93
- Athletes participated: 5,151 (4,473 men; 678 women)
- Events organised: 19 sports; 163 events
- Opened by: Emperor Hirohito

The Olympics in the Land of the Rising Sun

Japan was the first Asian host — and, indeed, the first non-Western host — of the Olympic Games and was determined to show the world that the atrocities of the Second World War were truly in the past. Tokyo's infrastructure was overhauled for the Games, with new train and subway lines, a super-speed train service, and a large highway building project, as well as modernisations to the international airport and the port, and a new undersea communications cable. The Japanese commitment to excellence showed through in the efficient organisation of the Games, which were well supported by the people of Japan — over two million tickets were sold.

The emblem for the Tokyo Games was composed of the Olympic rings and the Japanese national flag, representing *'the rising Sun'*

Participating Nations

A total of 93 nations took part in the Games, with 16 of them making their first Olympic appearance: Algeria, Cameroon, Chad, Congo, Côte d'Ivoire (as Ivory Coast), Dominican Republic, Libya, Madagascar, Malaysia, Mali, Mongolia, Nepal, Niger, Northern Rhodesia (now Zambia), Senegal and Tanzania.

These were the first Olympics in which South Africa was barred due to its racist policy of apartheid, and the Games also saw the absence of Indonesia and North Korea who withdrew when several of their athletes were disqualified for participating in the New Emerging Forces Games in Jakarta in 1963.

Venues

The Opening and Closing Ceremonies, and track and field events were held at the Olympic Stadium (known as the National Stadium), artistic gymnastics was held in the Tokyo Metropolitan Gymnasium, while swimming and basketball events took place in the Yoyogi National Gymnasium, south of the main Olympic Village.

Nippon Budokan, popularly known as Japan Martial Arts Hall, was built to house the judo events, and was used for demonstrations of traditional Japanese sports (*Budo*), such as *kendo* (fencing), *kyudo* (archery) and *sumo* (wrestling). It is now one of Tokyo's most famous concert venues.

In all, a total of 33 sports venues were used.

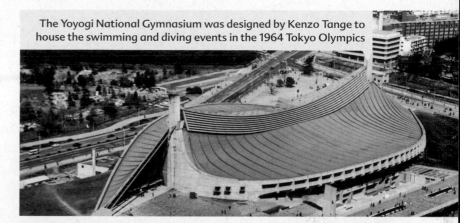

The Yoyogi National Gymnasium was designed by Kenzo Tange to house the swimming and diving events in the 1964 Tokyo Olympics

Facts

- The Games were telecast in the United States using Syncom 3, the first geostationary communication satellite, and from there to Europe using Relay 1, an older version of the satellite.
- Olympic pictograms, first seen at the 1948 Games, were used in Japan and became a feature at each subsequent Summer Olympics. In Tokyo there were 20 pictograms for the different sports and a further 39 general information pictograms.

The Olympic stadium in Tokyo, Japan during the Opening Ceremony

Additions and Innovations

• Judo and volleyball, both popular sports in Japan, made their Olympic debuts.
• The women's pentathlon was introduced.
• The 1964 Games saw the first use of computers to keep results.
• A fibreglass pole was used for the first time in the pole vaulting competition.
• In swimming, a new timing system started the clock by the sound of the starter gun and stopped it with touchpads.
• In athletics, the photo finish using a photograph with lines on it was introduced.
• The Games were telecast to the US using Syncom 3, the first geostationary communication satellite.

Memorable Winners

• Abebe Bikila of Ethiopia became the first athlete to win the marathon twice in a row — less than six weeks after having his appendix removed!
• Soviet gymnast Larisa Latynina brought her career medal total to an incredible 18, winning two gold medals, two silver and two bronze medals! She holds the record for winning the most Olympic medals.
• Greco-Roman wrestler Imre Polyak of Hungary finally won a gold medal after finishing second in the same division at the previous three Games.
• Billy Mills, a little-known American runner, won the gold in the men's 10,000 m. He was the first — and so far only — American to win this event.
• In swimming, Dawn Fraser of Australia won the 100 m freestyle for the third time in a row.
• New Zealand's Peter Snell won a gold medal in both the 800 m and 1,500 m.
• Although Al Oerter of the US was suffering from injuries incurred a week before the competition, he managed to defend his discus throw title, winning a gold for the third Games in a row.
• Hungarian water polo player Dezso Gyarmati became the most successful water polo player in Olympic history, winning his fifth consecutive medal — his third gold.
• Three out of the four titles in the new sport of judo went to the host nation, Japan, who had lobbied strongly for the inclusion of the sport.

The Olympic Stadium during the Opening Ceremony

However, Anton Geesink of the Netherlands won the Open category, which allowed competitors of any weight to enter. The judo competition was only open to men until 1992, although it was included as a demonstration sport for women in 1988.

• Mary Rand won the gold medal in the long jump, breaking the world record and becoming the first-ever British female to win an Olympic gold medal in a track and field event. Rand was also a silver medallist in the women's pentathlon, and won a bronze as a member of the women's 4 x 100 m relay team.

Fact

The first official Fair Play Trophy was awarded to Swedish yachtsmen Lars Gunnar Käll and Stig Lennart Käll. The Swedish brothers set an outstanding example of sportsmanship when they gave up their race to come to the aid of two other competitors whose boat had sunk.

The gold medal winning Japanese team in a women's volleyball match during the 1964 Games

Mary Rand of Great Britain during the shot put event of the modern pentathlon at the Olympic Games in Tokyo

• Lynn Davies won the men's long jump, making it a British double for the event. He was only the second non-American athlete to win the men's event since the revival of the Games in 1896.

Top 10 Ranking Nations	Gold	Silver	Bronze	Total
USA	36	26	28	90
Soviet Union	30	31	35	96
Japan	16	5	8	29
Germany	10	22	18	50
Italy	10	10	7	27
Hungary	10	7	5	22
Poland	7	6	10	23
Australia	6	2	10	18
Czechoslovakia	5	6	3	14
Great Britain	4	12	2	18

1968 Mexico Olympics

The Games of the XIX Olympiad, or the 1968 Summer Olympics, were held in Mexico City, Mexico, and were the first Olympic Games to be hosted by a Spanish-speaking country. They ran from October 12 to October 27. The Games were held at the highest ever altitude, leading to difficulties for some and opportunities for others.

The emblem of the 1968 Summer Olympics

Quick Facts

- Host city: Mexico City, Mexico
- Nations participated: 112
- Athletes participated: 5516 (4735 men; 781 women)
- Events organised: 20 sports; 172 events
- Opened by: President Gustavo Díaz Ordaz

Mexican athlete Norma Enriqueta Basilio de Sotelo, the first woman to light the Olympic flame

The Political Background

The political situation worldwide was tense in 1968. Throughout the US, peace and civil rights demonstrations were taking place and both Martin Luther King and Robert Kennedy had been assassinated, the war in Vietnam was still ongoing, Russia had invaded Czechoslovakia, the People's Republic of China was in the midst of the Cultural Revolution, and students were demonstrating against the government in France. Just ten days before the opening of the Games, the Mexican army fired on a group of students protesting against the Mexican government, killing many and wounding more. Some of this politics naturally spilled out onto the Olympic arena . . .

Politics and the Olympics

Standing on the podium to receive their medals, American athletes Tommie Smith and John Carlos, winners of the gold and bronze medals respectively in the 200 m race, each raised one hand, covered by a black glove, in a Black Power salute, in a gesture meant to bring attention to racism in the US. The silver medalist, Peter Norman of Australia, wore a civil rights badge in support of them. The two Americans also wore only black socks and no shoes, to represent black poverty. The IOC insisted that Smith and Carlos be suspended from the US team and banned from the Olympic Village and the IOC President, Avery Brundage, threatened to ban the entire US track team if this did not happen. The US OC then expelled the two athletes from the Games. Norman was subsequently left off the Australian 1972 Olympic team. The IOC stated that the basic principle of the Olympic Games is that politics plays no part whatsoever in them, and that the American athletes had gone against this principle.

One of the heroines of the 1968 Games was Vera Caslavska, a Czech gymnast, who won four gold medals and two silvers, defeating Soviet gymnasts in the process. Standing on the podium she turned her head down and away during the playing of the Soviet national anthem, in silent protest at the invasion of her homeland by the Soviets two months earlier. Caslavska was subsequently banned from sporting events for some years by the new regime in her country.

Tommie Smith and John Carlos raise their fists in a Black Power salute in protest against racism

Vera Cáslavská from Czechoslovakia won six medals in the 1968 Olympic Games

Olympic Firsts

• A woman lit the Olympic flame for the first time.
• Drug testing was introduced and Swedish pentathlete Hans-Gunnar Liljenwall, was the first to be disqualified — for alcohol use.
• These were the first Games in a developing country.
• A synthetic material (tartan) was used for the first time on the athletics track.
• Electronic timing was introduced in addition to manual timing and was used for official timing.
• For the first time, the Closing Ceremony was transmitted in colour to all the world.
• For the first time, athletes from East and West Germany competed in separate teams.
• Barbados competed for the first time as an independent country, and Singapore returned to the Games as an independent country, having competed with the Malaysian team in Tokyo, while 11 new NOCs joined the roll call.

The Height of Success

The choice of Mexico City to host the 1968 Olympics was a controversial one because of the city's high altitude, 2,300 m, which meant that the air contained 30% less oxygen than at sea level. Sure enough, the rarefied air proved disastrous to many athletes competing in endurance events. On the other hand, the high altitude led to world records in all of the men's races that were 400 m or shorter, including both relays, and in the 400 m hurdles, long jump and triple jump as well. Bob Beamon's spectacular long jump of 8.90 m still stands as the Olympic record.

Robert Beamon won the long jump with a spectacular record breaking jump

John Stephen Akhwari from Tanzania, who continued running in the 1968 Olympic marathon despite an injury, is honoured at the Closing Ceremony of the 2000 Sydney Olympics

Memorable Winners

• In the high jump Dick Fosbury from America won the gold medal with his unorthodox jumping technique, jumping over the bar backwards and head first. This form of jumping became known as the '*Fosbury flop*' and became the dominant technique in the event.

• Bob Beamon of the United States stunned the crowds with his spectacular long jump — a world record at 8.90 m — 55 cm further than the previous world record, and a record that would stand for 23 years, until broken by Mike Powell in 1991. When he was told that he had broken the world record, he collapsed to his knees in shock.

Al Oerter won his fourth consecutive gold medal in the discus throw

The American delegation during the Opening Ceremony of the 1968 Olympic Games

- American swimmer Debbie Meyer became the first swimmer to win three individual gold medals, in the 200 m, 400 m and 800 m freestyle events. Debbie was only 16 years old at the time.
- Fellow American swimmer, Charles Hickcox, also won three golds — for the 200 and 400 m individual medleys and as a member of the record breaking men's 4 x 400 medley relay team — and a silver for the 100 m backstroke.
- American discus thrower Al Oerter, who won his fourth consecutive gold medal in that event, became the second athlete to achieve this feat in an individual event, and the first in track and field.
- John Stephen Akhwari from Tanzania fell during the marathon and was badly injured. He continued running despite a dislocated knee and finished, but his sportsman spirit won him the title of "*king without a crown.*" When asked why he had carried on, with no chance of winning, he said, "My country did not send me to Mexico City to start the race. They sent me to finish."
- After winning the gold medal for heavyweight boxing, George Foreman of America walked around the ring waving a small American flag. He is considered one of the hardest hitters of all time.
- This Games saw the start of the dominance of Africans in long distance running — Africans won medals in all events from 800 m to the marathon.

Top 10 Ranking Nations	Gold	Silver	Bronze	Total
USA	45	28	34	107
Soviet Union	29	32	30	91
Japan	11	7	7	25
Hungary	10	10	12	32
East Germany	9	9	7	25
France	7	3	5	15
Czechoslovakia	7	2	4	13
West Germany	5	11	10	26
Australia	5	7	5	17
Great Britain	5	5	3	13

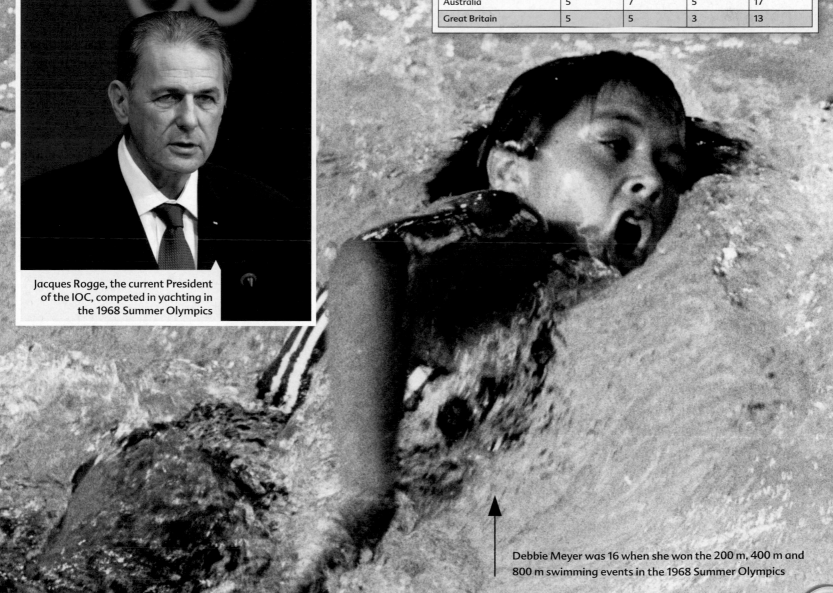

Jacques Rogge, the current President of the IOC, competed in yachting in the 1968 Summer Olympics

Debbie Meyer was 16 when she won the 200 m, 400 m and 800 m swimming events in the 1968 Summer Olympics

1972 Munich Olympics

The 1972 Summer Olympics, officially known as the Games of the XX Olympiad, were held in Munich, then a part of West Germany, from August 26 to September 11. The Games were successful and produced some outstanding champions, but sadly, they will forever be associated with tragedy for they were the scene of a deadly terrorist attack.

"The Games Must Go On!"

The West Germans hoped that, after the highly politicised Games in Berlin in 1936, the 1972 Games would show the world a new democratic and optimistic Germany — the official motto was '*the Happy Games.*' Indeed, the Games, the largest yet, were proceeding successfully when, on September 5th, eight Palestinian terrorists entered the Olympic Village and seized eleven members of the Israeli Olympic team, two of whom died as a result of the kidnap. The terrorists were demanding the release of Palestinians held in Israel. Competition was suspended, but by the end of the drama, and after a failed rescue attempt, all the Israelis, five terrorists and a German policeman had been killed, in a tragedy that rocked the world. The next day, a memorial service attended by 80,000 spectators and 3,000 athletes was held in the Olympic Stadium. Avery Brundage, IOC President, gave an address in which he famously stated, "*The Games must go on,*" to the disgust of some, but the approval of others. He retired following these Games.

More Controversy

The Munich Massacre was not the only political issue the Games had to contend with. At the start of the Games, the Rhodesian team was sent home due to pressure from other African nations which did not accept its legitimacy, while during the course of the competition, black American athletes once again protested on the podium — Vince Matthews and Wayne Collett had won gold and silver respectively in the men's 400 m race, but they turned away from the American flag, and when their anthem was played, chatted casually, and Collett subsequently made a Black Power salute. They were sent home and banned from future Olympics, but were allowed to keep their medals.

A Palestinian terrorist of the Black September group

The emblem of the Munich Games, '*Radiant Munich,*' represents a crown of rays of light, symbolising light, freshness and generosity — the spirit of the Munich Games. This was the first Summer Games when the emblem became a true standalone icon, a pattern that has been followed ever since

Munich1972

The front of the medal showed the Goddess of Victory, in a design used since 1928, but the reverse side broke with tradition, using a design created by Gerhard Marcks of the Bauhaus school. It showed Castor and Pollux, the twin sons of Zeus and Léda, the patrons of sports competitions and friendship, represented by two naked youths

The Venue

The main venue for the 1972 Summer Olympics was the *Olympiastadion* in the *Olympiapark*. The roof, with its large sweeping canopies of acrylic glass stabilised by steel cables — used for the first time on a large scale — was considered revolutionary and has become a Munich landmark.

The Olympic Stadium in Munich, Germany was built as the main stadium for the 1972 Games

The 1972 Games were the first to have an officially named mascot — Waldi, the dachshund (a popular breed of dog from Germany). Waldi was designed to represent the qualities that athletes need for success — resistance, tenacity and agility

Quick Facts

- Host city: Munich, West Germany
- Nations participated: 121
- Athletes participated: 7,134 (6,075 men; 1,059 women)
- Events organised: 21 sports; 195 events
- Opened by: President Gustav Heinemann

Opening Ceremony of the 1972 Games. The Olympic flag is being carried into the stadium

Memorable Winners

• In a truly amazing feat, Mark Spitz of the US dominated the swimming, winning seven gold medals to go with the two he had earned in 1968, and setting seven new world records in the process. As an American Jew, Spitz had to leave before the Closing Ceremony, as it was feared that he would be an additional target for Palestinian terrorists.

• One of the stars of the Games was Olga Korbut. The entire world fell in love with the tiny Soviet gymnast who was successful in the team competition, failed to win the individual all-around title after a fall, but then went on to win two gold for the apparatus — one for the balance beam and one for the floor exercise.

• 15 year old Australian Shane Gould won three golds, a silver and a bronze in the swimming events.

• Lasse Viren of Finland fell midway through the 10,000 m final, but rose and set a world record to win the first of his four career gold medals.

• In the Olympic 800 m final, American runner Dave Wottle came from the very back of the field at the 600 m mark, passing runner after runner to win by just 0.03 seconds ahead of the favourite,

Yevgeny Arzhonov from the Soviet Union. After this, Wottle was nicknamed '*The Head Waiter*!'

Slalom canoeing was contested for the first time and an artificial canal was constructed for it in the city of Augsburg

Facts

- For the first time an oath was sworn by an official.
- Archery returned to the Olympic programme after 52 years and handball after 36 years, while slalom canoeing and kayaking were included for the first time.
- Badminton and water skiing were demonstration sports.
- The events of the Munich Massacre were recorded in the Oscar-winning documentary, '*One Day in September*,' and were also the inspiration for Steven Spielberg's 2005 film '*Munich*.'

American swimmer Mark Spitz, who won seven medals and broke seven world records

Yet More Controversy

The basketball game between the Soviet Union and the United States (held late at night so that American TV audiences could watch it live!) was surely one of the most controversial basketball games of all time. With one second left on the clock, the score stood at 50-49 to the Americans. But there followed a period of confusion involving the clock being wrongly reset and a time-out supposedly called by the Soviet coach, but not acknowledged, and when, for the final time, the clock was again set back to three seconds, the Soviets scored, taking the score to 50-51 and leaving them with the gold medal. The Americans were outraged by what they saw as a complete injustice and refused to accept their silver medals.

Olga Korbut, a Soviet gymnast, was the darling of the Games

Top 10 Ranking Nations	Gold	Silver	Bronze	Total
Soviet Union	50	27	22	99
USA	33	31	30	94
East Germany (GDR)	20	23	23	66
West Germany (FRG)	13	11	16	40
Japan	13	8	8	29
Australia	8	7	2	17
Poland	7	5	9	21
Hungary	6	13	16	35
Bulgaria	6	10	5	21
Italy	5	3	10	18

Britain's judo team, left to right, Brian Jacks, Dave Starbrook and Angelo Parisi

1976 Montreal Olympics

The 1976 Summer Olympics, or the Games of the XXI Olympiad, ran from July 17 to August 1 in Montreal, in the province of Quebec in Canada. Unfortunately, like the previous Olympics at Munich, this event had its own set of controversies and was sadly marred by boycotts and drug allegations.

The Olympic emblem design consists of three symbolic elements: the Olympic rings, a running track (top centre), and an M for Montreal, which is also a graphic represents of an Olympic podium

A view of the Olympic Stadium

Quick Facts

- Host city: Montreal, Canada
- Nations participated: 92
- Athletes participated: 6,084 (4,824 men; 1260 women)
- Events organised: 21 sports; 198 events
- Opened by: Queen Elizabeth II

Boycotts

Over twenty African nations boycotted the Games because earlier in the year the New Zealand's All Blacks rugby union team had toured South Africa (which still practised its policies of apartheid) and the IOC, which had no control over the playing of rugby, refused to ban New Zealand from the Games. Iraq and Guyana also opted to join the boycott.

Taiwan withdrew after Canada informed them that they could not compete under the name 'Republic of China' (Canada officially recognised the People's Republic of China).

Amik, the beaver, was chosen as the mascot for 1976 Olympic Games. The beaver symbolises patience and hard work, and is also Canada's official national animal

The Big Owe

Her Majesty Queen Elizabeth II, as Head of State of Canada, officially opened the Olympic Games in 1976. The Olympic Stadium was still under construction at the Opening Ceremony because of bad management and corruption. Financially, the Games crippled Quebec. Huge amounts of money were spent on the stadium and related Olympic facilities and infrastructure, leaving Québec with around $1.5 billion of debt that took three decades to repay! In fact, as a result of this financial disaster, many nations and cities became wary of hosting the Olympics, so much so that Los Angeles' bid, a couple of years later, for the 1984 Games went uncontested.

The Olympic Stadium was nicknamed the '*Big O*,' in reference both to its name and the doughnut shaped permanent section of the roof. Later, it was often referred to as the '*Big Owe*,' for obvious reasons! The tower for it was only finished after the completion of the Games and it was not until 1988 that it was possible to retract the roof.

Drug Allegations

Drug and gender tests were carried out at these Games, and drug allegations were rife, although often not proven. Princess Anne of the United Kingdom, competing in equestrian events, was the only female competitor not to have to submit to a sex test.

Facts

- For the first and only time to date in Olympic history, the host country, Canada, left with no gold medals, winning five silver and six bronze medals.
- As a result of the Munich massacre, there was increased security at the Games.
- As a mark of respect for the hostages killed in Munich, Israeli competitors wore a green feather.
- A few days into the Games, the Olympic flame went out during a rainstorm. An official relit the flame using his cigarette lighter, but organisers quickly rushed to put it out and relit it using a backup of the original flame.
- Women's basketball, handball and rowing debuted.

The Olympic stadium in Montreal. The tower incorporated into the base of the stadium is the tallest inclined tower in the world at 175 metres

Memorable Winners

- In gymnastics, Nadia Comaneci from Romania made Olympic history - scoring an unprecedented perfect 10 for her performance on the uneven parallel bars. Not only that, but she went on to score another six 10s, winning herself three gold medals, a silver and a bronze in the process.
- Another star in women's gymnastics was Nellie Kim who scooped three gold medals and one silver for the Soviet Union.
- Her Soviet teammate, Nikolai Andrianov won four gold medals, including the all-around title, in the men's gymnastics.
- Winning their third consecutive gold medals were Viktor Saneyev of the Soviet Union in the triple jump, and Klaus Dibiasi of Italy in platform diving.
- Alberto Juantorena of Cuba became the first man to win both the 400 m and 800 m at the same Olympics.
- Another track double was achieved by Lasse Virén of Finland, who defended his titles in both the 5,000 m and the 10,000 m. However, in the marathon he could only manage fifth place,

and so Emil Zátopek's achievement in 1952 went unmatched.
- Women's volleyball was dominated by the Japanese team, who won all their matches in straight sets. Their opponents only reached a double figure score in one game out of fifteen!
- Irena Kirszenstein-Szewinska of Poland, won a gold medal in the 400 m run, who brought her career total to seven medals — in five different events.
- In boxing, America dominated the ring. Their team is seen as one of the strongest American boxing teams ever. Five of them — Sugar Ray Leonard, Leon Spinks, Michael Spinks, Leo Randolph and Howard Davis Jr. — won gold medals and of these five all but Davis went on to become professional world champions.

Sandra Handerson and Stéphane Prefontaine light the Olympic flame. The Olympic flame was electronically transmitted from Athens to Ottawa via satellite. From there it was carried to Montreal by hand

The parade of the Soviet delegation during the Opening Ceremony of the 1976 Olympic Games

Not Playing Fair

The East German women's swimming team dominated the pool, winning 11 of a possible 13 gold medals. They were accused by the US of using performance-enhancing drugs — one of the American swimmers, Shirley Babashoff, who won three silver medals in the pool, said in a newspaper interview that she felt as if she had been "*beaten by men.*" Years later, documents and court testimonies revealed that, between 1968 and 1988, East Germany operated a state-sponsored system of providing performance-enhancing drugs to as many as 10,000 athletes.

The Ultimate Team Player

In men's gymnastics, Shun Fujimoto of Japan broke his leg during the floor exercise. Despite this, in an incredible display of courage and will power, he hid the extent of his injury and fought off pain to compete again, first with a flawless performance on the pommel horse, and then on the rings, performing a perfect triple somersault dismount and barely flinching on the landing. With his score of 9.7, he helped to ensure that his team beat the Soviet Union to win gold.

Star of the Games, Nadia Comaneci of Romania, performs the floor exercise

Irena Kirszenstein-Szewinska won the 400 m running event in the 1976 Olympic Games

Top 10 Ranking Nations	Gold	Silver	Bronze	Total
Soviet Union	49	41	35	125
East Germany (GDR)	40	25	25	90
USA	34	35	25	94
West Germany (FRG)	10	12	17	39
Japan	9	6	10	25
Poland	7	6	13	26
Bulgaria	6	9	7	22
Cuba	6	4	3	13
Romania	4	9	14	27
Hungary	4	5	13	22

1980 Moscow Olympics

The 1980 Summer Olympics were held in Moscow, in the then Soviet Union, and were officially known as the Games of the XXII Olympiad. This was the first time the Games were held in Eastern Europe or in a socialist country. They are remembered now for being the Games with the biggest Olympic boycott. They began on July 19, and concluded on August 3.

The official Olympic mascot was Misha, the bear, designed by Victor Chizikov →

The Boycott

Once again, an Olympics became remembered for the wrong reasons. The 1980 Games saw the largest boycott of an Olympics in history. It was in protest at the December 1979 invasion of Afghanistan by Soviet troops, and their subsequent refusal to leave the country. The IOC condemned the boycott, saying that the Games should not be concerned with politics, but Canada, Japan, China, West Germany and a multitude of other countries also joined America in boycotting the Games. Several other countries officially supported the boycott, but allowed their athletes to compete if they so chose. As a result, athletes from several nations, including Australia, France, United Kingdom, Ireland, Italy, Portugal, Spain, and Switzerland, marched under the Olympic Flag, rather than their national flags, and the Olympic anthem was played during their medal ceremonies, while some athletes, including those from New Zealand, marched under their NOC's flag.

Quick Facts

- Host city: Moscow, USSR
- Nations participated: 80
- Athletes participated: 5,179 (4,064 men; 1,115 women)
- Events organised: 21 sports; 203 events
- Opened by: President Leonid Brezhnev

The Opening Ceremony of the Olympic Games in Moscow, with Misha, the bear

Venue

New stadia and sports facilities were built, and existing ones, such as the Lenin Stadium, were modernised. In preparation for world scrutiny the domes on top of the Kremlin and many churches were totally restored. The Games were held at about six different stadia in various places.

The Olympic Village in Moscow

The Olympic cauldron in the Olympic Stadium

Facts

- Eighty nations participated in the 1980 Olympics — the lowest participation since 1956.
- Just over a fifth of the competitors were female — a higher percentage than at any previous Olympics. Also, 20 events were held for them — more than at any other Olympics.
- For the first time, Rhodesia participated under its current name, Zimbabwe, and Ceylon competed as Sri Lanka.
- Misha, the bear, was the first sporting mascot to achieve large-scale commercial success as merchandise. It was used extensively during the Games, and appeared on several products. It even appeared in its own TV animated cartoon!
- At the Closing Ceremony, the Los Angeles city flag — rather than the United States flag — was raised to symbolise the next host of the Olympic Games.
- Also during the Closing Ceremony, Misha appeared with a tear in its eye!

The Luzhniki Stadium in Moscow, Russia. Luzhniki is the biggest sports stadium in Russia and has a seating capacity of 78,360

Competition

Without the Americans and the other boycotting nations, the Games lost a lot of their sparkle, and certainly their competitive edge — the Soviets dominated the Games, winning 195 medals (80 gold). East Germany came next, with 126 medals (47 gold), but after that, Bulgaria trailed with 8 golds and 41 medals overall. However, despite the absence of so many countries, 36 world records, 39 European records and 74 Olympic records were set.

Memorable Winners

• For the first time, a tournament was scheduled for women in field hockey. Unfortunately, because of the boycott, only the Soviet Union was left to compete, so five weeks before the Games a late invitation went out to Zimbabwe. The team was selected less than a week before the Games and rushed to Moscow, where — to everyone's surprise — they won the gold medal!

• Every Olympics produces its oddities: in the men's coxless pairs rowing event both the gold and silver medal winning teams were identical twins! Bernd and Jorg Landvoigt of East Germany took first place, while Yuri and Nikolai Pimenov of Russia finished second.

• At 28, Allan Wells of Scotland was considered old for a sprinter. He finished the 100 m neck and neck with Silvio Leonard of Cuba, and after a photo finish, was declared the winner. He later went on to take silver in the 200 m.

• Aleksandr Dityatin of the Soviet Union won a medal in every one of the men's gymnastics finals — becoming the first athlete to win eight medals at one Olympic Games. He won three golds, four silver and one bronze medal.

• Cuba's super-heavyweight boxer Teófilo Stevenson became the first boxer to win the same division three times.

• Daley Thompson of the UK won his first Olympic decathlon.

Olympic marathon runners cross Moscow's Red Square with St. Basil's Cathedral in the background

Australian swimmer Lisa Curry poses for a photo during the 1980 Games. Curry is now an Australian media celebrity

Battle of the Brits

Despite pressure from then Prime Minister Margaret Thatcher to boycott the Games, British middle-distance runners Steve Ovett and Sebastian Coe (Chairman of London's successful 2012 Olympic bid) went head-to-head in the 800 m and 1,500 m in one of the best track and field rivalries of all time. Coe was the world-record holder for the 800 m, but he had to settle for a silver medal when Ovett worked his way through the pack to take the lead seventy metres from the finish, holding off his rival to take gold by three metres. Six days later, the tables were turned. Ovett, unbeaten over the 1,500 m and mile for three years, was most people's favourite to win the 1,500 m, but a determined Coe redeemed himself, storming to victory, and leaving Ovett to claim the bronze medal, behind East German Jürgen Straub.

Sebastian Coe of Great Britain wins the men's 1,500 m

The delegations standing in front of the mascot Misha

Top 10 Ranking Nations	Gold	Silver	Bronze	Total
Soviet Union	80	69	46	195
East Germany (GDR)	47	37	42	126
Bulgaria	8	16	17	41
Cuba	8	7	5	20
Italy	8	3	4	15
Hungary	7	10	15	32
Romania	6	6	13	25
France	6	5	3	14
Great Britain	5	7	9	21
Poland	3	14	15	32

1984 Los Angeles Olympics

The 1984 Summer Olympics, or the Games of the XXIII Olympiad, were held in Los Angeles, California, in the USA. They began on July 28 and concluded on August 12, and were officially opened by US President Ronald Reagan. After the 1980 American boycott of Moscow, the Soviets and several other countries did not attend in 1984.

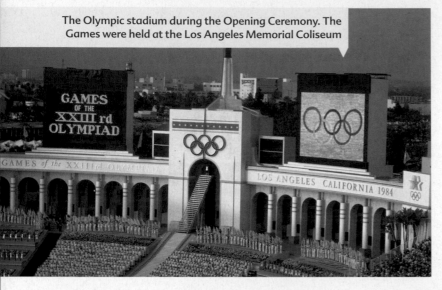

The Olympic stadium during the Opening Ceremony. The Games were held at the Los Angeles Memorial Coliseum

including Romania or Yugoslavia) boycotted the Games, leaving America to dominate the medal table. Iran and Libya boycotted for different reasons.

Though these countries boycotted the Games, the athletes of the People's Republic of China (China) participated in the Games after an absence of 32 years, competing alongside the Republic of China, (Chinese Taipei, commonly known as Taiwan). China won 32 medals, including 15 golds, on its return. The IOC is the only international organisation where the People's Republic of China and Chinese Taipei are jointly represented.

Out . . . and In

The Soviets, in retaliation for the US boycott of the 1980 Olympic Games, boycotted the 1984 Olympics. Along with the Soviet Union, East Germany and Cuba, fourteen other Communist countries (not

Quick Facts

- Host city: Los Angeles, California, USA
- Number of participating nations: 140
- Number of participating athletes: 6,829 (5,263 men; 1,566 women)
- Events organised: 21 sports; 221 events
- Opened by: President Ronald Reagan

A view of the Olympic stadium during the Opening Ceremony

Baseball was held as an exhibition sport for the sixth time. It finally debuted as a full medal discipline in Barcelona in 1992

An Olympic Model

Los Angeles was the only city to bid for the 1984 Games — probably as a result of the financial problems of 1976 in Montreal. There were plenty who criticised its bid, however, since instead of promising to build lots of new facilities and invest lots of money in the Games, it proposed reusing existing facilities wherever possible, and relied heavily on corporate sponsorship — these Games had 43 companies who were licensed to sell '*official*' Olympic products — and not on government investment. Nevertheless, despite those early concerns, the Los Angeles Games were well run, and because of the corporate sponsorship proved very successful financially. Indeed, they were the first Games since 1932 to generate a profit (around $225 million), and they became the model for future Olympics.

The mascot for the Games was Sam, the eagle. The cartooned eagle was designed by Walt Disney. He wears the costume of legendry Uncle Sam and holds the Olympic torch

The Effects of the Boycott

Some sports were worse hit by the boycott than others. Weightlifting was greatly affected by it: out of the world's top 100 ranked lifters, 94 were absent, as were all ten of the defending world champions in the ten weight categories.

Facts

- The Olympic torch was continuously carried by runners on foot for the last time.
- California was the home state of President Reagan.
- John Williams composed the theme song '*Olympic Fanfare and Theme*' for the Games. It became very popular and John Williams won a Grammy award for it. He also composed music for many films including, among others, *Jaws*, the *Star Wars* saga, *Superman*, the *Indiana Jones* films, and three *Harry Potter* films!
- Countries participating in the Olympics for the first time included Bangladesh, Bhutan, Mauritius and United Arab Emirates (UAE).
- Boycotting countries organised another major event in July-August 1984, called the '*Friendship Games.*'
- 11 athletes failed drug tests.
- Synchronised swimming and rhythmic gymnastics were added to the Olympic programme, as was men's wind surfing and a women's cycling road race. Tennis and basketball were held as exhibition sports.

Memorable Winners

• The star of the Olympics was Carl Lewis, who emulated Jesse Owens' 1936 feat by winning four golds in a single Olympiad — and in the same events! Making his first of four appearances in the Olympics, he won gold medals in the 100 m, 200 m, 4 x 100 m relay and the long jump.

• Taking a gold medal in the 400 m hurdles, Nawal El Moutawakel of Morocco became the first female Olympic champion of an Islamic nation, and the first athlete of her country to win a gold medal.

• British rower Steven Redgrave won his first Olympic gold — the first of five.

• Britain's Daley Thompson won his second consecutive decathlon gold, apparently just missing the world record. When photo finishes were checked his score was retroactively raised, giving him shares in the world record.

• Mary Lou Retton from the US became the first American — and the first gymnast outside Eastern Europe — to win the gymnastics all-around competition, with two perfect 10s.

The 400 m hurdle race for women was introduced in 1984 and Morocco's Nawal El Moutawakel won the gold

• Archer Neroli Fairhall of New Zealand was the first paraplegic athlete to take part in a medal event.

• The first Olympic women's marathon was won by Joan Benoit of the US. Swiss runner Gabi Andersen-Schiess, suffering from heat exhaustion, took five

Mary Lou Retton of the US took the all-around title in the women's gymnastics

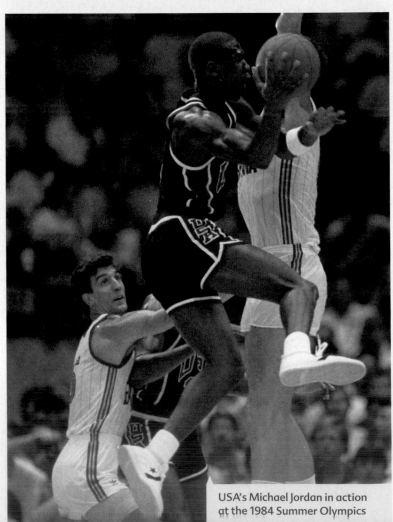
USA's Michael Jordan in action at the 1984 Summer Olympics

Li Ning from China won three gold, two silver and one bronze medal in different gymnastic events

minutes and 44 seconds to complete the final lap. She finished 37th, ahead of seven other runners.

• Sebastian Coe became the first repeat winner of the men's 1,500 m.

• Edwin Moses won the gold medal in the 400 m hurdles eight years after winning in 1976.

• Li Ning from the People's Republic of China won six medals in gymnastics, including three gold medals. He was nicknamed '*Prince of Gymnasts*' in China.

Controversy

In the women's 3,000 m track final, two of the main gold medal contenders collided. Zola Budd, an 18 year old from South Africa who had recently gained British citizenship, moved to the inside causing American Mary Decker to stumble and fall. Amid the boos of the crowd, Budd eventually finished in seventh place. She was initially disqualified but was later reinstated after officials reviewing a recording of the race concluded that she had not purposely done anything to stop Decker.

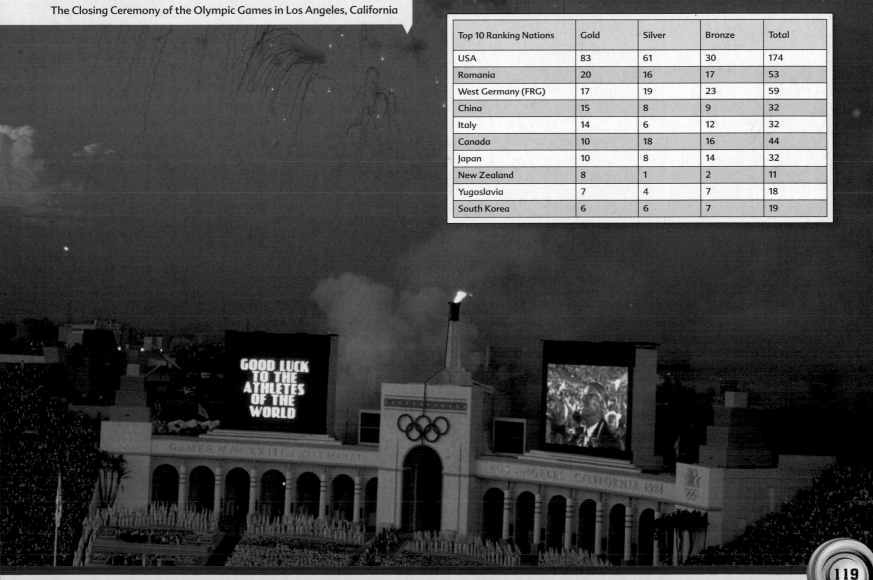

The Closing Ceremony of the Olympic Games in Los Angeles, California

Top 10 Ranking Nations	Gold	Silver	Bronze	Total
USA	83	61	30	174
Romania	20	16	17	53
West Germany (FRG)	17	19	23	59
China	15	8	9	32
Italy	14	6	12	32
Canada	10	18	16	44
Japan	10	8	14	32
New Zealand	8	1	2	11
Yugoslavia	7	4	7	18
South Korea	6	6	7	19

GOOD LUCK TO THE ATHLETES OF THE WORLD

1988 Seoul Olympics

The 1988 Summer Olympics, officially known as the Games of the XXIV Olympiad, were held in Seoul, South Korea, the second time the Games were held in Asia. They began on September 17 and ended on October 2. They were unmarked by the extensive boycotts of the previous two Games and were well organised.

The official emblem for the Seoul Olympics featured a *samtaeguk* pattern — a traditional pattern used in Korean artefacts and folk crafts

Politics and the Games

The Games had an impact on internal politics within South Korea, and were undoubtedly a catalyst for the transition of the country to a democracy. They allowed the world to see past the country's conflicts with its neighbour North Korea, to explore its culture and history, and opened up foreign trade.

There was no organised boycott of the 1988 Summer Olympics. They were boycotted by seven socialist nations, including Cuba, Seychelles, Nicaragua, North Korea, Ethiopia, Albania and Madagascar. Some of those stayed away in support

City of Seoul

The Olympic stadium during the Opening Ceremony. The stadium was designed by Kim Swoo Geun

Quick Facts

- Host city: Seoul, South Korea
- Nations participated: 159
- Athletes participated: 8,391 (6,197 men; 2,194 women)
- Events organised: 23 sports; 237 events
- Opened by: President Roh Tae-woo

of North Korea (officially at war with South Korea, they refused to participate when the IOC would not allow them to co-host the Games). Despite that, these Games saw the largest Olympic participation up till then. Records were set with 159 nations participating, 52 winning medals and 31 taking home gold medals.

Amateur Ruling

The ruling that only amateur athletes could compete in the Games was overturned in 1986 and at Seoul sporting bodies could now determine themselves whether or not 'professionals' could compete. This opened up the Seoul Games to professional athletes and enabled tennis to return to the Olympics after an absence of 64 years. Leaders of world tennis could now participate and Steffi Graf of West Germany added the Olympic title to her four Grand Slam victories of the year, beating Argentina's Gabriela Sabatini in the final.

The official Olympic torch used during the 1988 Summer Olympics in Seoul

A True Gentleman

In a wonderful example of good sportsmanship, Canadian sailor Lawrence Lemieux, was set to win a silver medal in the Finn class when he abandoned the race to save an injured competitor, finishing in 21st place. He was given a special award by the IOC in honour of his bravery and sacrifice.

Facts

- The Soviet Union and East Germany participated for the last time. The states of East Germany were included in the Federal Republic of Germany (FRG) in 1990, while the Soviet Union collapsed in 1991.
- Table tennis was introduced for the first time.
- These were the last Summer Games to hold an Opening Ceremony during the daytime due to hot summer weather.
- The Olympic torch was carried into the stadium by 76 year old Sohn Kee-chung, the winner of the 1936 marathon. When he had won that title, Sohn had been forced to enter using a Japanese name because Korea was occupied by Japan.
- The motto of these Games was 'harmony and progress.'
- Peace was the motif for the reverse of the medals. The front followed the standard design, while on the reverse side was a dove, flying with a laurel branch in its mouth.
- The official mascot for the 1988 Games was Hodori, the tiger. In Korean, ho means tiger and dori is a diminutive for boy. Hodori's female counterpart was called Hosuni.
- For the first time, the Paralympic Games took part in the same venue as the Olympics.

Hodori, the tiger, the Olympic Mascot for the 1988 Games, wearing a traditional Korean dance hat and holding the torch above his head

A Tragic Accident

In a tragic accident, a number of the live doves that were released during the Opening Ceremony as a symbol of world peace, were burned alive by the lighting of the Olympic cauldron. As a result of this, live doves are no longer used.

Controversy

Canadian Ben Johnson won the 100 m in a world record time of 9.79 seconds, but was disqualified and stripped of his gold medal two days later after he tested positive for stanozolol. He was the first well known athlete to be disqualified for using drugs. Carl Lewis was awarded the 100 m gold medal.

When American boxer Roy Jones Jr. lost the gold medal to South Korean fighter Park Si-Hun, there were allegations made that Korean officials had fixed the judging. Three of the judges were eventually suspended, and Jones Jr. was awarded the Val Barker Trophy, an award for the most impressive boxer of the Games.

The lighting of the Olympic cauldron

Aerial view of the Closing Ceremony of the 1988 Olympic Games in Seoul

Memorable Winners

• In the pool Kristin Otto of East Germany won 6 gold medals, while Matt Biondi of the USA won seven medals, including five gold in the 50 m freestyle, 100 m freestyle and all three relays, while he finished second in the 100 m butterfly (in which he was beaten by just .01 of a second by Anthony Nesty of Suriname who won his country's first Olympic medal and was also the first black to win individual swimming gold) and third in the 200 m freestyle.

In 1988 Christa Luding-Rothenburger won medals in both the Summer and Winter Games

Ben Johnson won the 100 m sprint in a world record time of 9.79 seconds, but was later disqualified

Jackie Joyner-Kersee throws a javelin during the 1988 Seoul Olympics, in which she set the still-standing heptathlon world record

• US sprinter Florence Griffith Joyner, nicknamed 'Flo-Jo,' won three golds in the 100 m, 200 m and 4 x 100 m relay and a silver in the 4 x 400 m relay, setting an Olympic record in the 100 m and a world record in the 200 m. Her sister-in-law, Jackie Joyner-Kersee, won the long jump and heptathlon.

• US diver Greg Louganis defended his springboard and tower diving titles, but only after hitting the springboard with his head in the 3 m event final.

• East Germany's Christa Luding-Rothenburger became the only athlete to win Olympic medals at the Winter and Summer Olympics in the same year, winning a silver in cycling to add to the two medals she had won in speed skating in Calgary. After that, the Winter and Summer Games were staggered.

Top 10 Ranking Nations	Gold	Silver	Bronze	Total
Soviet Union	55	31	46	132
East Germany (GDR)	37	35	30	102
USA	36	31	27	94
South Korea	12	10	11	33
West Germany (FRG)	11	14	15	40
Hungary	11	6	6	23
Bulgaria	10	12	13	35
Romania	7	11	6	24
France	6	4	6	16
Italy	6	4	4	14

1992 Barcelona Olympics

The 1992 Summer Olympic Games, officially known as the Games of the XXV Olympiad, were celebrated in Barcelona in Catalonia, Spain. They began on July 25 and concluded on August 9. They were unmarked by boycotts and were a spectacular success.

A New Era

The 1992 Games were the first in three decades without a boycott. There were some significant changes to the lineup. Athletes from most of the new countries of the former Soviet Union competed as the '*Unified Team*,' — although the winners were honoured under the flags of their own republics, while Lithuania, Estonia and Latvia made independent appearances. Following the fall of the Berlin Wall and the reunification of West and East Germany, Germany competed as a unified country under one flag for the first time since 1964, and a now apartheid-

Montjuic Communications Tower at Olympic Park, Barcelona, Spain

Herminio Menendez-Rodrigo of Spain with the torch at the Opening Ceremony of the 1992 Olympic Games held at Montjuic Stadium in Barcelona, Spain

free South Africa (constitutionally at least) was also welcomed back. The only sour note concerned Yugoslavia, which was banned from taking part in any team sports because of its military aggression against Croatia and Bosnia-Herzegovina, although individual athletes from the country were allowed to compete as '*independent Olympic participants*.'

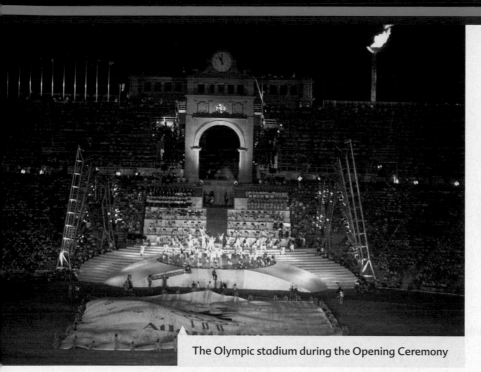
The Olympic stadium during the Opening Ceremony

A Message of Hope

In the 10,000 m final, Derartu Tulu, a black runner from Ethiopia, took the lead in the last lap and went on to win. At the finishing line, she waited for her opponent Elana Meyer, a white South African. They ran their lap of honour hand in hand in a message of hope for a new Africa.

Ceremonies

The Barcelona Olympics were seen as incredibly successful, both sportswise and culturally, and helped confirm Barcelona as a top tourist destination. The Games were opened in a dramatic fashion as Paralympic archer Antonio Rebollo lit the Olympic cauldron by firing a burning arrow towards the cauldron. His arrow passed over the cauldron, and ignited the gas which was emanating from it, so lighting the flame. The Opening Ceremony was both spectacular and stylish, with performances from legends Placido Domingo, Jose Carreras, and Montserrat Caballé who performed '*Barcelona*' — which had been written by Queen singer Freddie Mercury before

his death from AIDS in 1991. He had originally planned to sing it with her. The main song of the Closing Ceremony was written by Andrew Lloyd Webber and Don Black: '*Amigos Para Siempre*' (*Friends for Life*) was sung by Lloyd Webber's ex-wife Sarah Brightman and José Carreras.

Facts

- Barcelona was the birthplace of the then IOC President, Juan Antonio Samaranch.
- The IOC launched an appeal for the observance of the Olympic Truce for the first time.
- This was the last Olympics in which there were demonstration sports — Basque pelota, roller hockey, and taekwondo — as it was felt by the IOC that the Olympic programme had become too big to accommodate them adequately.
- Baseball was added as a full Olympic medal sport having appeared as an exhibition or demonstration sport at six previous Games.
- Badminton and women's judo were also added to the Olympic programme, while slalom canoeing returned after a 20 year absence.
- Cobi, a Catalan Sheepdog in Cubist style created by Javier Mariscal, was the official mascot of the 1992 Summer Olympics. He was used in advertisements by many of the Olympic sponsors and even had his own TV series. He appeared on souvenirs, referred to as '*Cobiana.*'

Barcelona'92

The 1992 emblem, designed by Josep Maria Trias from Barcelona, consisted of lines representing a human figure jumping an obstacle (made up of the five Olympic rings)

Cobi, the Catalan Sheepdog was the official mascot of the 1992 Summer Olympics

A basketball match between USA and Croatia during the 1992 Olympic Games. The USA team nicknamed the 'Dream Team' won the gold medal

The Professionals

The change in the amateur ruling truly came into play in 1992, as Coubertin's original Olympic ideal of amateurism became a thing of the past. Basketball saw the arrival of the legendary 'Dream Team.' Now that professional athletes were allowed to attend the Games, the US basketball team was made up of some of the most famous professional basketball players, such as Charles Barkley, Magic Johnson, Michael Jordan and Larry Bird. Not surprisingly, they dominated the competition to win gold!

A Helping Hand

In the first round of the men's 400 m race, Derek Redmond posted the fastest time. He also won his quarter-final. But in the semi-final, 175 m from the finish, Redmond tore his hamstring. As he struggled to finish, his father, Jim Redmond, came onto the track and helped Derek complete the race, letting him cross the line on his own. Sadly, as he had had assistance, he was disqualified, but he received a standing ovation from the crowd who admired his bravery and determination.

Derek Anthony Redmond injured himself during the 400 m semi-finals, but completed the full lap of the track with the help of his father

Fireworks set out during the Closing Ceremony

Gwen Torrence (l) of the US stands with teammates Carlette Guidry, Esther Jones and Evelyn Ashford after winning the gold medal in the 4 x 100 m relay during the Summer Olympics

Vitaly Scherbo, shown here performing on the rings, won six gold medals in the 1992 Summer Olympics

Memorable Winners

• Carl Lewis earned two gold medals with his third consecutive Olympic win in the long jump, and as a member of the world record breaking American 4 x 100 m relay team.

• Belarus's Vitaly Scherbo became the first gymnast to win six gold medals in the same Olympiad — four of them on the same day! This made him the top medal winner of the Games.

• At 32, Britain's Jamaican-born Linford Christie became the oldest champion of the Olympic 100 m.

• American Jackie Joyner-Kersee won her second consecutive heptathlon gold.

• In the pool, 18 year old Krisztina Egerszegi of Hungary won gold in the 100 and 200 m backstroke, and the 400 m individual medley.

• The winner of the women's 100 m sprint was American Gail Devers — two years previously doctors had nearly amputated her feet as a result of radiation treatment for Graves' disease.

Top 10 Ranking Nations	Gold	Silver	Bronze	Total
Unified Team	45	38	29	112
USA	37	34	37	108
Germany	33	21	28	82
China	16	22	16	54
Cuba	14	6	11	31
Spain	13	7	2	22
South Korea	12	5	12	29
Hungary	11	12	7	30
France	8	5	16	29
Australia	7	9	11	27

1996 Atlanta Olympics

The 1996 Summer Olympics of Atlanta were officially known as the Games of the XXVI Olympiad, but were also unofficially known as the Centennial Olympics, as it was 100 years since the first modern Games in Athens. They began on July 19 and concluded on August 4.

The Centennial Olympics

Some felt Athens should have had the right to host the Games because it marked the 100th anniversary of the modern Olympic Games, but some members of the IOC had concerns regarding the infrastructure of Athens and whether it could be ready in time. Athens would eventually be chosen to host the 2004 Games.

Atlanta used no public money to finance the Games, relying instead on ticket sales, commercial endorsements, advertising, and private money. Because of this, some felt the Games were over-commercialised affecting the atmosphere of the event. The Games cost around US$1.7 billion to host and helped greatly to modernise the city.

The torch base is made of the five Olympic rings. The flames evolve into a star symbolising the pursuit of excellence

Quick Facts

- Host city: Atlanta, Georgia, USA
- Nations participated: 197
- Athletes participated: 10,318 (6,806 men and 3,512 women)
- Events organised: 26 sports; 271 events
- Opened by: President Bill Clinton

Opening Ceremony at the Centennial Olympic Stadium, Atlanta

Record-Breaking Games

Despite issues with over-commercialism, technology problems and transportation issues, the Games nevertheless showcased many great athletes. For the first time in Olympic history, all the recognised National Olympic Committees at the time took part in the Games, making them the largest yet, with a record 197 nations attending of which a record-breaking 79 nations won medals and 53 won gold. The Games saw the participation of a large number of new countries, including Palestine and many of the Soviet countries now competing under their own name.

Delegations at the Olympic stadium

Facts

- Some 19.6 billion people (spectators and TV viewers) watched the Games.
- Five athletes failed drug tests and were disqualified.
- Softball (as a women-only sport), beach volleyball and mountain biking all debuted on the Olympic programme, as did women's soccer/football and lightweight rowing.
- In football, each team was allowed to include three professionals, regardless of age.
- There were no demonstration sports.
- One of the Olympiad's official themes, '*Summon the Heroes*,' was written by John Williams, making it the third Olympiad for which he has composed. It was sung at the Opening Ceremony by Celine Dion, while Gloria Estefan jointly composed the song '*Reach*' which she sung at the Closing Ceremony.
- Critics complained that the Olympic cauldron looked like a holder for french fries!
- The motto of the Games was '*The Celebration of the Century*.'

Muhammad Ali holding the torch before lighting the Olympic flame

Tragedy

On July 27, half-way through the Games, a terrorist's home-made bomb exploded in the Centennial Olympic Park in Atlanta, killing two people (one indirectly of a heart attack) and injuring 111. The world was filled with horror, but, as in Munich, the Games continued.

A Sporting Legend

In an emotional start to the Games, boxing legend Muhammad Ali lit the Olympic torch during the Opening Ceremony. He was suffering from Parkinson's Disease. He was later presented with a replacement gold medal — he had allegedly thrown the gold medal that he had won in the 1960 Summer Olympics into the Ohio River after being refused entry to a '*whites-only*' restaurant.

Memorable Winners

- America's Michael Johnson won an anticipated double in the 200 and 400 m men's races — breaking the world record in the 200 m, while Marie-Jose Perec of France achieved the same victories in the women's events.
- At the age of 35, Carl Lewis of the US collected his ninth Olympic gold medal when he won the long jump for the fourth consecutive time.
- Donovan Bailey of Canada set a world record to win the 100 m, and was part of the winning 4 x 100 m relay team which beat the US to win gold.
- The US women were on the verge of an historic win in the gymnastics team competition in Atlanta, but when one of their gymnasts fell on both her final vaults they were relying on Kerri Strug to nail her vault. Unfortunately, Kerri fell too, damaging an ankle. She bravely overcame the pain to take her final attempt, which was good enough to secure her team the gold medal!
- Amy Van Dyken became the first American woman to win four titles in a single Olympics when she won four gold medals in the pool.
- Turkish weightlifter Naim Suleymanoglu became the first weightlifter in history to win three consecutive Olympic titles.
- Kurt Angle won the gold medal in 100 kg (220 lb) freestyle wrestling for America even though he was suffering from a fractured neck that he had injured during the trials six months earlier.

Legendary athlete Carl Lewis won his final Olympic long jump gold medal

American wrestler Kurt Angle holds the American flag during the Games. Kurt won a gold medal in men's heavyweight freestyle wrestling

Izzy, short for 'Whatizit,' the official mascot for the 1996 Olympics, was a computer-generated figure that could morph into various shapes. It received a lot of criticism

- In tennis, Andre Agassi became the first male player to win the career Golden Slam by winning the men's singles tournament. His wife is the women's Grand Slam champion, Steffi Graf.

Marie-Jose Perec (r) with Merlene Ottey (l). Perec won gold in the 200 m and 400 m. Ottey won silver in the 100 m and 200 m

- In what was both the first and last time that Hong Kong won a medal as a British colony, Lee Lai Shan won a gold medal in sailing.
- Sailor Hubert Raudaschl from Austria became the first person ever to compete in nine Olympics.

Top 10 Ranking Nations	Gold	Silver	Bronze	Total
USA	44	32	25	101
Russia	26	12	16	63
Germany	20	18	27	65
China	16	22	12	50
France	15	7	15	37
Italy	13	10	12	35
Australia	9	9	23	41
Cuba	9	8	8	25
Ukraine	9	2	12	23
South Korea	7	15	5	27

American Michael Johnson won both the 200 m and 400 m events, becoming the first male Olympian to do so. He set a new world record of 19.32 seconds in the 200 m

(l to r) Leander Paes, Sergi Bruguera and Andre Agassi took the bronze, silver and gold respectively in men's singles

2000 Sydney Olympics

The 2000 Summer Games, although officially known as the Games of the XXVII Olympiad, were also known as the Millennium Games, or the Games of the New Millennium. They were celebrated in Sydney, New South Wales, Australia, the second time the Games had been held in the Southern Hemisphere, and ran from September 15 till October 1, which was early spring there.

The logo for the Sydney Games was also known as the '*Millennium Athlete.*' It featured the figure of an athlete using symbols like the boomerang and colours associated with Australia

The Millennium Games

The Sydney Games were the largest yet, with 10,651 athletes from 199 NOCs competing in 300 events. There were also four '*Individual Olympic Athletes*' from Timor. Korea (South Korea) and the Democratic People's Republic of Korea (North Korea) marched together under the same flag, and all the nations who had taken part in the previous Games attended, except for Afghanistan which was banned due to its discrimination against women under Taliban rule as well as its ban on sports of any kind.

The Games were well organised and successful, but are remembered above all for the friendliness and helpfulness of the host nation. In fact, the IOC awarded Sydney and its inhabitants with the '*Pierre de Coubertin Trophy*' in recognition of the collaboration and happiness shown by the people of Sydney during the event to all the athletes and visitors from around the world.

Quick Facts

- Host city: Sydney, Australia
- Nations participated: 199 + 4 individual athletes
- Athletes participated: 10,651 (6,582 men and 4,069 women)
- Events organised: 28 sports; 300 events
- Opened by: Sir William Deane, Governor General of Australia

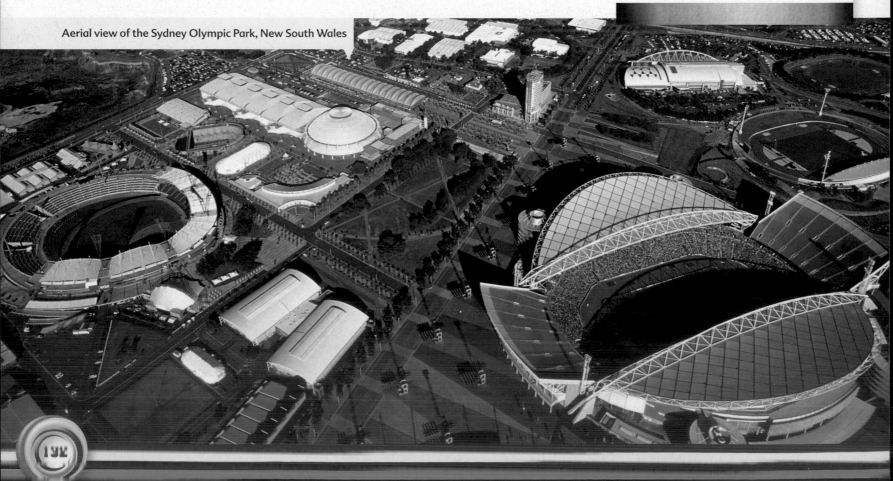

Aerial view of the Sydney Olympic Park, New South Wales

The three official Olympic mascots for Sydney 2000 were all native Australian animals, representing earth, air and water.

'Syd' (from Sydney) is a platypus. Syd represents the environment and captures the vigour and energy of Australia and its people

'Millie'(from Millennium) is an echidna. Millie has all the up to date information and is great with technology

'Olly' (from Olympic) is a kookaburra and epitomises the Olympic spirit of generosity

Facts

- The official motto of the Games was *Share the Spirit*.
- The Games reportedly cost AU$6.6 billion to host.
- The Games were a ratings disaster for American television because of the time zone.
- The World Anti-Doping Agency (WADA), an independent body, was at the Games to monitor all the procedures followed by the IOC, and the first tests to detect EPO (erythropoietin, a performance-enhancing drug) were carried out.
- Triathlon and taekwondo were two new additions to the Olympic programme.
- Women took part in the modern pentathlon and weightlifting for the first time in Olympic history.

Lighting the Flame

The 2000 Summer Games began with an impressive Opening Ceremony that highlighted Australian history from the aboriginal people to the settlers of the outback. Australian aboriginal Cathy Freeman lit the Olympic flame at the Opening Ceremony, a symbol of the nation's desire to reconcile its white and aboriginal populations. Ten days later, she won the 400 m gold medal in front of an ecstatic home crowd, the first athlete to light the Olympic flame and then win an Olympic gold medal in the same Games. The win was historical for the Australians: not only was it the first ever individual gold medal won by an Australian of aboriginal ancestry, but it was also the 100th Australian gold medal since the beginning of the modern Olympic Games in 1896.

Australian sprinter Cathy Freeman with the Olympic torch

Drugs Scandal

Marion Jones of the US became the first women to win five athletics medals at an Olympic Games, winning the 100 m / 200 m sprint double, as well as the 4 x 400 m relay together with bronzes in the long jump and 4 x 100 m relay. However, seven years later, she admitted that she took performance-enhancing drugs and has had to forfeit all those medals.

Vaulting Controversy

Halfway through the women's all-around competition, it was discovered that the vaulting horse, which should have been set at a height of 125 cm, had been set 5 cm too low. It was raised and those gymnasts who had already vaulted were given the opportunity to vault again. Unfortunately, the damage had already been done for some - 18 gymnasts had already vaulted, and many had performed poor vaults or even fallen, and had had their confidence shattered. Annika Reeder, a British gymnast, had to leave the arena in a wheelchair due to an injury. Olympic favourite, Svetlana Khorkina of Russia, had performed a poor vault and, believing that she had ruined her chances, had performed poorly on her next event, the uneven bars. Even though she had a chance to re-do her vaults, with a low score on bars too, her all-around hopes had already been eliminated.

Memorable Winners

• 17 year old Australian swimmer Ian Thorpe, nicknamed '*The Thorpedo*,' thrilled the home crowd when he won the gold medal in the

Marion Jones from the US won a gold in the 4 x 400 m relay in the 2000 Olympic Games but her medal was later taken away

The dazzling display of fireworks during the 2000 Sydney Olympics Opening Ceremony

Australian swimmer Ian Thorpe won the gold for the 400 m freestyle event. Italian Massimiliano Rosolino (l) won the silver and American Klete Keller (r) came third

400 m freestyle by breaking his own world record. His second gold came in the men's 4 x 100 m freestyle, and a third gold as part of the winning 4 x 200 m freestyle relay team. He completed his collection with a silver medal in the 200 m freestyle.

• Great Britain's Steve Redgrave became the first rower to win gold medals at five consecutive Olympics.

• Taking her medal tally to eight, Australia's champion swimmer Susie O'Neill (affectionately nicknamed 'Madame Butterfly') collected a gold and three silver medals at the Games. Paradoxically, she won the race she didn't expect to (the 200 m freestyle), and finished second in the one she expected to win (the 200 m butterfly), an event in which she had been unbeaten for six years.

• Birgit Fischer of Germany earned two gold medals in kayaking — the first woman to win medals 20 years apart.

• Michael Johnson of the US defended his 400 m title to bring his total number of Olympic gold medals to four. It would have been five, but the 4 x 400 m American winning relay team were later disqualified for taking performance enhancing drugs, although Johnson was not implicated.

British rower Steve Redgrave won his fifth gold medal in the 2000 Olympic Games

Top 10 Ranking Nations	Gold	Silver	Bronze	Total
USA	37	24	31	92
Russia	32	28	28	88
China	28	16	15	59
Australia	16	25	17	58
Germany	13	17	26	56
France	13	14	11	38
Italy	13	8	13	34
Netherlands	12	9	4	25
Cuba	11	11	7	28
Great Britain	11	10	7	28

Fireworks erupt over the Opera House during the Closing Ceremony, at which many popular singers and bands performed, including Kylie Minogue, INXS, Midnight Oil and Savage Garden. A river of lightning coursing down Parramatta River from Homebush Bay to Sydney Harbour marked the end of the Games

2004 Athens Olympics

The 2004 Summer Olympic Games, officially known as the Games of the XXVIII Olympiad, returned to Athens, Greece — the birthplace of both the ancient and modern Olympic Games — for the first time since the inaugural Games in 1896 (excluding the 1906 Intercalated Games). The Games began on August 13 and ran till August 29.

Aerial view of the Athens Olympic sports complex

Ready in Time

The Greeks had been disappointed that they had not been chosen to host the 1996 Games, but their bid for the 2004 Games addressed the IOC's concerns regarding whether or not they could have the infrastructure ready in time, and relied less heavily on the emotional angle that the Games should return to the home of both the ancient and the modern Games. Their bid was successful, but nevertheless, leading up to the 2004 Summer Games, there were still concerns about whether Athens would be ready on time. By late March 2004, some Olympic projects were still behind schedule. The main Olympic Stadium, due to hold the Opening and Closing Ceremonies, was completed only two months before the Games opened. However, despite worries from

The main Olympic stadium during the 2004 Olympic Games

Quick Facts

- Host city: Athens, Greece
- Nations participated: 201
- Athletes participated: 10,625 (6,296 men and 4,329 women)
- Events organised: 28 sports; 301 events
- Opened by: President Konstantinos Stefanopoulos

onlookers, the Greeks never doubted that they would deliver what they had promised, and by August 2004, all venues were ready: new tram and rail lines linking Athens with various sporting venues, upgrades to the ring road, expressway and Metro, a new international airport and various sporting facilities were all completed in time for the start of the Games, which were held at a mixture of modern and ancient venues, including the ancient Stadium at Olympia.

The official mascots for the 2004 Games were two figures, a sister and brother named Athena and Phevos. They were based on an ancient doll found at an archaeological site in Greece and are named after Athena, the Greek Goddess of Wisdom, Strategy and War, and Phoebos, the God of Light and Music, yet are children of modern times and so are supposed to be a link between Greek history and the modern Olympic Games.

The medal design was changed for the first time since the 1928 Games in Amsterdam. The design of the medal was created by Elena Votsi and showed the Goddess Nike inside the Panathinaiko stadium, where the first modern Games were held, bringing victory to the best athlete

The Olympic Flame

The lighting ceremony of the Olympic flame took place on March 25 in Ancient Olympia. For the first time, the torch relay passed through all five continents represented by the Olympic rings, following a route through 27 countries and 34 cities, including all former Summer Olympic host cities, carried by over 3,600 torch bearers.

Athenà Phèvos

Jacques Rogge (l), President (IOC), and Gianna Angelopoulos, the head of the Athens 2004 Olympic Games Organising Committee, unveil the Olympic torch for the 2004 Games

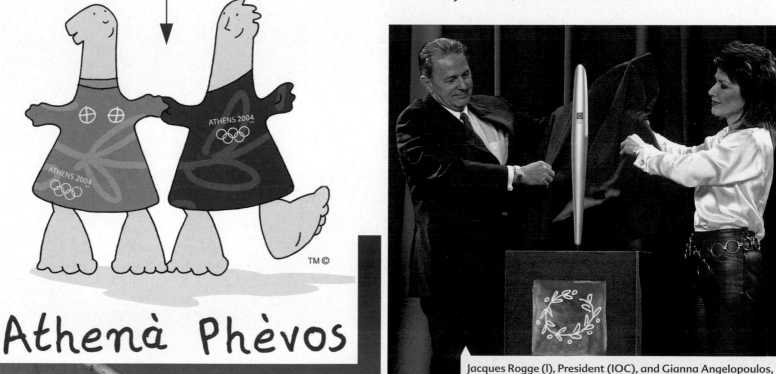

Facts

- Traditionally, in the Parade of Nations Greece leads the parade and the host team goes last. As Greece was the host, weightlifter Pyrros Dimas opened the Parade and the rest of the Greek athletes entered at the end.
- An official pop album of the Athens Olympics was released, titled '*Unity.*' It featured songs by popular artists such as Sting, Lenny Kravitz and Avril Lavigne.
- Afghanistan returned after its 2000 ban.
- The emblem of the 2004 Summer Games was a crown made from an olive tree branch. In the ancient Olympic Games, such crowns were awarded to Olympic winners. The olive tree is also the sacred tree of Athens.
- Women's wrestling was included in the program for the first time and in the fencing competition women competed in the sabre.
- The shot put events were held in Olympia, the site of the ancient Olympic Games.
- The archery competitions were staged in the Panathinaiko Stadium used for the 1896 Games.
- There was a demonstration of wheelchair racing in a joint Olympic/Paralympic event.

Kelly Holmes of Britain secures gold in the 1,500 m. Russian Tatyana Tomashova follows in second place

The lit-up Olympic rings at the Athens stadium during the Opening Ceremony, which began with a 28 second countdown — in honour of the fact that this was the 28th Olympiad — before a firework display. The Ceremony mainly showcased traditional Greek culture and history

Memorable Winners

- American swimmer Michael Phelps won 6 gold medals and set a single-Games record with 8 total medals!
- Hicham El Guerrouj of Morocco became the first runner since Paavo Nurmi in 1924 to win both the 1,500 m and the 5,000 m.
- Kelly Holmes won two athletic golds for Great Britain in the 800 m and the 1,500 m.
- Birgit Fischer of Germany came out of retirement to collect a gold medal in the K-4 500 m and a silver in the K-2 500 m, becoming the first woman to win gold medals in 6 different Olympics, the first woman to win gold 24 years apart and the first person in Olympic history to win two or more medals in five different Games. She has been both the youngest and oldest Olympic canoeing champion, and it is not surprising that she is considered to be the greatest woman canoeist of all time.
- Argentina's men's basketball team put an end to the domination of the US professionals, defeating them 89-81 in the semifinals, and

Liu Xiang of China won a gold in the 110 m hurdles. China had its most successful Olympics ever, winning 63 medals including 32 golds over 14 sports, including first-time titles in tennis, men's athletics, wrestling and canoeing

Nurcan Taylan of Turkey won gold and set a new world record in the women's 48 kg category weightlifting event. She was the first Turkish woman to win an Olympic gold

Hicham El Guerrouj celebrates his victory

The winning German kayaking team with Birgit Fischer (right)

going on to win against Italy in the final. Argentina also won men's football without conceding a goal, but in softball it was America who took the gold — outscoring their opponents by an aggregate of 51-1.

• Fani Halkia of Greece came out of retirement to thrill a home crowd by winning gold in the 400 m hurdles, shattering her own personal record and setting a new Olympic record in the process.

• The marathon race followed the same route as the 1896 race, beginning in Marathon and ending in Athens' Panathinaiko Stadium. Less than 7 km to go to the end of the race, the leader, Vanderlei de Lima of Brazil, who was hoping to win his country's first marathon gold, was pushed off the course by a spectator. Helped back onto the track, De Lima still managed to finish in third place, winning a bronze medal and was awarded the Pierre de Coubertin Medal in recognition of his Olympic spirit.

• The US women's 4 x 200 m swimming team won the gold medal. They broke the world record set by the German Democratic Republic in 1987.

Adriana Carmona (r) of Venezuela and Natalia Silva of Brazil during the women's over 67 kg Taekwondo repechage match

Winners of the 4 x 100 m swimming freestyle relay

Heightened Security

The 2004 Games were the first since the terror attacks of September 11, 2001, and so concerns about terrorism were much higher. The Greek budget for security at the Olympics was €970 million (US$1.2 billion). Approximately 70,000 police officers patrolled Athens and the Olympic venues during the Olympics.

Watched by Billions

The popularity of the Games soared to new heights as 3.9 billion people were able to watch the action on television, while, for the first time, audiences could watch video coverage of the Olympics over the Internet, although there were restrictions placed on it to protect broadcasting contracts in other areas. In America, coverage of the Games was censored during the Opening Ceremony: a topless Minoan priestess was shown only briefly — the breasts having been pixelated digitally and men dressed as ancient Greek statues were only shown above the waist!

Top 10 Ranking Nations	Gold	Silver	Bronze	Total
USA	36	39	28	103
China	32	17	14	63
Russia	27	27	38	92
Australia	17	16	16	49
Japan	16	9	12	37
Germany	13	16	20	49
France	11	9	13	33
Italy	10	11	11	32
South Korea	9	12	9	30
Great Britain	9	9	12	30

A light show at the Closing Ceremony of the Paralympic Games. The 2004 Paralympics were held from September 17 to September 28. Around 3,800 athletes took part from 136 nations in 519 events

2008 Beijing Olympics

The 2008 Summer Olympics, or the Games of the XXIX Olympiad, took place in Beijing, China — the third time that the Summer Olympic Games had been held in Asia, but the first to be held in China, the world's most populous nation with over 1.3 billion people. The Games began on August 8 and ran till August 24.

Record Breaking Games

Out of a possible total of 205 NOCs, all but one — Brunei — participated, some for the first time, and many of them won medals for the first time — an unprecedented 86 countries won at least one medal during the Games. More than 40 world records and over 130 Olympic records were broken. The Games were extremely well organised and 4.7 billion viewers worldwide tuned in to some of the TV coverage.

Beijing invested heavily in infrastructure prior to the Games, in preparation for the arrival of both athletes and hordes of visitors. Beijing's airport saw the addition of the new Terminal 3, the world's largest airport terminal, designed by renowned architect Norman Foster, while the city's subway doubled its capacity and size. Some existing sporting facilities were used, while others were new, such as the National Stadium, nicknamed the 'Bird's Nest,' where much of the athletics and the Opening

Inside view of the National Stadium

and Closing Ceremonies were held, and the environmentally friendly National Swimming Centre, known as the 'Water Cube' — both stunning symbols of the new Beijing. Although the Beijing Organising Committee claimed that its total

Quick Facts

- Host city: Beijing, China
- Nations participated: 204
- Athletes participated: 10,942 (6,305 men, 4,637 women)
- Events organised: 28 sports; 302 events
- Opened by: President Hu Jintao

The Beijing National Stadium, nicknamed the Bird's Nest, was designed for the Games and the Paralympics. Its capacity during the Games was 91,000. It cost US$423 million to build

Jade was used for the first time for the Olympic medals. All Olympic medals must be at least 60mm in diameter and 3mm thick, but the ones given out at Beijing in 2008 had a diameter of 70mm and were 6mm thick, with the front displaying the winged goddess of victory in the Panathinaiko Stadium and the back showed the Beijing Games emblem surrounded by an inset jade circle. The winners' medal was made of gold weighing not less than six grams and the runner's-up medal was made of pure silver. The medals were noble and elegant, blending traditional Chinese culture and Olympism

spending on the Games was in line with that of Athens in 2004, there were rumours that the Games had cost as much as US$ 40 billion to host!

Concerns

In an effort to improve the air quality of Beijing — a major concern in the lead up to the Games — restrictions were placed on construction sites, gas stations, and on the use of commercial and passenger vehicles in the city. Nevertheless, because of worries about air quality affecting athletes, some countries set up offshore training camps to avoid the pollution in Beijing. In an attempt to reduce air pollution and also to try to ensure rain free Closing and Opening Ceremonies, China launched rockets with silver iodide over Beijing to induce rain storms. In the event, the air quality, although the worst in Olympics history, was not as bad as many had feared beforehand.

The official emblem of Beijing 2008 entitled 'Chinese Seal, Dancing Beijing' combined the traditional Chinese seal and calligraphy with sporting features, transforming the elements into a human figure running forward and embracing triumph

The mascots of Beijing 2008 Olympics were five *Fuwa* — *Fuwa* means 'good-luck doll' in Chinese. Designed for children, the Fuwa represent four of China's most popular animals and the Olympic Flame, and each has one of the five colours of the Olympic rings as their main colour. Beibei is the Fish, Jingjing is the Panda, Huanhuan is the Olympic Flame, Yingying is the Tibetan Antelope and Nini is the Swallow, and when you put the first syllable of each of their names together — Bei Jing Huan Ying Ni — they say "*Beijing Welcomes You*"

The five Fuwa, mascots for the Beijing 2008 Olympics: l-r, Beibei, Jingjing, Huanhuan, Yingying and Nini

Facts

- The slogan for the Games was 'One World, One Dream.'
- The 2008 Games were the first to be produced and broadcast entirely in high definition (HD) by the host broadcaster.
- Some swimming and gymnastics events were scheduled early in the morning so that they could be broadcast live during television prime time in the US.
- In cycling, the road race followed the Great Wall of China and passed in front of the Forbidden City.

Chris Hoy became the first British athlete in 100 years to win three golds in a single Olympiad, when he won the men's keirin, the men's team sprint and also the men's individual sprint

The Torch Relay

The relay, with the theme 'Journey of Harmony,' proved anything but! It followed a route passing through every continent except Antarctica (being carried to the top of Mount Everest in the process) — around 137,000 km (85,000 miles), the longest Olympic torch relay — but it was plagued with protests about China's human rights record, particularly in Tibet and became highly politicised. The Olympic torch was designed to remain lit in 65 km per hour winds, and in heavy rain, but they had not reckoned on protestors: in Paris, police had to extinguish the torch on a number of occasions, although the flame itself was kept alight in a safety lantern.

South African swimmer Natalie Du Toit, whose left leg was amputated after a motor scooter accident, was one of two Paralympians to compete at the 2008 Summer Olympics in Beijing. She finished 16th in the women's 10 km marathon. Natalia Partyka of Poland, born without a right forearm, competed in table tennis

The Opening Ceremony

The Opening Ceremony officially began at 8:08 pm on August 8, 2008 (08.08.08) in the Beijing National Stadium — the number 8 is associated with prosperity and confidence in Chinese culture. It was a celebration of ancient Chinese art and culture, involving more than 15,000 performers.

Fireworks lit up the sky at the spectacular Opening Ceremony of the Beijing Olympics on August 8, 2008

A Swimming Sensation

On the first day of competition, swimmer Michael Phelps of the US set a world record in the first round of the men's 400 m individual medley, starting as he meant to go on. By the end of the Games, he had set world records in seven out of his eight events and an Olympic record in the 100 m butterfly. With his Games tally of eight golds, he also broke Mark Spitz' 1972 record for most gold medals in one Olympics, and for most career gold medals (14) for an Olympian. His medal total (16) is second only to the 18 which Soviet gymnast Larissa Latynina won, including nine gold.

Memorable Winners

• Jamaica's Usain Bolt secured the popular title of 'World's Fastest Man' when he set new world records to win both the 100 m and 200 m sprints. He claimed a third gold medal and record as a member of the Jamaican 4 x 100 m relay team. Michael Johnson described his run as "the greatest 100 m performance in the history of the event." Jamaica's women were also successful in the women's 100 m, with Shelly-Ann Fraser taking gold, and Sherone Simpson and Kerron Stewart tying for silver.

• Rebecca Adlington's 400 m freestyle win was Britain's first Olympic swimming title since 1988. She then smashed the world record to win the 800 m freestyle, and became the first British swimmer to win more than one gold medal at a single Olympic Games since 1908.

• China had it all their own way in the table tennis, winning every medal that was available to them: gold, silver and bronze in the men's and women's singles, and gold in the men's and women's team tournaments.

• The British team of Tom James, Steve Williams, Peter Reed and Andrew Triggs-Hodge won the men's coxless fours, making it the third time in a row that Great Britain has won gold in this event.

Michael Phelps with his gold medal. Phelps won eight medals in swimming events in the 2008 Games

Ben Ainslie of Britain successfully defended his Olympic sailing title, winning gold in the Finn class

Jamaican athlete Usain Bolt wins the men's 200 m race

Rebecca Adlington of Great Britain, poses with her gold medal after winning the women's 800 m freestyle

Yelena Isinbayeva of Russia successfully defended her 2004 pole vault gold, setting a world record of 5.05 m on her third attempt

• In tennis, Switzerland's Roger Federer teamed up with Stanislas Wawrinka to win his first Olympic medal in the men's doubles, while Rafael Nadal defeated Chile's Fernando González to win the men's singles, taking home Spain's first Olympic tennis gold.
• Britain's Rebecca Romero won a cycling gold to become one of the few athletes with medals in two distinct disciplines, the 2008 medal being added to her 2004 rowing silver.

The Sports

Several new events were added to the Olympic programme in Beijing, including a totally new cycling discipline — BMX (Bicycle Motorcross) — with men's and women's individual races. Women's events increased from 125 to 127 (out of 302), including the women's 3,000 m steeplechase, women's team events in the foil and sabre fencing disciplines, and the gruelling 10 km marathon swim (this event was also new for men). In table tennis, team events replaced doubles. Altogether, two sports were open only to men — baseball and boxing — while one sport and one discipline were open only to women — softball and synchronised swimming.

The Closing Ceremony

The 2008 Closing Ceremony, beginning at 8.00pm on August 24, 2008, was as spectacular as the Opening Ceremony had been, although it was generally seen as being more lighthearted. Part of the Ceremony included the hand over of the Games from Beijing to London. Guo Jinlong, the Mayor of Beijing handed over the Olympic flag to the Mayor of London, Boris Johnson. This was followed by a performance organised by the London Organising Committee for the Olympic Games, featuring guitarist Jimmy Page and singer Leona Lewis, footballer David Beckham . . . and a double decker bus!

Nelson Evora of Portugal won a gold in the men's triple jump

Top 10 Ranking Nations	Gold	Silver	Bronze	Total
China	51	21	28	100
USA	36	38	36	110
Russia	23	21	28	72
Great Britain	19	13	15	47
Germany	16	10	15	41
Australia	14	15	17	46
South Korea	13	10	8	31
Japan	9	6	10	25
Italy	8	9	10	27
France	7	16	18	41

Fireworks over the National Stadium during the Closing Ceremony of the Games

2012 London Olympics

The 2012 Summer Olympic Games will be officially known as the Games of the XXX Olympiad. They are scheduled to take place in London, United Kingdom, from July 27 to August 12, 2012. With these Games, London will become the first city to officially host the modern Olympic Games three times.

Hosting the Games

London, bidding against Moscow, New York City, Madrid and Paris, was elected as the host city for the Summer Olympics in 2012 on 6 July 2005. The successful bid was headed by former Olympic champion Sebastian Coe. The London 2012 Olympic Games will feature 26 sports, which break down into 38 disciplines and around 300 events. (The 2012 Paralympic Games programme has 20 sports and 21 disciplines.) When London originally bid, there were 28 sports on the programme, but the IOC voted to drop baseball and softball from the 2012 Games two days after it selected London as the host city. Since then, women's boxing has been added to the programme for the very first time.

Venues

The 2012 Olympics will take place in London, mostly in Stratford, an area of East London, in the newly constructed Olympic Park, which will contain many new sports venues, as well as the Olympic Village itself. Certain events will take place elsewhere in the capital, such as the Greenwich Millennium Dome for gymnastics and Horse Guards Parade in central London for beach volleyball, while some sports will be held outside Greater London, including the sailing, which will be held in Weymouth and Portland on the English south coast, rowing and the canoe sprint, which will be held at Eton Dorney near Windsor Castle, and the football tournament, which will be staged at several grounds around the UK.

Wellington Arch, Hyde Park. Hyde Park will be used as a venue for the triathlon and the 10 km marathon swim

The Aquatics Centre

The Aquatics Centre in the Olympic Park features a spectacular wave-like roof that is 160 m long and up to 80 m wide, giving it a longer single span than Heathrow Terminal 5. For the Games, two temporary wings will accommodate extra spectators. It has a 50 m competition pool, a 25 m competition diving pool, a 50 m warm-up pool and a 'dry' warm-up area for divers. It will be used after the Games by the local community, clubs and schools, as well as elite swimmers.

The design for the Aquatics Centre where swimming and diving events will be held

The Olympic Stadium

The Olympic Stadium will be the 2012 centrepiece, staging the Opening and Closing Ceremonies as well as the track and field events. Located in the south of the Olympic Park on an 'island' site, with waterways on three sides, it will be accessed via five bridges. For the Games, it will have a capacity of 80,000: 25,000 spectators will be seated in its permanent lower tier, while a demountable upper tier will hold a further 55,000. The Stadium can be scaled back to 25,000 seats later as required. English Premier League football club, West Ham United, has been selected as the preferred bidder to assume ownership of it after the Games. The club has stated that it is happy for the athletics track to be kept and for the venue to be used for a variety of sporting events and concerts.

A simulation of the London Olympic Stadium

The Velodrome

The Velodrome will have seating for 6,000 spectators, with 3,500 seats located around the track in the lower tier, and a further 2,500 seats suspended in two upper tiers within the two curves of the venue's roof. The glass wall between the lower concrete and upper tiers gives spectators a 360-degree view across the Olympic Park and allows people outside to see the sporting action taking place inside. A new 400 m BMX circuit will stage the BMX competition, and a new mountain bike course and road-cycle circuit will subsequently be added to create the VeloPark — a new cycling 'hub' for East London, sports clubs and elite athletes.

Olympic Park Venues

Hockey will be played on pitches in a temporary Hockey Centre located in the Olympic Park. They will also be used for Paralympic 5-a-side and 7-a-side football. Other temporary facilities will include a Water Polo Arena next to the Aquatics Centre, with competition and warm-up pools for the water polo tournament. One of the largest-ever temporary venues built for any Games will be the Basketball Arena, which will host not only the basketball, but also some of the handball (early rounds will take place in a new Handball Arena) and, during the Paralympics, will be the venue for wheelchair basketball and wheelchair rugby.

Wembley Stadium

Wembley Stadium, with a capacity of 90,000, will host the finals of the women's and men's football tournaments. The new stadium's arch soars over 130 m into the sky, more than four times the height of the towers of the old stadium. It is the biggest of the six stadiums staging the 2012 Olympic Football competition. The others are Old Trafford in Manchester, Millennium Stadium in Cardiff, St James' Park in Newcastle, Hampden Park in Glasgow, and City of Coventry Stadium.

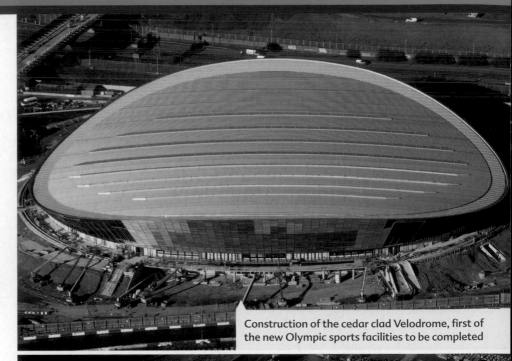

Construction of the cedar clad Velodrome, first of the new Olympic sports facilities to be completed

The temporary Basketball Arena — it is hoped that it will be reused elsewhere in the UK after the Games.

Wembley Stadium, venue for the gold medal events in both the men's and women's football

Other Venues

Other iconic London landmarks will also feature in the 2012 Summer Games. Horse Guards Parade will have more sand brought in and a temporary arena erected to stage the beach volleyball events; the Royal Artillery Barracks will be the venue for shooting; the Mall will see the start and finish of both the marathon and the road cycling races; Hyde Park will host the triathlon and the marathon; and Hampton Court will host the start and finish of the road cycling time trials. Tennis will be held at Wimbledon, the only remaining major grass-court tennis venue in the world and the setting for the famous Wimbledon tennis tournament since 1877, while archery will be held at Lord's Cricket Ground. Other events will be held at Earls Court, Greenwich Park, ExCeL in London's Docklands, Wembley Arena and North Greenwich Arena.

The British beach volleyball teams test out their Olympic Venue at Horse Guards Parade in 2008, as members of the Household Cavalry Mounted Regiment change guard

The Logo

The logo for the London Games was designed by Wolff Olins and is a representation of the number 2012, with the Olympic Rings embedded within the zero. For the first time, the same essential logo will be used for both the Olympic and Paralympic Games. The logo has been used in a variety of colours, even including the Union Jack flag, but the standard colours are green, magenta, orange and blue. There were protests raised by Iran, who believed that the logo spelt out the word Zion and found that offensive, but they have nevertheless agreed to participate in the Games.

The Mascots

The official mascots for the 2012 Summer Olympic and Paralympic Games were unveiled on 19 May 2010. Wenlock (named after the Shropshire town of Much Wenlock, which held a forerunner of the current Olympic Games) and Mandeville (after Stoke Mandeville in Buckinghamshire where the Paralympic Games were first held) are animations depicting two drops of steel from a steelworks in Bolton — supposedly the last two drops of British steel used for the London 2012 Olympic Stadium. The 'back-story' behind the mascots was written by the author Michael Morpurgo.

Money Matters

In March 2007, a budget of £5.3 billion was announced by the Minister for Olympics to cover building the venues and infrastructure for the Games. (A budget for the wider regeneration of the Lower Lea Valley of £1.7 billion was announced alongside this.) Other costs were also announced, including an overall additional contingency fund of £2.7 billion, security and policing costs of £600 million, VAT of £800 million and elite sport and Paralympic funding of nearly £400 million. Including the money for the regeneration of Lower Lea Valley, the total budget for the Games was £9.345 billion.

The costs of mounting the Games are separate from those for building the venues and infrastructure, and redeveloping the land for the Olympic Park. While the Games are privately funded, with money raised by a combination of sponsorship, merchandising, ticketing and broadcast rights, the venues and Park costs are to be met largely by public money.

The National Lottery will contribute almost £2.2 billion towards London 2012, of which £750 million will come from specially designated lottery games. The money will help to fund the new sports facilities including the Olympic Stadium, VeloPark, Aquatics Centre, Handball Arena and Hockey Centre.

Legacy

One of the keystones of the London 2012 bid was the concept of legacy — ensuring that when the Games were over, the people of the country were left with improved infrastructure, new housing and recreational areas, and better sporting facilities and opportunities.

Stratford in East London, as one of the capital's most economically deprived areas, was already earmarked for redevelopment. It will benefit immensely from the new Olympic Park, which will provide not only new sports facilities, transportation improvements and parkland, but will also eventually provide much needed housing.

After the Games, the Olympic Park will become the Queen Elizabeth Olympic Park and it is planned that 8,000 new family homes will be built on the park alongside new schools, health centres and commercial businesses. The northern area of the park, where development will first start, will be more park-like, with canals, while the southern end near the Olympic Stadium and the ArcelorMittal Orbit tower will be more town-like, and will have plazas that will host concerts and events.

During the Games, the Athletes' Village in the Olympic Park will accommodate around 17,000 athletes and officials, along with shops, restaurants, medical, media and leisure facilities and large areas of open space, while after the Games, it will be transformed into 2,800 new homes.

Infrastructure

Plans for improvement in public transport include the expansion of the London Overground's East London Line, upgrades to the Docklands Light Railway and the North London Line, and the introduction of a new high-speed rail service. Transport for London also proposed the construction of a cable car across the River Thames, to link 2012 Olympics venues, carrying 2,500 people an hour 50 m above the river — although this raised safety concerns as it was to cross through an enlarged public safety '*crash zone*' around London City Airport.

An impression of the 2012 Olympic Games in London

Simulation of the ArcelorMittal Orbit, in the Olympic Park in Stratford, London, designed by artist Anish Kapoor and structural designer Cecil Balmond — a gigantic observation tower, around 115 m high, which will allow visitors to view the whole Olympic Park and London's skyline from two observation platforms. The steel sculpture will be Britain's largest piece of public art, with a continuous looping lattice of tubular steel at the cutting edge of architecture and engineering

GREAT OLYMPIANS

Profiles of some of the greatest Olympians of all time

Robert Garrett (1896-1900)

The first American Olympic Champion in discus and shot put was born in Baltimore County, Maryland. An undergraduate at Princeton University, he excelled in track and field athletics. Although he planned to participate only in shot put and jumping events, his professor convinced him to give the Greek sport of discus throwing a try. Garrett got a blacksmith to design a discus to practice with, but it weighed too much to throw properly. However, when Garrett discovered that a real discus was much lighter, he decided to participate. After a couple of clumsy tries, his final throw won him the gold medal. He beat the Greeks at their own game and became a hero back home! He won three other medals that year, and two more in the 1900 Games, making him the greatest Princeton Olympian of all time.

Robert Garrett

Winning Streak

Olympic medals: 6

1896 (Athens)

- Gold Medal: shot put, discus throw
- Silver Medal: high jump, long jump

1900 (Paris)

- Bronze Medal: shot put, standing triple jump

Other Highlights

- Won the IC4A (Intercollegiate Association of Amateur Athletes of America) Championship for shot put in 1897

Raymond Ewry (1900-1908)

Ray Ewry had polio when he was a child, and doctors feared he would be paralysed for life. Instead, Ewry went on to become one of the great Olympians. He worked tremendously hard to overcome polio, often practising leg exercises from morning till evening. After graduating from University, he became a member of the New York Athletic Club and an excellent standing jumper. In the 1900 Olympics held in Paris, Ewry won gold medals in all three standing jumps. He eventually won a total of 10 gold medals in his Olympic career.

* The IOC no longer recognises medals or records won at the Intercalated Games held in Athens in 1906.

Winning Streak

Olympic medals: 10

1900 (Paris)

- Gold Medal: standing high jump, standing long jump, standing triple jump

1904 (St. Louis)

- Gold Medal: standing high jump, standing long jump, standing triple jump

1906 (Intercalated Games, Athens)*

- Gold Medal — standing high jump, standing long jump

1908 (London)

- Gold Medal — standing high jump, standing long jump

Other Highlights

- Won 15 National Championships for standing jump events between 1898 and 1910
- Set world records for standing high jump and standing long jump

John Flanagan (1900-1908)

Winning Streak

Olympic medals: 4

1900 (Paris)
- Gold Medal: hammer throw

1904 (St Louis)
- Gold Medal: hammer throw
- Silver Medal: 56-pound weight throw

1908 (London)
- Gold Medal: hammer throw

Other Highlights
- Broke at least 16 world records for hammer throw from 1895-1909
- Won 13 AAU titles — 7 for hammer throw and 6 for the 56-pound weight throw

John Flanagan was born in Ireland and was already Britain's hammer throw Champion when he moved to the US in 1896. The American sport had significant differences — in Britain, Flanagan had been used to using a wooden-handled hammer in a 9-foot circle, whilst in the US he had to get used to using one with a pliable handle in a 7-foot circle. It didn't stop him! This burly policeman went on to win three gold medals for hammer throw and one silver medal for 56-pound weight throw. He also competed in discus throw and tug-of-war events. In the 1908 Olympics, he broke his own world record with a hammer throw of 170 ft, 4.5 inches. At the age of 41, he broke his own record again, becoming the oldest person to break a world record in athletics at the time.

Eric Lemming (1900-1912)

This Swedish athlete had many talents, but he became famous as the first great javelin champion of the modern Olympics. He competed in a variety of events, including high jump, long jump, pole vault, triple jump and discus throw. His journey began in the 1900 Olympics where he competed in four events but did not win a medal (at the time, javelin throw was not an Olympic event). At the 1906 Intercalated Games he won medals for javelin, tug-of-war, pentathlon and shot put.

Winning Streak

Olympic medals: 7

1906 (Intercalated Games, Athens)
- Gold Medal: javelin throw (freestyle)
- Bronze Medal: tug-of-war, shot put, pentathlon

1908 (London)
- Gold Medal: javelin throw, javelin throw (freestyle)

1912 (Stockholm)
- Gold Medal: javelin throw

Other Highlights
- Set the world record for javelin throw in 1899, when he was 19.
- Set 14 javelin throw world records in total.

Meyer Prinstein (1900-1906)

Born in Poland and brought up in New York City, Meyer (or Myer) Prinstein was the greatest long jumper of his time. He held the world record for the long jump and won gold medals in the 1900 and 1904 Olympics. In 1900 he took gold in the triple jump, but had to settle for silver in the long jump as he would not compete in the the final as it was held on a Sunday. Four years later, he took gold in both events, the only athlete to win both events in the same Games. He also competed in two running races — the 60 m and 400 m — coming fifth in both. In the 1906 Intercalated Games, he again won the long jump, beating world record holder, Peter O'Connor.

Winning Streak

Olympic medals: 5

1900 (Paris)
- Gold Medal: triple jump
- Silver Medal: long jump

1904 (St Louis)
- Gold Medal: long jump, triple jump

1906 (Intercalated Games, Athens)
- Gold Medal: long jump

Other Highlights
- Set 2 world records for long jump: 7.235 m in 1898, and 7.5 m in 1900
- Was National Long Jump Champion 4 times

Étienne Desmarteau (1904)

A policeman from Montreal, Canada, Étienne Desmarteau lost his job because he decided to participate in the 1904 Olympics! His boss didn't want to give him a leave of absence, but Desmarteau went to St. Louis in the US anyway. Fortunately, the results were worth it. A member of the Montreal Athletic Club, Desmarteau took part in the 56-pound (26 kg) weight throwing competition. He was a top contender, as he had come first in the Amateur Athletic Union (AAU) weight-throwing event in 1902. Desmarteau repeated this performance in the Olympic Games and beat record-holder John Flanagan. After his victory, Desmarteau got his job back, too, but sadly, he died the following year.

Winning Streak

Olympic medals: 1

1904 (St Louis)
- Gold Medal: 56-pound weight throw

Other Highlights
- Defeated Olympic Champion John Flanagan, and won the AAU weight throwing title in 1902
- Set a world record for the 56-pound weight throw in 1905

Archie Hahn (1904-1906)

Archie Hahn was one of the best sprinters of the 20th century. He first shot to fame in 1903 when he won the American and Canadian Championships. That was just the beginning of stardom for him. In the 1904 Olympics he thrilled his many fans by winning the 60 m, 100 m and 200 m gold medals. He repeated his 100 m victory in the 1906 Intercalated Games held in Athens, a feat which was not equalled until 1988 when Carl Lewis won the 100 m for the second consecutive Games (after the disqualification of Ben Johnson).

Winning Streak

Olympic medals: 4

1904 (St Louis)
- Gold Medal: 60 m, 100 m, 200 m

1906 (Intercalated Games, Athens)
- Gold Medal: 100 m

Other Highlights
- Broke world record for 100-yard dash in 1901 (9.8 secs) and 200 m (straight track) (21.6 secs) in 1904
- Won the AAU title for the 100-yard dash in 1903 and for 220 yards in 1903 and 1904

Martin Sheridan (1904-1908)

Winning Streak

Olympic medals: 9

1904 (St Louis)
- Gold Medal: discus throw

1906 (Intercalated Games, Athens)
- Gold Medal: discus throw, shot put
- Silver Medal: standing high jump, standing long jump, stone throw

1908 (London)
- Gold Medal: discus throw, discus throw (Greek Style)
- Bronze Medal: standing long jump

Other Highlights
- Set 15 'world's best' records for discus throw. His 1905 record went unbroken for 7 years
- Won 11 national titles and the AAU discus throwing event 4 times
- Was declared the All-round AAU Champion 3 times

Born in Ireland, Martin Sheridan moved to the US and went on to win a total of five gold medals for his new country. He was known as the best all-around athlete of the Irish American Athletic Club and, indeed, the entire country, which is not surprising when you consider that he won gold medals for shot put, discus throw and Greek discus, as well as other medals for stone throw, standing high jump and standing long jump. This New York Police Department officer was known as one of the greatest track and field athletes in the world.

Ralph Rose (1904-1912)

A towering 6 feet and 5 inches in height, the burly Ralph Rose was an American track and field athlete with many talents. He was the first shot putter to set a world record of 50 ft, which was not broken for 16 years. He compiled a medal record of three gold, two silver and one bronze in three Olympic Games. In the 1904 Olympics, he won the shot put, stood second in the discus throw, third in the hammer throw and was sixth in the 56-pound weight throw. In the 1908 Olympics, he won gold for shot put and in the 1912 Olympics, he won the Two-Handed shot put. He died of typhoid fever at just 28.

Winning Streak

Olympic medals: 6

1904 (St Louis)
- Gold Medal: shot put
- Silver Medal: discus throw
- Bronze Medal: hammer throw

1908 (London)
- Gold Medal: shot put

1912 (Stockholm)
- Gold Medal: shot put (two handed)
- Silver Medal: shot put

Other Highlights
- Won 7 AAU titles: four for shot put, two for discus and one for javelin
- Set the first official world record for shot put (15.54 m [51 ft]) in 1909 — a record unbeaten for almost 10 years

G. Alberto Braglia (1906-1912)

A self-taught gymnast, Alberto Braglia was known as the '*human torpedo*' for the amazing stunts he was able to perform. In fact, he eventually became a circus performer! Before this, however, he made a name for himself internationally. He first performed in the 1906 Intercalated Games, where he won two silver medals. He went on to bag three Olympic gold medals, one in 1908 and two in 1912. He almost didn't get to perform in the 1912 Games because he was declared a professional. Luckily, he succeeded in regaining his amateur status before the Games. Though he never took part in the Olympics after 1912, he coached the Italian team for the 1932 Olympics and led them to victory.

Winning Streak

Olympic medals: 5

1906 (Intercalated Games, Athens)
- Silver Medal: individual all-around, individual all-around (5 Events)

1908 (London)
- Gold Medal: individual all-around

1912 (Stockholm)
- Gold Medal: individual all-around, team all-around

Other Highlights
- Won the World Championship in 1909

Melvin Sheppard (1908-1912)

American athlete Melvin Sheppard won four gold medals in the 1908 and 1912 Olympics. Born in New Jersey, he was rejected by the New York Police as he had a slightly enlarged heart. Despite his health problems, he continued running and became the favourite in middle-distance events in the 1908 Olympics, where he went on to win the 1,500 m, 800 m and the relay race, running fully half of the 1,600 m race. Later, he held the world indoor records for 600 yards, 800 yards, 1,000 yards and a mile. He remained involved with athletics even after he retired.

Winning Streak

Olympic medals: 5

1908 (London)
- Gold Medal: 800 m, 1,500 m, 1,600 m medley relay

1912 (Stockholm)
- Gold Medal: 4 x 400 m relay
- Silver Medal: 800 m

Other Highlights
- Broke the 1 mile relay world record along with his team members
- Broke world records in 600 yards and 1,000 yards (indoors)
- Won 7 AAU titles for various middle-distance running events

Hannes Kolehmainen (1912-1924)

Winning Streak

Olympic medals: 5

1912 (Stockholm)
- Gold Medal: 5,000 m, 10,000 m, cross country (individual)
- Silver Medal: cross country (team)

1920 (Antwerp)
- Gold Medal: marathon

Other Highlights
- Set world record for 3,000 m and broke world records for 5,000 m, 25 km and 30 km
- Won all the 22 races in which he participated in 1911, including the British AAA Championship
- Won the AAU title 3 times — in 1912, 1913 and 1915

A Finnish long-distance runner, Hannes Kolehmainen is said to be the first of the 'Flying Finns,' a nickname given to a generation of top Finnish athletes. He belonged to a family of sportspersons. Both his brothers were accomplished runners, and one was an Olympian. Kolehmainen's remarkable performance at the 1912 Olympics — when he won three gold medals — made him a star. His performance in the 5,000 m race that year remained one of his most memorable and exciting victories. The neck-to-neck race to the finish line between Kolehmainen and Frenchman Jean Bouin was extremely close — Kohlemainen won by less than half a metre. The very next day, although his team failed to win a medal, the Flying Finn set a world record during the 3,000 m team race.

Matthew McGrath (1908-1924)

An officer in the New York Police Department, Matthew McGrath won medals both for his sporting skills and bravery. He won the NYPD's '*Medal of Valor*' twice and bagged three Olympic medals for hammer throw. He is considered to be one of the greatest weight throwers of all time. He represented the US in four Olympics — 1908 (in tug-of-war), 1912, 1920 and 1924. He was in the world's top ten for hammer throwing till the age of 50 and won seven AAU Championships in that discipline.

Winning Streak

Olympic medals: 3

1908 (London)
- Silver Medal: hammer throw

1912 (Stockholm)
- Gold Medal: hammer throw

1924 (Paris)
- Silver Medal: hammer throw

Other Highlights
- Won 14 AAU Championships (7 for hammer throw and 7 for 35-lb weight throw)
- Set 2 world records, while the Olympic record he set at Stockholm remained unbroken for 24 years

Nedo Nadi (1912-1920)

This Italian swordsman is believed to be one of the most skilled fencers of all time, and also one of the most versatile —he is the only fencer to have won a gold medal in each of the three fencing weapons at a single Games. His father, also a famous fencer, trained him when he was a young boy. He went on to set a record by winning five gold medals for the sabre, foil and épée fencing events in the 1920 Olympics. It wasn't the first time he'd shone at the Olympics — when he was just 18, he won the foil fencing event in the 1912 Olympics. His brother, Aldo, was also an accomplished fencer and an Olympic Champion.

Winning Streak

Olympic medals: 6

1912 (Stockholm)
- Gold Medal: foil fencing (individual)

1920 (Antwerp)
- Gold Medal: foil fencing (individual), foil fencing (team), sabre fencing (individual), sabre fencing (team), épée fencing (team)

Other Highlights
- Was World Épée Champion in 1930

Suzanne Lenglen (1920)

French tennis player Suzanne Lenglen was born in 1899. She was a sickly child who started playing tennis in order to build up her strength. She quickly went on to become one of the best female tennis players ever to come from France, winning Wimbledon six times! She was just as successful in the 1920 Olympics. On her way to winning the gold medal, she lost only four games in ten sets. She also partnered Max Decugis for the Mixed Doubles Championship and again walked away with a gold medal. She later turned professional, the first top female tennis star to do so. She was nicknamed *La Divine* (the divine one) by the French press. Lenglen died at the age of 39.

Winning Streak

Olympic medals: 3

1920 (Antwerp)

- Gold Medal: women's singles, mixed doubles
- Bronze Medal: women's doubles

Other Highlights

- Won 4 World Hard Court Championships (1914, 1921, 1922 and 1923) and 2 French Open Singles Championships
- Won 6 Wimbledon Championships, 5 of them consecutively
- Won 31 Grand Slam titles between 1914 and 1926

Paavo Nurmi (1920-1928)

One of the most outstanding long-distance runners of his time, Paavo Nurmi was one of the legendary '*Flying Finns*.' Over the course of three Olympic Games, he won nine gold medals and three silver. He also set 22 world records. One of his most amazing feats was during the 1924 Paris Olympics, when he won the 1,500 m and 5,000 m races within just an hour of each other! He was not allowed to compete in the 1932 Olympics because of allegations that he earned money for running. He did, however, carry the torch for the Opening Ceremony of the 1952 Olympics.

Winning Streak

Olympic medals: 12

1920 (Antwerp)

- Gold Medal: 10,000 m, cross country (individual), cross country (team)
- Silver Medal: 5,000 m

1924 (Paris)

- Gold Medal: 1,500 m, 3,000 m (team), 5,000 m, cross country (individual), cross country (team)

1928 (Amsterdam)

- Gold Medal: 10,000 m
- Silver Medal: 3,000 m steeplechase, 5,000 m

Other Highlights

- Set over 20 official world records for a range of track events. His record for the 10,000 m was unbroken for almost 13 years
- Was the first to win 5 golds in athletics at a single Olympic Games

Edvin Wide (1920-1928)

Edvin Wide

A Swedish national, this Finland-born long-distance runner made an impression at three Olympic Games and set three world records. He is most famous for breaking Paavo Nurmi's record for the 3,000 m in 1925. He was also the US 2 Mile Indoor Champion in 1929. Although Wide never won an Olympic gold, his performances in the Games were memorable. It's widely believed that he would have bagged the gold medal had he not had to always compete against the '*Flying Finns*' — Paavo Nurmi and Ville Ritola.

Winning Streak

Olympic medals: 5

1920 (Antwerp)
- Bronze Medal: 3,000 m (team)

1924 (Paris)
- Silver Medal: 10,000 m
- Bronze Medal: 5,000 m

1924 (Paris)
- Bronze Medal: 5,000 m, 10,000 m

Other Highlights
- Was the US Champion for the Indoor 2 mile event in 1929

Giulio Gaudini (1924-1936)

An Italian foil and sabre fencer, Giulio Gaudini began his Olympic career when he was just 19 years old, at the 1924 Games in Paris. Unfortunately, he didn't win a medal because the Italian team withdrew from the competition to protest a decision made by the judges. However, Gaudini made up for lost time in the 1928 Games, where he won his first gold medal. He went on to give remarkable performances in two more Olympic Games. He won three silver medals and one bronze at the 1932 Games. His performance only grew better at the 1936 Games. He won a gold medal for individual foil fencing and another for the team event. The Italian team had registered 104 wins against only 19 losses. Gaudini's final Olympic medal was for the sabre team event.

Winning Streak

Olympic medals: 9

1928 (Amsterdam)
- Gold Medal: foil (team)
- Bronze Medal: foil (individual)

1932 (Los Angeles)
- Silver Medal: foil (team), sabre (individual), sabre (team)
- Bronze Medal: foil (individual)

1936 (Berlin)
- Gold Medal: foil (individual), foil (team)
- Bronze Medal: sabre (team)

Other Highlights
- Best remembered for leading the Italian foil team to victory in the 1928 Olympics, with a remarkable record of 30 wins against 2 losses

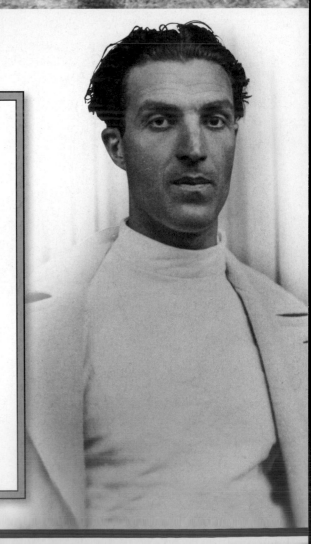

Georges Miez (1924-1936)

Swiss gymnast Georges Miez was only 19 when he took part in the 1924 Olympics. Though he competed in nine different events, he won only a bronze medal. This did not dampen his spirits — by the 1928 Olympics he was the world's leading gymnast and went on to win three gold and one silver medal. In the 1932 Games, he was the only Swiss gymnast to participate, and won a silver medal in the Floor exercises. In the 1936 Games, he did even better and won a gold medal. He retired from competition after this and devoted the rest of his long life to the promotion of gymnastics as a sport. He died in 1999.

Winning Streak

Olympic medals: 8

1924 (Paris)
- Bronze Medal: team all-around

1928 (Amsterdam)
- Gold Medal: individual all-around, team all-around, horizontal bar
- Silver Medal: men's pommel horse

1932 (Los Angeles)
- Silver Medal: men's floor exercise

1936 (Berlin)
- Gold Medal: men's floor exercise
- Silver Medal: men's team

Other Highlights
- Was World Champion in 1934

Ville Ritola (1924-1928)

This '*Flying Finn*' was one of the most outstanding long-distance runners to emerge from Finland. He migrated to the US when he was 17 and joined the Finnish-American Athletic Club. Another top Finnish runner, Hannes Kolehmainen, trained with him and tried to convince him to participate in the 1920 Olympics, but Ritola wanted to practice more. His plan worked, even though at 28 he was older than most other runners.

He won four gold medals and two silver at the 1924 Olympics. He also bettered his record for the 10,000 m event. Ritola quickly gained a reputation that was equal to track star Paavo Nurmi. Nurmi beat Ritola at the 5,000 m in the 1924 Games, but Ritola got his revenge in the 1928 Games. In that 5,000 m event, he managed to get ahead of Nurmi in the final curve, winning by a margin of 12 m. Today, a Finnish phrase translates as "*to pull a Ritola*" — it means to make a quick exit! Ritola retired from athletics after the 1928 Games.

Winning Streak

Olympic medals: 8

1924 (Paris)
- Gold Medal: 10,000 m, 3,000 m steeplechase, 3,000 m (team), cross country (team)
- Silver Medal: 5,000 m, cross country (individual)

1928 (Amsterdam)
- Gold Medal: 5,000 m
- Silver Medal: 10,000 m

Other Highlights
- Set 2 world records for 10,000 m in 1924
- Won several AAU Championships for a number of events including 10 miles, cross country and steeplechase

Betty Robinson (1928-1936)

Elizabeth 'Betty' Robinson was the first woman to win the 100 m race in the Olympics. It was 1928 — the first time the event was introduced for women at the Games — and she was only 16 years old. She also won a silver medal for the 4 x 100 m relay event. With these victories under her belt, the track and field star went on to set several world records. However, she was badly hurt in a plane crash in 1931 which left her in a coma for seven months. It took her two more years to begin walking by herself again. Despite her injuries, Betty participated in the 1936 Olympics in Berlin and won her second gold medal. She retired soon after but remained involved with the Amateur Athletic Union (AAU). She died in 1999.

Winning Streak

Olympic medals: 3
1928 (Amsterdam)
- Gold Medal: 100 m
- Silver Medal: 4 x 400 m relay

1936 (Berlin)
- Gold Medal: 4 x 400 m relay

Other Highlights
- Set a world record of 11.0 secs for the 100 yard dash in 1928
- Set 2 more world records in 1931

Fanny Blankers-Koen (1936-1952)

Born on April 26, 1918, this Dutch athlete became a household name at 30, when she was already a mother of two. Nicknamed the '*Flying Housewife*,' she failed to win any medals in the 1936 Olympics and did not participate again until 1948, when she won four gold medals — the first woman to win four gold medals at a single Olympics. She was a talented sprinter, hurdler and long jumper. She broke 16 world records and was declared '*Female Athlete of the Century*' by the International Association of Athletics Federations (1999). She later became the captain of the Dutch female track and field team. She was married to Jan Blankers, a former Olympian and coach. She died in 2004.

Winning Streak

Olympic medals: 4
1948 (London)
- Gold Medal: 100 m, 200 m, 80 m hurdles, 4 x 400 m relay

Other Highlights
- Won 58 Dutch Championships
- Won 5 European titles

Jesse Owens (1936)

Born in Alabama and raised in Ohio, Owens is one of the greatest American track and field athletes of all time. Although his given name was James Cleveland Owens, his teacher misheard "J.C." as Jesse, and the name stuck. Owens started training with the help of his high school coach, Charles Riley. Owens' achievements include four gold medals in the 1936 Olympics, eight individual NCAA Championships, and four World Records. Owens became a symbol of black pride after his victory in Berlin at a time when Hitler was trying to prove that white Aryans were a 'superior' race. Unfortunately, Jesse had to endure racism in America as well and he struggled for many years. He was honoured in 1955 when US President Dwight Eisenhower named him 'Ambassador of Sports.'

Winning Streak

Olympic medals: 4

1936 (Berlin)

- Gold Medal: 100 m, 200 m, 4 x 100 m relay, long jump

Other Highlights

- Set 3 world records at the Big Ten Championships in 1935 within an hour — in the long jump (his 8.13 m record was unbroken for 25 years), the 220 yard sprint and the 220 yard low hurdles, and tied the record in the 100 yard sprint.
- In his junior year at Ohio State, he took part in 42 track events and won them all
- In the Berlin Games, he set Olympic records for 200 m (20.7 secs) and long jump (8.06 m). A world record was also set in the relay (39.8 secs)

John Davis (1948-1952)

This former US Army soldier won every weightlifting championship he took part in between 1938 and 1953, including 7 World Championships, 12 National Championships and 2 Olympic gold medals. He was also the first weightlifter to lift over 180 kg (400 lb). In fact, Davis was defeated only once in his career, and that was due to an injury. When he wasn't weightlifting, Davis worked as an officer with the New York Department of Corrections, where he was well known for his calm and gentle personality!

Winning Streak

Olympic medals: 2

1948 (London)

- Gold Medal: men's heavyweight

1952 (Helsinki)

- Gold Medal: men's heavyweight

Other Highlights

- Set 16 world records in both the light heavyweight and super heavyweight categories

Harrison Dillard (1948-1952)

This American athlete is one of only two Olympians who have won both the sprinting and hurdling gold medals. However, Dillard had to really sweat for his success at the hurdling event. Even though he'd won dozens of hurdling competitions, he failed to qualify for the event at the 1948 Olympics. That year, he had also lost the AAU hurdling title despite having won 82 events in a row. Though he had better luck with sprinting and won two gold medals, Dillard was not satisfied. He loved hurdling, and when he was a child, he'd practice with old car springs as barriers! So, when the 1952 Olympics arrived, he tried yet again. This time he qualified for the hurdling event — and won. He was delighted and said, "*Good things come to those who wait.*" He also won a gold for the 4 x 100 m relay in the 1952 Games.

Winning Streak

Olympic medals: 4
1948 (London)
- Gold Medal: 100 m, 4 x 100 m relay

1952 (Helsinki)
- Gold Medal: 110 m hurdles, 4 x 100 m relay

Other Highlights
- Won 14 AAU and 6 NCAA titles
- Tied 2 world records in different hurdles events

Micheline Ostermeyer |··········●

Micheline Ostermeyer (1948)

A concert pianist as well as a talented all-around athlete, Micheline Ostermeyer (who was also the great-niece of the French author Victor Hugo) once famously remarked that she gave her arms a workout by playing the piano. This popular French athlete won two gold medals at the 1948 Olympics for discus throw and shot put. She also won a bronze medal for high jump. She is the only female French athlete to have won three medals at a single Games. Though Ostermeyer claimed she practised the piano for five hours a day and athletics for only five hours a week, she managed to bag several titles for running, jumping and shot put events over the years, making her France's most versatile female athlete. She devoted herself to playing the piano in her later years.

Winning Streak

Olympic medals: 3
1948 (London)
- Gold Medal: shot put, discus throw
- Bronze Medal: high jump

Other Highlights
- At the European Championships in 1946, she won silver in the shot put
- By the time she retired she had won 13 French titles in five separate disciplines: shot put, high jump, 60 m dash, hurdles and the Heptathlon

László Papp (1948-1956)

The Hungarian champion has the distinction of being the first boxer to win three gold medals in three consecutive Olympics. Papp had to face many challenges along the way, as Hungary was a Communist country at the time and had a lot of restrictions. Nonetheless, he became a middleweight champion and even defeated future World Champion José Torres in the 1956 Olympics. He later turned professional, fighting in Europe even though professional boxing wasn't allowed in Hungary. In 1965 he was not given permission to compete in the World Championship and was forced to retire. He was given a place in the International Boxing Hall of Fame in 2001. He had not lost one game in his professional career.

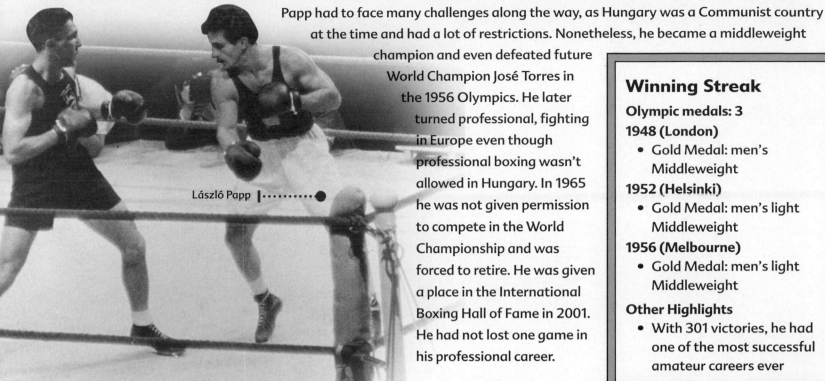

László Papp |··········●

Winning Streak

Olympic medals: 3
1948 (London)
- Gold Medal: men's Middleweight

1952 (Helsinki)
- Gold Medal: men's light Middleweight

1956 (Melbourne)
- Gold Medal: men's light Middleweight

Other Highlights
- With 301 victories, he had one of the most successful amateur careers ever

Robert Richards (1948-1956)

Born in 1926 in Illinois, USA, Richards was a multi-talented athlete who was part of three Olympic teams in two events. Popularly known as the '*Vaulting Vicar*,' he made a mark in pole vaulting and the decathlon. He is the only man to have won a gold medal twice in pole vaulting. He was featured in the US Olympic Hall of Fame in 1983 and also made it to the US National Track and Field Hall of Fame in 1975. In 1984, he stood as a candidate for the US presidential elections, and got more than 65,000 votes. That wasn't enough for him to win the election, so he settled down to a life breeding miniature horses at the Olympian Ranch in Texas.

Winning Streak

Olympic medals: 3
1948 (London)
- Bronze Medal: men's pole vault

1952 (Helsinki)
- Gold Medal: men's pole vault

1956 (Melbourne)
- Gold Medal: men's pole vault

Other Highlights
- Was the second person ever to pole vault over 15 ft (4.57 m)
- Won decathlon Championships in the 1951, 1954 and 1955 AAU Meets

Shirley Strickland de la Hunty (1948-1956)

This Australian track and field athlete's won seven Olympic medals, a record unequaled until 1976 (it has since been bettered by Merlene Ottey). Born in 1925, Strickland was soon introduced to track and field — her father was a sprinter too — and won almost every event she participated in as a schoolgirl. She studied and taught physics, but never stopped running and hurdling. After winning several Australian events, she made her first Olympic appearance in London 1948, where she won one silver and two bronze medals. She then won three gold medals at the British Empire Games in 1950, and later, her first gold at the 1952 Olympics. Two more Olympic gold medals followed in 1956. She carried the Olympic torch for the Sydney Games in 2000, but was criticised in 2001 for auctioning her medals. Strickland said she needed the funds for her grandchildren's education. She died in 2004.

Winning Streak

Olympic medals: 7

1948 (London)
- Silver Medal: 4 x 100 m relay
- Bronze Medal: 100 m, 80 m hurdles

1952 (Helsinki)
- Gold Medal: 80 m hurdles
- Bronze Medal: 100 m

1956 (Melbourne)
- Gold Medal: 80 m hurdles, 4 x 100 m relay

Other Highlights
- Won 3 gold medals in the 1950 British Empire Games in Auckland
- Broke or matched 5 world records, 4 for hurdling and 1 for 100 m

Károly Takács (1948-1956)

The Hungarian shooter overcame great odds to compete in the Olympics. Takács was a soldier in the Hungarian Army. By 1936, he was a world-class pistol shooter, but as he was a sergeant and not a commissioned officer he was denied a place in the Hungarian shooting team for the 1936 Olympics. This law was changed in time for the 1940 Olympics, but Takács was injured during army training in 1938 when a faulty grenade exploded in his right hand. Takács refused to give up and taught himself to shoot with his left hand, practising in secret and surprising every-one when he won the Hungarian National Pistol Shooting Championship in 1939. Unfortunately, the Second World War meant that Takács had to wait until the 1948 Olympics in London to achieve his Olympic dream, when at the age of 38, he beat the reigning World Champion to win gold in the rapid-fire shooting event, setting a new world record in the process. He won a second gold medal in the event in Helsinki in 1952 — the first person to do so. The IOC granted him the status of 'Olympic hero.'

Winning Streak

Olympic medals: 2

1948 (London)
- Gold Medal: men's 25 m rapid-fire pistol

1952 (Helsinki)
- Gold Medal: men's 25 m rapid-fire pistol

Other Highlights
- Won a bronze medal at the 1958 ISSF World Shooting Championships in 25 m centre-fire pistol

Malvin Whitfield (1948-1952)

Born on October 11, 1924, this American athlete was the first black athlete to win the United States AAU's annual James E. Sullivan Award. Popularly known as '*Marvellous Mal*,' he was a two-time winner of the 800 m at the Olympic Games and also won an Olympic gold as part of the 4 x 400 m relay team. Considered the best 400-800 m runner of his time, Marvellous Mal reached the peak of his career between 1948 and 1954, a period in which he lost only three (out of 69) 800 m races. After retirement, Whitfield worked for the US State Department. He made it his mission to encourage and support African athletes by establishing scholarships and training programmes for them.

Winning Streak

Olympic medals: 5

1948 (London)
- Gold Medal: 800 m, 4 x 400 m relay
- Bronze Medal: 400 m

1952 (Helsinki)
- Gold Medal: 800 m
- Silver Medal: 4 x 400 m relay

Other Highlights
- Won the AAU title in 800 m from 1949 to 1951
- Won the 400 m, 800 m and 4 x 400 m relay in the 1951 Pan-American Games in Buenos Aires
- Set a world record for the 800 m in 1950 and broke it again in 1952

Emil Zátopek (1948-1956)

Known as the '*Czech Locomotive*,' Zátopek made headlines with his triple gold medal win in the 1952 Olympics in Helsinki. Known for his very strict training regime, he amazed the world by winning the 5,000 m, 10,000 m and marathon events, breaking the Olympic record each time. Interestingly, this was the first time he had competed in a marathon event. In the 5,000 km race, he was in fourth position until he suddenly sped up and overtook the other runners. Post athletics he joined the Communist Party in Czechoslovakia, but his support for its democratic wing landed him in trouble. He was removed from his position and made to work in a Uranium mine. His ordeal only ended in 1990. Zátopek was married to javelin champion Dana Zátopková, who also won a gold medal at the Helsinki Olympics. He is the only Olympic athlete to have his statue at the Olympic Museum in Switzerland.

Winning Streak

Olympic medals: 5

1948 (London)
- Gold Medal: 10,000 m
- Silver Medal: 5,000 m

1952 (Helsinki)
- Gold Medal: 5,000 m, 10,000 m, marathon

Other Highlights
- Broke the 10 km world record in 1949; broke his own record 3 times in the following seasons
- Won the 5,000 m and 10,000 m in the European Championships in 1950

Margit Korondi (1952-1956)

This Hungarian gymnast was born in 1932. Margit Korondi vaulted into the limelight in the 1952 Olympics in Helsinki. She also competed in the 1956 Olympics in Melbourne. Korondi won two gold medals, two silver medals and four bronze medals in all, making her one of Hungary's best gymnasts. She was the first Olympic Champion at uneven bars, as this gymnastic event was introduced only in 1952. She was granted political asylum and eventually moved to the United States.

Winning Streak

Olympic medals: 8

1952 (Helsinki)
- Gold Medal: uneven bars
- Silver Medal: team all-around
- Bronze Medal: floor exercise, balance beam, individual all-around, team portable apparatus

1956 (Melbourne)
- Gold Medal: team portable apparatus
- Silver Medal: team all-around

Dawn Fraser (1956-1964)

As a child, Fraser suffered from asthma and began swimming to help with her breathing. She went on to become the greatest female sprint swimmer ever. She became the first swimmer ever to win Olympic titles in the same event at three consecutive Olympic Games, in the 100 m freestyle — an achievement she now shares with Hungarian Krisztina Egerszegi — in the years 1956, 1960 and 1964. She broke 41 world records and was the first woman to swim the 100 m freestyle sprint distance in under one minute. However, she was suspended for ten years after allegations of misbehaviour at the 1964 Summer Olympics in Tokyo. Still considered to be one of Australia's greatest sportspersons, Fraser has been given a number of titles and honours including the *'Member of the Order of the British Empire'* in 1967. In 1988, she was named Australia's *'Greatest Female Athlete of the Century.'*

Winning Streak

Olympic medals: 8

1956 (Melbourne)
- Gold Medal: 100 m freestyle, 4 x 100 m freestyle relay
- Silver Medal: 400 m freestyle

1960 (Rome)
- Gold Medal: 100 m freestyle
- Silver Medal: 4 x 100 m freestyle relay, 4 x 100 m medley relay

1964 (Tokyo)
- Gold Medal: 100 m freestyle
- Silver Medal: 4 x 100 m freestyle relay

Other Highlights
- Her record time of 58.9 secs for 100 m set in 1964 was unbroken until 1972
- Won the gold for 100 m freestyle in the 1958 Commonwealth Games, and gold in 100 m and 400 m freestyle in the 1962 Commonwealth Games

Winning Streak

Olympic medals: 18

1956 (Melbourne)
- Gold Medal: floor exercise, horse vault, individual all-around, team all-around
- Silver Medal: uneven bars
- Bronze Medal: team portable apparatus

1960 (Rome)
- Gold Medal: floor exercise, individual all-around, team all-around
- Silver Medal: uneven bars, balance beam
- Bronze Medal: horse vault

1964 (Tokyo)
- Gold Medal: floor exercise, team all-around
- Silver Medal: horse vault, individual all-around
- Bronze Medal: uneven bars, balance beam

Other Highlights
- Won 6 titles at the 1958 and 1962 World Championships in individual events
- At the 1957 European Championships, she won all 5 individual events

Larisa Latynina (1956-1964)

With nine gold medals, Larissa Latynina is the woman with the most Olympic golds, and is second only to Michael Phelps (along with Carl Lewis, Mark Spitz and Paavo Nurmi). She holds more Olympic medals (18) than anyone else, has the most individual Olympic medals in history (14), and won a medal in every Olympic event in which she competed bar one (and in that she only missed out by one place!) She retired after the 1966 World Championships and took up coaching the Soviet National Gymnastics Team in 1977. She helped organise the gymnastics at the 1980 Moscow Olympics.

Al Oerter (1956-1968)

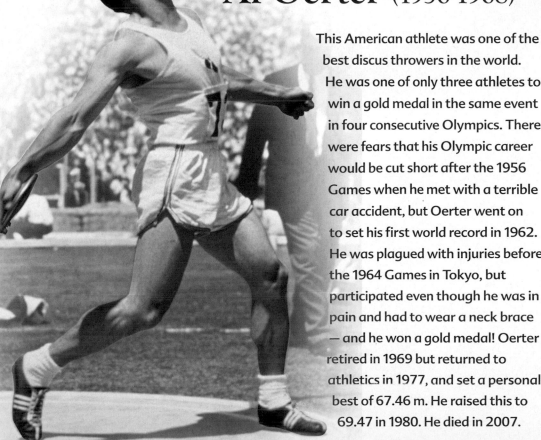

This American athlete was one of the best discus throwers in the world. He was one of only three athletes to win a gold medal in the same event in four consecutive Olympics. There were fears that his Olympic career would be cut short after the 1956 Games when he met with a terrible car accident, but Oerter went on to set his first world record in 1962. He was plagued with injuries before the 1964 Games in Tokyo, but participated even though he was in pain and had to wear a neck brace — and he won a gold medal! Oerter retired in 1969 but returned to athletics in 1977, and set a personal best of 67.46 m. He raised this to 69.47 in 1980. He died in 2007.

Winning Streak

Olympic medals: 4

1956 (Melbourne)
- Gold Medal: discus throw

1960 (Rome)
- Gold Medal: discus throw

1964 (Tokyo)
- Gold Medal: discus throw

1968 (Mexico City)
- Gold Medal: discus throw

Other Highlights
- Won the AAU title 6 times and set the world record 4 times
- Was honoured as the first athlete recipient of 'The Olympic Order' — the highest award issued by the IOC

Wilma Rudolph (1956-1960)

Nicknamed '*The Tornado*' for her incredible speed, Rudolph was the first American woman to win three track and field events at a single Games. Yet, when Rudolph was a child, she had polio. She only started walking properly when she was about 11 years old. Rudolph first participated in the Olympics in 1956 when she was 16 years old, winning a bronze medal. After this, she trained harder than ever and became famous as the '*fastest woman in the world*,' setting several world records and earning Championship titles. However, she retired at the age of just 22. She turned her focus to the Wilma Rudolph Foundation to help underprivileged children. She died in 1994.

Winning Streak

Olympic medals: 4

1956 (Melbourne)
- Bronze Medal: 4 x 100 m relay

1960 (Rome)
- Gold Medal: 100 m, 200 m, 4 x 100 m relay

Other Highlights
- Won the AAU 100 m for 4 successive years from 1959. In 1960 she also won the 200 m

Boris Shakhlin (1956-1964)

The winner of seven gold Olympic medals, this Soviet champion began gymnastics at 12. His first appearance at the 1956 Olympics won him two gold medals, one of which, the pommel horse event, became his strongest individual event. In his career, he won 13 Olympic medals and 14 medals at World Championships. He became known as the '*Man of Iron*' both for his physical strength and his determination. After retiring in 1966, he served as a gymnastics official and a senior lecturer on gymnastics at Kiev's National University of Physical Training and Sports. Inducted into the International Gymnastics Hall of Fame in 2002, Shakhlin died in 2008.

Winning Streak

Olympic medals: 13

1956 (Melbourne)
- Gold Medal: pommel horse, team all-around

1960 (Rome)
- Gold Medal: pommel horse, parallel bars, individual all-around, horse vault
- Silver Medal: team all-around, rings
- Bronze Medal: horizontal bar

1964 (Tokyo)
- Gold Medal: horizontal bar
- Silver Medal: individual all-around, team all-around
- Bronze Medal: rings

Other Highlights
- Was All-around Champion at the 1955 European Championships and at the 1958 World Championships
- Won 14 World Championship medals

Muhammad Ali (1960)

The American boxer and heavyweight champion was born Cassius Marcellus Clay, Jr. in 1942. In 1964 he joined the Nation of Islam and took on the name Muhammad Ali. He is known the world over as the greatest heavyweight Championship boxer in history. He was the first boxer to win the lineal heavyweight Championship three times. Ali was given the title of '*Sportsman of the Century*' in 1999 by Sports Illustrated and '*Sports Personality of the Century*' by the BBC. In his career he won 56 boxing matches and lost only five. Ali has said the secret of his success was his ability to "*float like a butterfly and sting like a bee!*" Ali suffers from Parkinson's Disease, but still travels around the world to participate in various humanitarian missions.

Winning Streak

Olympic medals: 1
1960 (Rome)
- Gold Medal: light-heavyweight

Other Highlights
- Earned the nickname, '*The Greatest*' in 1960, when he won Kentucky Golden Gloves titles, 2 national Golden Gloves titles, an AAU National Title, and the light heavyweight gold medal in the Rome Olympics

Abebe Bikila (1960-1968)

The Ethiopian runner is considered a hero in his country, and with good reason. He was the first black African to win an Olympic gold medal. Bikila only joined the 1960 Ethiopian Olympic team at the last moment, when another runner was injured. The story goes that when Bikila went to try out running shoes, Adidas, the shoe sponsor, did not have a pair left that fitted him properly, and so Abebe decided to run barefoot. He went on to beat his nearest rival by 25 seconds, setting a world record and winning the gold medal. After the race, when asked why he had run barefoot, Bikila replied, "*I wanted the world to know that my country, Ethiopia, has always won with determination and heroism.*" After his win, he ran many more marathons, winning most of them. Shortly before the 1964 Summer Olympics in Tokyo, Bikila was operated on for acute appendicitis. Nevertheless, he started training again even when recovering in hospital. Although not expected to compete in Tokyo, he did enter the marathon, this time wearing Puma shoes, and went on to set another world record time, becoming the first athlete in history to win the Olympic marathon twice. Unfortunately, he was injured in 1967 and could not complete the 1968 marathon. In 1969, he was badly hurt in a car accident and lost the use of his legs. He never lost his fighting spirit, and even participated in archery competitions, but died in 1973 from complications relating to the accident. His funeral was attended by 75,000 and a national day of mourning was proclaimed.

Winning Streak

Olympic medals: 2
1960 (Rome)
- Gold Medal: marathon

1964 (Tokyo)
- Gold Medal: marathon

Reiner Klimke (1960-1988)

One of the most accomplished dressage riders of all time, this German equestrian won six Olympic gold and two bronze medals and achieved unmatched success in the World Championship and the European Championship, too. He also made a mark in Eventing, especially in the early part of his career, although he did not earn any Olympic medals for it. In his two-decade gallop across the Olympics, Klimke was often accompanied by Ahlerich, his favourite horse. Ahlerich saw Klimke to victory in both the Los Angeles and Seoul Olympics. Klimke died in 1999. Reiner Klimke's daughter, Ingrid Klimke is also a noted dressage rider: she won a gold medal in the 2008 Olympics at Beijing, twenty years after her father won his last Olympic Gold.

Winning Streak

Olympic medals: 8

1964 (Tokyo)
- Gold Medal: mixed dressage (team)

1968 (Mexico City)
- Gold Medal: mixed dressage (team)
- Bronze Medal: mixed dressage (individual)

1976 (Montreal)
- Gold Medal: mixed dressage (team)
- Bronze Medal: mixed dressage (individual)

1984 (Los Angeles)
- Gold Medal: mixed dressage (individual), mixed dressage (team)

1988 (Seoul)
- Gold Medal: mixed dressage (team)

Other Highlights
- Was Individual Champion at the European Championships in 1967, 1973 and 1985
- Won 5 gold and 1 bronze medal in European Championships team dressage
- Won 2 individual and 4 team gold medals in the World Championships

Ingrid Krämer (1960-1968)

Born in Dresden, Germany, this diving champion was only 17 years old when she participated in the 1960 Olympics. She ended up winning the gold medal for both platform and springboard diving — she was the first non-American woman to win both diving events. Her last platform dive in the 1960 Olympics was the highest scoring dive of the event. Ingrid won one gold and one silver in the 1964 Olympics, but did not win any event in the 1968 Games. She competed under three different names at the Olympics. She appeared under her maiden name of Krämer in 1960, while in 1964 she used the name of her first husband (Engel) and in 1968 that of her second husband (Gulbin). In 1960 Krämer was elected Sportswoman of the Year in both parts of Germany, the only time this has been achieved, and in 1962-64 she was elected *'Sportswoman of the Year'* in East Germany. Later, she retired and trained some of Germany's best divers, becoming an internationally renowned coach. She was given a place in the International Swimmers Hall of Fame in 1975.

Winning Streak

Olympic medals: 4

1960 (Rome)
- Gold Medal: springboard, platform

1964 (Tokyo)
- Gold Medal: springboard
- Silver Medal: platform

Tamara Press (1960-1964)

Born in 1937, in Ukraine, Press represented the Soviet Union in discus throw and shot put. Apart from her stint at the 1960 and 1964 Olympics, Press had several victories in the European Championships. Her younger sister Irina was a track athlete and together Tamara and Irina were referred to as the '*Press Sisters*' — or sometimes as the '*Press Brothers*'! Tamara set six world records. However, both Tamara and Irina abruptly retired from sports when gender testing was made compulsory for International sporting events in 1966. This led to speculation that the '*sisters*' were not actually female, or were taking male hormones in order to make them stronger, though no such thing was ever proved. Tamara later wrote several books about sports.

Winning Streak

Olympic medals: 4
1960 (Rome)
- Gold Medal: shot put
- Silver Medal: discus throw

1964 (Tokyo)
- Gold Medal: shot put, discus throw

Other Highlights
- In the 1958 European Championship in Stockholm she won the gold in the discus throw and bronze in shot put
- Won gold medals in both shot put and discus throw in the 1962 Belgrade European Championships
- Set six world records

Ildikó Újlaky-Rejto (1960-1976)

Ildikó Újlaky-Rejto is one of the greatest female fencers in the history of the Olympics. She was born deaf and communicated with her coach through written instructions. She started her career early, at the age of 15, and won seven Olympic medals from 1960-1972. This invincible Hungarian fencer added another feather to her cap when she won the women's title in the World Veterans Championships. She was 62 years old at the time!

Winning Streak

Olympic medals: 7
1960 (Rome)
- Silver Medal: foil fencing (team)

1964 (Tokyo)
- Gold Medal: foil fencing (individual), foil fencing (team)

1968 (Mexico City)
- Silver Medal: foil fencing (team)
- Bronze Medal: foil fencing (individual)

1972 (Munich)
- Silver Medal: foil fencing (team)

1976 (Montreal)
- Bronze Medal: foil fencing (team)

Other Highlights
- Has the unusual distinction of winning Olympic medals in three different names: as Miss Rejto in 1960, as Mrs. Ujlaky -Rejto in 1964 and 1968, and as Mrs. Ságiné-Ujlaky-Rejto in 1972 and 1976

Vera Cáslavská (1960-1968)

Winning Streak

Olympic medals: 11

1960 (Rome)
- Silver Medal: team all-around

1964 (Tokyo)
- Gold Medal: horse vault, balance beam, individual all-around
- Silver Medal: team all-around

1968 (Mexico City)
- Gold Medal: Floor exercise, uneven bars, horse vault, individual all-around
- Silver Medal: balance beam, team all-around

Other Highlights
- At the World Championship in 1962 she won gold in the vault, and in 1966 she won the vault again and gold in both the individual and team all-around
- Was All-around European Champion in 1965 and 1967, and in 1965 she won the title in all the individual events
- Won 15 gold, 6 silver and 2 bronze medals in European and World Championships

Cáslavská's good looks and charisma made her a favourite with the public. This Czech gymnast has claimed 22 international titles and holds the honour of being the only gymnast to have won a gold in every individual title in the Olympics. Her condemnation of the Soviet-led invasion of Czechoslovakia forced her into retirement and she was denied the right to attend sporting events, work, write and travel abroad. In the 1990s, she held a term as the president of the Czech Olympic Committee. She was also inducted into the International Gymnastics Hall of Fame.

Peter Snell (1960-1964)

This New Zealand athlete had only a brief career as a sportsman, but in this short span he achieved enough fame to become New Zealand's '*Sports Champion of the 20th Century.*' Over the course of his short career, he achieved three Olympic and two Commonwealth gold medals, along with five individual world records. Snell was only 21 when he won his first Olympic gold, for which he broke the world record and defeated the world record-holder. His record for the 800 m and 880 m went unbeaten in New Zealand for four decades. He was at the height of his success in the mid-1960s, but retired in 1965.

Winning Streak

Olympic medals: 3

1960 (Rome)
- Gold Medal: 800 m

1964 (Tokyo)
- Gold Medal: 800 m, 1,500 m

Other Highlights
- Set world records for 800 m, 880 yards, 1,000 m and mile
- Won gold for the 880 yards and the mile at the 1962 Commonwealth Games

Irena Szewinska
(1964-1980)

With six world records and seven Olympic medals to her credit, this Polish athlete became the first woman to hold world records in 100 m, 200 m and 400 m races simultaneously. She went on to gather 26 titles of '*Champion of Poland*' between 1965 and 1979, setting 38 Polish records in a number of events. She was appointed the head of the Polish Federation of Athletes in 2004 and also became a member of the IOC. Szewinska entered the International Jewish Sports Hall of Fame for her excellence in athletics.

Richard Fosbury
(1968)

Winning Streak

Olympic medals: 7

1964 (Tokyo)
- Gold Medal: 4 x 100 m relay
- Silver Medal: long jump, 200 m

1968 (Mexico City)
- Gold Medal: 200 m
- Bronze Medal: 100 m

1972 (Munich)
- Bronze Medal: 200 m

1976 (Montreal)
- Gold Medal: 400 m

Other Highlights
- In the 1966 Budapest European Championships she won golds in the 200 m, 4 x 100 m relay and long jump; in 1974 in Rome she bagged the gold in the 100 m and the 200 m
- Broke six world records, becoming the first woman to hold records for 100 m, 200 m and 400 m at the same time

Fosbury's tryst with high jumping started at the age of 16 when he began competing in high jump at school level. Unable to perform the '*straddle method*' of high jumping, he altered the '*upright scissor method*' and adapted it to suit himself. He was widely criticised as the world's laziest high jumper for his new style of jump which came to be called the '*Fosbury Flop.*' His win in the 1968 Olympics silenced many of his critics. His unique method of high jump came to be accepted widely and became popular. Today, the '*Fosbury Flop*' is one of the most popular techniques in modern high jumping.

Winning Streak

Olympic medals: 1

1968 (Mexico City)
- Gold Medal: high jump

Other Highlights
- Set a world record for high jump (2.24 m) in 1968

Deborah Meyer (1968)

American swimmer Debbie Meyer was only 15 years old when she set world records in the 400 m and 800 m freestyle events during the Pan-American Games in 1967. The fact that she had asthma never stopped her from pushing herself. That same year, Meyer — who was

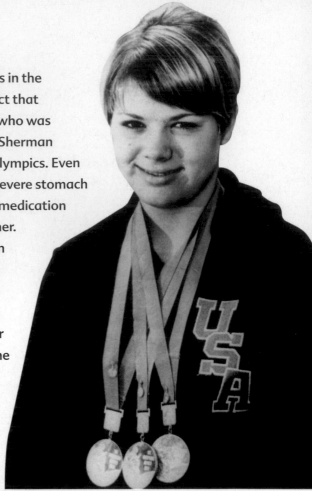

Winning Streak

Olympic medals: 3
1968 (Mexico City)
- 200 m freestyle, 400 m freestyle, 800 m freestyle

Other Highlights
- Set 15 world records between 1967 and 1970 for freestyle races over 200 m, 400 m, 800 m and 1,500 m
- She broke 24 US records
- Won AAU titles for 400 m and 1,500 m from 1967 to 1970. She won the 400 m individual medley event in 1969

trained by US Olympic coach Sherman Chavoor — qualified for the Olympics. Even though Debbie contracted a severe stomach infection, she refused to take medication as it would have disqualified her. Despite her illness, Meyer won the 200 m, 400 m and 800 m freestyle events, breaking the Olympic record for each. She was the first woman swimmer to win three gold medals in one Olympics. Meyer retired from competitive swimming when she was only 18 years old.

Mark Spitz (1968-1972)

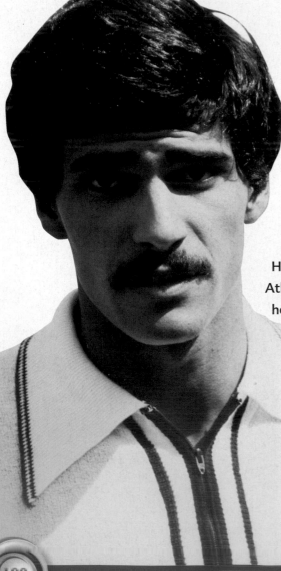

Born in 1950, Mark Spitz is one of the greatest swimmers in history. In the 1972 Olympics at Munich he won seven gold medals, setting a new world record for each event. This wasn't the first time that Spitz had made a major splash. in 1971 he became the first swimmer to win four AAU individual events at a single meet. He also won eight National Collegiate Athletic Association (NCAA) titles while he was a student at the University of Indiana. It was no surprise, then, that he was named 'World Swimmer of the Year' in 1969, 1971 and 1972. The International Olympic Committee, too, has recognised him as one of the 'Five Athletes of the Century.' Spitz's butterfly stroke remains legendary and he still has many fans worldwide.

Winning Streak

Olympic medals: 11
1968 (Mexico City)
- 4 x 100 m freestyle relay, 4 x 200 m freestyle relay
- Silver Medal: 100 m butterfly
- Bronze Medal: 100 m freestyle

1972 (Munich)
- Gold Medal: 100 m freestyle, 200 m freestyle, 4 x 100 m freestyle relay, 4 x 200 m freestyle relay, 100 m butterfly, 200 m butterfly, 4 x 100 m medley relay

Other Highlights
- Won 24 AAU titles
- Won five gold medals at the Pan-American Championships in 1967
- Set over 30 world records including 26 individual records

Alberto Juantorena (1972-1980)

Born in 1950, this Cuban track champion started out as a basketball player but was later advised to take up running as a career. Juantorena took the advice and qualified for the 1976 Olympics, where — having only seriously taken up running the 800 m earlier that year — he became the first and so far only athlete to win both the 400 m and 800 m Olympic titles. He became known as '*El Caballo*' (the horse) because of his three-metre stride, and '*White Lightning*' for his amazing speed. He just missed out on a medal in the 400 m at the 1980 Summer Olympics in Moscow, coming fourth. Juantorena went on to serve as the Vice Minister of Sports for Cuba.

Winning Streak

Olympic medals: 2
1976 (Montreal)
- Gold Medal: 400 m, 800 m

Other Highlights
- Ranked first in the world for 400 m in 1974, 1976, 1977 and 1978; in 1976 and 1977, he was ranked first for 800 m

Don Quarrie
(1972-1984)

With a track and field career spanning four Olympics, Quarrie is one of Jamaica's most celebrated athletes. The entrance to the National Stadium at Jamaica features a statue of him and he has even had songs written about him! He is regarded as one of the finest sprinters in the history of track and field and is considered the greatest runner around the bend. Quarrie won medals at three Olympic Games — an exceptional accomplishment for a sprinter. In Montreal in 1976, he won the 200 m and was only 0.01 seconds behind the winner of the 100 m. He was involved in a car accident in the run up to the 1980 Olympics in Moscow, but still managed to recover and win the bronze medal in the 200 m. He was the first male athlete to earn six gold medals in the Commonwealth Games, taking gold in the 100 m for three consecutive Games. He was also admired and respected for his good nature and behaviour both on and off the track.

Winning Streak

Olympic medals: 4
1976 (Montreal)
- Gold Medal: 200 m
- Silver Medal: 100 m

1980 (Moscow)
- Bronze Medal: 200 m

1984 (Los Angeles)
- Silver Medal: 4 x 100 m relay

Other Highlights
- Became the first athlete to retain the two titles for 100 m and 200 m at the Commonwealth Games

Lasse Virén (1972-1980)

A former police officer, this Finnish long-distance runner won a total of four Olympic gold medals, and set three world records in 1972. His win in the 10,000 m event at the Munich Games was one of his most memorable, since he fell down in the twelfth lap. While Viren focused much of his career on the Olympics and on rigorous training (rather than on various championships), he was twice elected '*Sportsman of the Year*' in Finland. In 1980, he announced retirement from active competitive running. He went on to become a well-known politician in Finland.

Winning Streak

Olympic medals: 4
1972 (Munich)
- Gold Medal: 5,000 m, 10,000 m

1976 (Montreal)
- Gold Medal: 5,000 m, 10,000 m

Other Highlights
- Set three world records in 1972 for 5,000 m, 2 miles and with his gold medal winning run in the 10,000 m

Evelyn Ashford (1976-1992)

Described as "*one of the greatest track and field runners ever*" by the National Track and Field Hall of Fame, this American athlete was the first woman to run under 11 seconds in an Olympic Games. She was conferred the title of '*Athlete of the Year*' by *Track and Field News* twice. In 1985, she parted ways with her coach Pat Connolly and ever since then trained herself, winning a gold medal in both the 1988 and 1992 Olympics. She was the flag bearer for the United States team in the Opening Ceremony at the 1988 Olympics.

Winning Streak

Olympic medals: 5
1984 (Los Angeles)
- Gold Medal: 100 m, 4 x 100 m relay

1988 (Seoul)
- Gold Medal: 4 x 100 m relay
- Silver Medal: 100 m

1992 (Barcelona)
- Gold Medal: 4 x 100 m relay

Other Highlights
- Won two World Cup titles for 100 m and 200 m sprints in 1979, and retained them in 1981
- Set a world record of 10.76 seconds for 100 m in 1984

Nadia Comaneci (1976-1980)

Winning Streak

Olympic medals: 9

1976 (Montreal)

- Gold Medal: individual all-around, balance beam, uneven bars
- Silver Medal: team all-around
- Bronze Medal: floor exercise

1980 (Moscow)

- Gold Medal: floor exercise, balance beam
- Silver Medal: individual all-around, team all-around

Other Highlights

- Won 3 gold medals in the pre-Olympic Junior Meet in 1972
- Was the all-around winner in the European Championships in 1975, 1977 and 1979, winning a total of 12 medals (9 gold) over the 3 competitions
- Won the American Cup in New York City in 1976

This Romanian gymnast was only 14 years old when she won three gold medals at the Montreal Olympics. She was also the first gymnast to get a perfect score of 10 for her performance on the uneven parallel bars. In all, she got a perfect score seven times during the Games! While her Olympic performance won Comaneci fans all over the world, she was already famous back in Romania, where she was the youngest person to win the Romanian nationals. Comaneci went on to win two more gold medals at the 1980 Olympics. Her original skills and techniques ensured that she won many events before her retirement in 1981. Nadia eventually married an American gymnast, Olympic gold medalist Bart Conner, and settled down in the US.

Edwin Moses
(1976-1988)

One of the greatest hurdlers of all time, this American athlete was not defeated even once between 1977 and 1987. Moses burst on to the track and field arena in 1976 when he won the Olympic gold medal for the 400 m hurdles. There was no stopping for him from that point on and he became known for his unique style of running. This physics and industrial engineering student went on to set many world records and was named '*Athlete of the Year*' by *Track and Field News* in 1980. After he retired, Moses became Chairman of the Laureus World Sports Academy, which works towards using sports as a tool for social change.

Winning Streak

Olympic medals: 3

1976 (Montreal)

- Gold Medal: 400 m hurdles

1984 (Los Angeles)

- Gold Medal: 400 m hurdles

1988 (Seoul)

- Bronze Medal: 400 m hurdles

Other Highlights

- Set his first world record of 47.64 secs in the 1976 Games and his last world record of 47.02 secs in 1983
- Had 122 consecutive wins

Steve Ovett (1976-1984)

A middle-distance runner, Steve Ovett is one of the most talented athletes to emerge from the United Kingdom. He won the European Junior 800 m title in 1973, kicking off a great career. While he stood fifth in his first Olympic event in 1976, he was back in much better form in 1980. He had won several AAA titles and had made a name for himself in Europe. At the Olympics, he won the 800 m race, and came third in the 1,500 m race. In fact, he won 45 1,500 m races in a row before his defeat at Moscow. Although Ovett qualified for the 1984 Olympics, he could not perform well due to health problems. He had to be hospitalised after he collapsed in the middle of a race. He retired a few years later, having set six world records in his career.

Winning Streak

Olympic medals: 2
1980 (Moscow)
- Gold Medal: 800 m
- Bronze Medal: 1,500 m

Other Highlights
- Won the European Cup in 1975 and 1977, and the World Cup in 1977 and 1981
- Won the 5,000 m at the 1986 Commonwealth Games

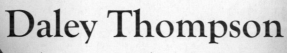

Daley Thompson
(1976-1988)

Born Francis Morgan Oyodélé Thompson, but known commonly as Daley Thompson, this English decathlete has four world records, three Commonwealth titles and two Olympic Gold medals to his credit. When, in 1983, Daley was crowned the all-round king at the inaugural World Championships, he became the first decathlete to hold the European, World and Olympic titles simultaneously. He is revered as one of the greatest decathletes in history. A prolonged hamstring injury forced him into retirement from athletics in 1992. He moved on to work as a fitness coach for the football clubs at Luton Town and Wimbledon FC. Daley was awarded the MBE in 1982, the OBE in 1986, and the CBE in 2000 and was chosen as an ambassador for the London 2012 Olympics.

Winning Streak

Olympic medals: 2
1980 (Moscow)
- Gold Medal: men's decathlon
1984 (Los Angeles)
- Gold Medal: men's decathlon

Other Highlights
- Won the World Championship for decathlon in 1983 and the European Championships in 1982 and 1986

Winning Streak

Olympic medals: 12

1980 (Moscow)
- Gold Medal: kayak singles 500 m

1988 (Seoul)
- Gold Medal: kayak doubles 500 m, kayak fours 500 m
- Silver Medal: kayak singles 500 m

1992 (Barcelona)
- Gold Medal: kayak singles 500 m
- Silver Medal: kayak fours 500 m

1996 (Atlanta)
- Gold Medal: kayak fours 500 m
- Silver Medal: kayak doubles 500 m

2000 (Sydney)
- Gold Medal: kayak doubles 500 m, kayak fours 500 m

2004 (Athens)
- Gold Medal: kayak fours 500 m
- Silver Medal: kayak doubles 500 m

Other Highlights
- Her Olympic career spans 7 Olympiads
- Won 38 different ICF Canoe Sprint World Championships medals between 1978 and 2005, including 28 golds

Birgit Fischer
(1980-2004)

Birgit Fischer was only 18 when she won her first Olympic gold medal. It was the beginning of a long and successful Olympic career for the talented kayaker who won 8 golds and 4 silver medals. At 42, she was the oldest canoeing champion. In fact, she has been the youngest as well as oldest Olympic canoeing champion. In addition to this, she has earned 38 canoe sprint World Championship medals between 1978 and 2005. She was declared the '*German Sportswoman of the Year*' in 2004. She retired in 2000 but made a comeback in the 2004 Olympics and won a gold and silver medal.

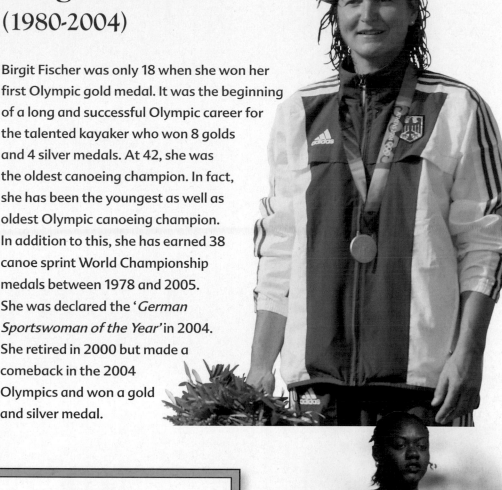

Merlene Ottey
(1980-2004)

Jamaican-born Merlene Ottey ranks among the greatest 100 m and 200 m female athletes of all time. Her total of nine Olympic medals is yet to be exceeded by any other female track and field athlete. However, Merlene Ottey also earned the nickname '*Bronze Queen*' as she never won an Olympic gold medal — she lost out to Gail Devers in the 100 m at Atlanta in 1996 by five-thousandths of a second! Nevertheless, Ottey won several gold medals in other events, including the Commonwealth Games. She was named '*Jamaican Sports-woman of the Year*' 15 times between 1979 and 1997, although she became a citizen of Slovenia in 2002. Ottey has set many world records in one of the longest track and field careers in the world.

Winning Streak

Olympic medals: 9

1980 (Moscow)
- Bronze Medal: 200 m

1984 (Los Angeles)
- Bronze Medal: 100 m, 200 m

1992 (Barcelona)
- Bronze Medal: 200 m

1996 (Atlanta)
- Silver Medal: 100 m, 200 m
- Bronze Medal: 4 x 100 m relay

2000 (Sydney)
- Silver Medal: 4 x 100 m relay
- Bronze Medal: 100 m

Other Highlights
- Holds the record for running 100 m in under 11 seconds 67 times
- Holds 14 World Championship medals

Sebastian Coe (1980-1984)

One of the greatest middle-distance runners of all time, Coe became the first athlete to win the 1,500 m Olympic title twice. This British athlete also set several national and world records. Ironically, some of his best performances were for the 800 m, but he won only one Olympic gold for this event. His rivalries with fellow Britons Steve Ovett and Steve Cram dominated middle-distance racing for much of the 1980s. After retirement he went into politics, later successfully leading London's bid for the 2012 Summer Olympics. He was awarded the MBE in 1982, the OBE in 1990, and the KBE in 2006.

Winning Streak

Olympic medals: 4

1980 (Moscow)
- Gold Medal: 1,500 m
- Silver Medal: 800 m

1984 (Los Angeles)
- Gold Medal: 1,500 m
- Silver Medal: 800 m

Other Highlights
- Set 9 outdoor world records and 3 indoor ones in the 800 m, 1,000 m, 1,500 m and mile and held records for 800 m, 1,500 m and mile concurrently
- Won the 800 m European Championships in 1986

Carl Lewis (1984-1996)

Termed '*Olympian of the Century*' by *Sports Illustrated* and '*Sportsman of the Century*' by the IOC, this track and field athlete was a remarkable sprinter and long jumper who set world records in the 100 m, 4 x 100 m and 4 x 200 m relays. He bagged a total of 65 consecutive wins in the long jump which is one of the longest winning streaks in athletics, although has never set a world record in the outdoor long jump. Lewis is one of only three athletes to win the same individual Olympic event four times.

Winning Streak

Olympic medals: 10

1984 (Los Angeles)
- Gold Medal: 100 m, 200 m, 4 x 100 m relay, long jump

1988 (Seoul)
- Gold Medal: 100 m, long jump
- Silver Medal: 200 m

1992 (Barcelona)
- Gold Medal: 4 x 100 m relay, long jump

1996 (Atlanta)
- Gold Medal: long jump

Other Highlights
- Won 10 World Championship medals, of which 8 were gold
- His world record in the indoor long jump has stood since 1984
- Had 65 consecutive victories in the long jump over 10 years — one of the sport's longest undefeated streaks

Jackie Joyner-Kersee (1984-1996)

Born in 1962 in St. Louis, Illinois, Jackie Joyner-Kersee is considered to be amongst the greatest athletes in women's Heptathlon and long jump. She won the first of four straight National Junior Pentathlon Championships when she was just 14. Jackie went on to win a silver medal at the 1984 Olympics. In 1986, she went on to set a new world record in the Heptathlon at the Goodwill Games in Moscow, becoming the first woman to pass 7,000 points. She beat her own record just three weeks later, in the US Olympic Festival in Houston, Texas, scoring 7,158 points. She retired in February 2001.

Winning Streak

Olympic medals: 6

1984 (Los Angeles)
- Silver Medal: Heptathlon

1988 (Seoul)
- Gold Medal: long jump, Heptathlon

1992 (Barcelona)
- Gold Medal: Heptathlon
- Bronze Medal: long jump

1996 (Atlanta)
- Bronze Medal: long jump

Other Highlights
- Holds the world record in Heptathlon since 1988 with 7,291 points

Dara Torres (1984-2008)

Dara Grace Torres is the first American swimmer to compete in five Olympics, and the first woman to swim in the Olympics past the age of 40. Although she first thought of retiring at the age of 25, she later stated that "*age is just a number*" and pushed for more victories. She won 12 Olympic medals in all. Trained by renowned coach Darlene Bible, she earned 28 All-American swimming honours — the maximum number possible in a college career. Torres, along with Amanda Beard and Natalie Coughlin, was elected as one of the captains of the US Olympic Women's Swimming team for Beijing in 2008.

Winning Streak

Olympic medals: 12

1984 (Los Angeles)
- Gold Medal: 4 x 100 m freestyle relay

1988 (Seoul)
- Silver Medal: 4 x 100 m medley relay
- Bronze Medal: 4 x 100 m freestyle relay

1992 (Barcelona)
- Gold Medal: 4 x 100 m medley relay

2000 (Sydney)
- Gold Medal: 4 x 100 m freestyle relay, 4 x 100 m medley relay
- Bronze Medal: 50 m freestyle, 100 m freestyle, 100 m butterfly

2008 (Beijing)
- Silver Medal: 4 x 100 m freestyle relay, 4 x 100 m medley relay, 50 m freestyle

Other Highlights
- Is one of only a handful of Olympians to earn medals in five different Games

Matt Biondi
(1984-1992)

Born in 1965, American Matt Biondi is a phenomenal Olympic swimmer. He swam in the 1984, 1988 and 1992 Olympics, and won a gold medal each time. Over the course of his career, he earned dozens of national, international and collegiate titles and set 12 world records. He reached his peak at the 1988 Olympics in Seoul, winning seven medals to tie the record set by swimming legend Mark Spitz in 1972. The first swimmer to win seven medals at a World Championship, Matt also became the first swimmer in more than a half-century to sweep the 50, 100, and 200-yard freestyle races in the NCAA Championships. He is a member of the US Olympic Hall of Fame and the International Swimming Hall of Fame.

Winning Streak

Olympic medals: 11
1984 (Los Angeles)
- Gold Medal: 4 x 100 m freestyle relay

1988 (Seoul)
- Gold Medal: 50 m freestyle, 100 m freestyle, 4 x 100 m freestyle relay, 4 x 200 m freestyle relay, 4 x 100 m medley relay
- Silver Medal: 100 m butterfly
- Bronze Medal: 200 m freestyle

1992 (Barcelona)
- Gold Medal: 4 x 100 m freestyle relay, 4 x 100 m medley relay
- Silver Medal: 50 m freestyle

Other Highlights
- Set 7 individual world records (3 at 50 m freestyle and 4 at 100 m freestyle)
- At the 1986 World Championships he won 3 gold medals, 1 silver and 3 bronzes to set a record of 7 medals at one World Championship meet *

* since equalled by Michael Phelps

Steve Redgrave (1984-2000)

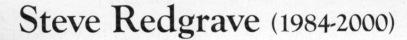

Sir Stephen Geoffrey Redgrave was born in 1962, in Marlow, England. This British rower has won gold medals at five consecutive Olympic Games — the only Briton ever to achieve this feat — and is considered by some to be Britain's greatest Olympian. He has won nine rowing World Championship gold medals, and three gold medals at the 1986 Commonwealth Games. In 1989, he started bobsledding competitively and was part of a championship-winning team. What is most remarkable is that this great sportsman has battled several illnesses throughout his career, including diabetes. Since retiring from competitive sport, Redgrave has participated in various events for charity. He was made an MBE in 1987, a CBE in 1997, and was awarded the title of Knight Bachelor in 2001.

Winning Streak

Olympic medals: 6
1984 (Los Angeles)
- Gold Medal: Coxed Fours

1988 (Seoul)
- Gold Medal: Coxless Pairs
- Bronze Medal: Coxed Pairs

1992 (Barcelona)
- Gold Medal: Coxless Pairs

1996 (Atlanta)
- Gold Medal: Coxless Pairs

2000 (Sydney)
- Gold Medal: Coxless Fours

Other Highlights
- Won 9 gold medals, 2 silvers, and a bronze at the rowing World Championships and 3 Commonwealth golds

Hassiba Boulmerka (1988-1996)

This middle-distance Algerian athlete specialised in 800 m and 1,500 m races. Her first breakthrough came in 1991 when she won the 1,500 m World Championship, becoming the first African woman to win the world title. An inspiration to Muslim women the world over for her courage and determination, Boulmerka remained under surveillance of fundamentalist groups in Algeria for showing too much skin while racing. She later moved to Europe to train. Boulmerka won a gold medal for the 1,500 m at the 1992 Summer Olympics in Barcelona, setting a an African record time.

Winning Streak

Olympic medals: 1
1992 (Barcelona)
- Gold Medal: 1,500 m

Other Highlights
- Won 2 World Championship gold medals for the 1,500 m (in 1991 and 1995) and 3 Mediterranean Games golds — two for the 800 m (in 1991 and 1993) and one for the 1,500 m in 1991
- Was honoured with Algeria's prestigious Medal of Merit

Gwen Torrence (1988-1996)

Gwen Torrence was born in 1965, in the US city of Georgia. The only slow part of Gwen's life, her mother once said, was when she was born with the umbilical cord around her neck, which left her spending the first few days of her life in an incubator. Torrence grew up to become one of the most celebrated runners in history. She has won a medal in almost every major athletics competition including three Olympic gold medals and three golds in the World Championships. Torrence became a hairdresser after she retired from athletics.

Winning Streak

Olympic medals: 5
1992 (Barcelona)
- Gold Medal: 200 m,
  4 x 100 m relay
  Silver Medal: 4 x 400 m relay

1996 (Atlanta)
- Gold Medal: 4 x 100 m relay
- Bronze Medal: 100 m

Other Highlights
- At the 1995 World Championships she won gold in the 100 m and the 4 x 100 m relay
- Won many medals in World and National Championships and in National Indoor Championships over 60 m, 100 m and 200 m

Heike Drechsler (1988-2000)

Heike Gabriela Drechsler is a German athlete who has won medals in both track and field events. In her first Olympics in 1988, she took silver in the long jump and bronze in the 100 m and 200 m events. Considered one of the most successful female long jumpers, she went on to win gold in the 1992 and 2000 Olympics. She also won many gold medals at various European, German and World Championships. Drechsler set five outdoor and eight indoor world records: ten in the long jump and three in the 200 m. She was conferred with the *'Distinguished Career Award'* by the IAAF in 2000 and *'Female Long Jumper of the Century'* by *Track & Field News* magazine. She has retired from athletics.

Winning Streak

Olympic medals: 5

1988 (Seoul)
- Silver Medal: long jump
- Bronze Medal: 100 m, 200 m

1992 (Barcelona)
- Gold Medal: long jump

2000 (Sydney)
- Gold Medal: long jump

Other Highlights
- Won gold for long jump in the World Championships in 1983 and 1993
- Won gold for long jump and 200 m in the World Indoor Championship in 1987 and in the European Championships won 4 long jump golds and another for the 200 m

Krisztina Egerszegi (1988-1996)

Born in 1974, this Hungarian swimmer was only 14 years old when she won her first two Olympic medals. She was then the youngest athlete ever to win a swimming gold. Egerszegi became known as one of the best backstroke swimmers of all time, and won a total of four gold medals for the event. She held the record for the 100 m backstroke between 1991 and 1994, and her record for the 200 m backstroke remained unbroken for 17 years. She was also named *'World Swimmer of the Year'* in 1991, 1992 and 1995. Along with Dawn Fraser, she is one of only two women to win the gold medal for the same event in three consecutive Olympics. She has now retired from swimming.

Winning Streak

Olympic medals: 7

1988 (Seoul)
- Gold Medal: 200 m backstroke
- Silver Medal: 100 m backstroke

1992 (Barcelona)
- Gold Medal: 100 m backstroke, 200 m backstroke, 400 m individual medley

1996 (Atlanta)
- Gold Medal: 200 m backstroke
- Bronze Medal: 400 m individual medley

Other Highlights
- Won 2 golds in the 1991 World Championship and 9 golds in the 1991, 1993 and 1995 European Championships

Yolanda Gail Devers (1988-2004)

Gail Devers was born in 1966, in Seattle, Washington. Devers first became interested in running as a child. One of the fastest female runners in the world, she achieved fame by winning the 100 m sprint at the Barcelona Olympics in 1992. Also an accomplished hurdler, Devers faced the toughest hurdle in her life when she was diagnosed with Graves' disease, a dangerous illness that affects the thyroid gland. Devers overcame the disease to become one of the leading track and field performers in the world.

Winning Streak

Olympic medals: 3

1992 (Barcelona)
- Gold Medal: 100 m

1996 (Atlanta)
- Gold Medal: 100 m, 4 x 100 m relay

Other Highlights
- Won the 100 m high hurdles title in the World Championships in 1993, 1995 and 1999
- Won the 100 m at the 1993 World Championships and 1996 Olympics, both times narrowly defeating Jamaican runner, Merlene Ottey

Cathy Freeman (1992-2000)

Winning Streak

Olympic medals: 2

1996 (Atlanta)
- Silver Medal: 400 m

2000 (Sydney)
- Gold Medal: 400 m

Other Highlights
- Won gold at the 1990 Commonwealth Games as part of the 4 x 100 m relay team at the age of 16
- Won 2 World Championship gold medals for the 400 m (1997 and 1999) and 1 bronze (1995) for the 4 x 400 m relay

This Australian-Aboriginal sprinter is known for her determination. When she failed to win a medal at the 1992 Olympics in Barcelona, she scribbled her plans down on a paper bag *"48.60 Atlanta."* She reached her goal. At the Atlanta Olympics she won her first Olympic medal. She came second after finishing the women's 400 m race in 48.63 seconds! She was also the first Aborigine to win an individual medal at the Olympics. A hero in her country, she lit the Olympic torch for the Sydney Games in 2000. She won her first gold medal in the 400 m event that year, having recently won many other 400 m events, including the World Championship. She was named *'Australian of the Year'* in 2008 and was awarded the Order of Australia medal in 2001. She is now retired from athletics.

Michael Johnson
(1992-2000)

Born in 1967, in Dallas, Texas, Michael Johnson reached his peak as a runner in the 1990s, when he was almost unbeaten in the 200 m and 400 m races. He won four Olympic gold medals and was the World Champion eight times. Carl Lewis was the only other runner who won as many World Championships. In 1999 he set a new world record of 43.18 seconds in the 400 m. In the 2000 Olympics he again won two gold medals. Known for his unique running style (with stiff upright stance and very short steps), he was the first man to top both the 200 m and 400 m rankings simultaneously. Not just that, he achieved this feat five times!

Winning Streak

Olympic medals: 4

1992 (Barcelona)
- Gold Medal: 4 x 100 m relay

1996 (Atlanta)
- Gold Medal: 200 m, 400 m

2000 (Sydney)
- Gold Medal: 400 m

Other Highlights
- Ranked first in the world in the 200 m and 400 m sprints in 1990
- Won 8 World Championship golds between 1991 and 1999 in 200 m (2), 400 m (4) and 4 x 400 m relay (2)
- Set many world records over 200 m, 400 m and 4 x 400 m relay

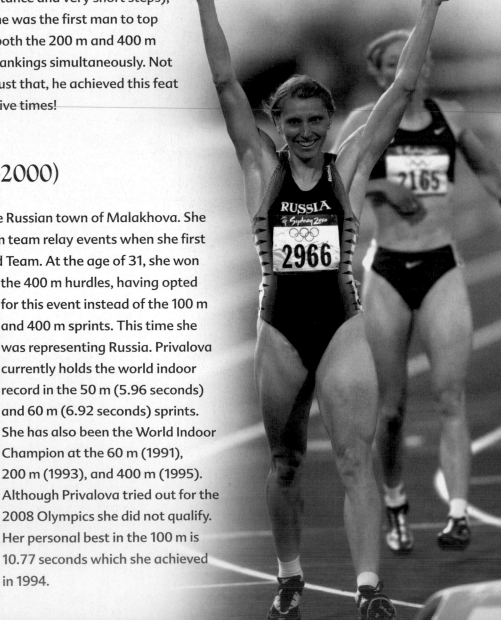

Irina Privalova (1992-2000)

Irina Anatoljewna Privalova was born in 1968, in the Russian town of Malakhova. She won two Olympic medals in the 100 m and 4 x 100 m team relay events when she first participated in 1992, whilst representing the Unified Team. At the age of 31, she won the 400 m hurdles, having opted for this event instead of the 100 m and 400 m sprints. This time she was representing Russia. Privalova currently holds the world indoor record in the 50 m (5.96 seconds) and 60 m (6.92 seconds) sprints. She has also been the World Indoor Champion at the 60 m (1991), 200 m (1993), and 400 m (1995). Although Privalova tried out for the 2008 Olympics she did not qualify. Her personal best in the 100 m is 10.77 seconds which she achieved in 1994.

Winning Streak

Olympic medals: 4

1992 (Barcelona)
- Silver Medal: 4 x 100 m relay
- Bronze Medal: 100 m

2000 (Sydney)
- Gold Medal: 400 m hurdles
- Bronze Medal: 4 x 400 m relay

Other Highlights
- Won a gold in the 100 m and 200 m in the 1994 European Championships and a 200 m gold in 1998
- Was declared '*Women's European Athlete of the Year*' in 1994

Jennifer Thompson (1992-2004)

Born in 1973, this American has won 12 Olympic medals, including eight gold medals (more than any other female swimmer), in the 1992, 1996, 2000, and 2004 Games. She won all her gold medals in relay events, losing out in some individual events by a fraction. She started swimming at the age of seven and first appeared on the international scene when she was 14. Thompson won the 50 m freestyle and stood third in the 100 m freestyle in 1987. She won her first World Championship in 1991, as part of the USA's winning 4 x 100 m freestyle relay team, and held the world record in the 50 m and 100 m freestyle in the 1992 Olympics.

Jennifer Thompson

Winning Streak

Olympic medals: 12

1992 (Barcelona)
- Gold Medal: 4 x 100 m relay (freestyle), 4 x 100 m relay (medley)
- Silver Medal: 100 m (freestyle)

1996 (Atlanta)
- Gold Medal: 4 x 100 m relay (freestyle), 4 x 100 m relay (medley), 4 x 200 m relay (freestyle)

2000 (Sydney)
- Gold Medal: 4 x 100 m relay (freestyle), 4 x 100 m relay (medley), 4 x 200 m relay (freestyle)
- Bronze Medal: 100 m (freestyle)

2004 (Athens)
- Silver Medal: 4 x 100 m relay (freestyle), 4 x 100 m relay (medley)

Other Highlights
- 18 World Championship gold medals
- Won 25 gold medals in the Pan Pacific Championships

Amy Van Dyken (1996-2000)

Amy Van Dyken was yet another athlete who didn't allow asthma to prevent her from becoming one of America's best swimmers. Born in 1973, she started swimming at the age of six and has won her country many accolades. She won four of her six Olympic gold medals at the Atlanta Olympics in 1996. She made history when she became the first American woman to win four golds at a single Olympics. She won gold in the 50 m freestyle, 100 m butterfly, 4 x 100 m freestyle relay, and the 4 x 100 m medley relay. At the 2000 Olympic Games in Sydney, Dyken won two more gold medals, and finished fourth in the 50 m freestyle.

Winning Streak

Olympic medals: 6

1996 (Atlanta)
- Gold Medal: 50 m freestyle, 4 x 100 m freestyle relay, 100 m butterfly, 4 x 100 m medley relay

2000 (Sydney)
- Gold Medal: 4 x 100 m freestyle relay, 4 x 100 m medley relay

Other Highlights
- Won 3 gold medals in the 1988 Perth World Championship in the 50 m, 4 x 100 m freestyle relay and 4 x 100 m medley relay

Kelly Holmes (1996-2004)

Born to a Jamaican father and a British mother in 1970, Kelly started training when she was 12. Now retired, this immensely successful British woman broke a number of national records. She enrolled in the British Army and only turned to professional athletics in the early 1990s. She specialised in the 800 m and 1,500 m and in 2004 in Athens became the third woman in history to win the middle-distance Olympic double. She was awarded the title '*Dame*' for her achievements and was '*European Woman Athlete of the Year*' in 2004.

Winning Streak

Olympic medals: 3
2000 (Sydney)
- Bronze Medal: 800 m

2004 (Athens)
- Gold Medal: 800 m, 1,500 m

Other Highlights
- Won the 1,500 m gold in the 1994 and 2002 Commonwealth Games

Winning Streak

Olympic medals: 12
1996 (Atlanta)
- Gold Medal: team all-around, horse vault
- Silver Medal: individual all-around
- Bronze Medal: floor exercise, pommel horse, horizontal bar

2000 (Sydney)
- Gold Medal: individual all-around, horizontal bar
- Silver Medal: floor exercise
- Bronze Medal: team all-around, pommel horse, parallel bars

Other Highlights
- Won 3 individual gold medals at the European Championships
- Won 13 medals at the World Championships including 5 individual gold medals

Alexei Nemov (1996-2000)

Alexei Yurievich Nemov was born in 1976, in Mordovia, Russia. The winner of 12 Olympic medals, Nemov has won six bronze — more than any other gymnast except Finland's Heikki Savoleninen. At the age of 16, Nemov participated in the 1993 World Championship, his first senior event. His career as an all-rounder took off and he went on to win six medals in the 1996 Olympics. He became famous for his complicated routines, but was not expected to do so well at the Sydney Olympics as he had suffered injuries and his performance had been declining. He surprised everyone by winning six medals, including the all-around title.

Maurice Greene (2000-2004)

Born in 1974, this American sprinter reached the peak of his career between 1997 and 2001. His greatest strengths were the 100 m and 200 m. He was the record holder for the 100 m in 1999 and in the same year won the National Championship for the 200 m. He was ranked first for seven years until 2003. His career was marred by a motorbike accident which affected his form. He remains the world record holder in the 60 metre dash and the joint-fastest man over 50 metres. Now retired, he once said, *"If you want to be number one, you have to train like you're number two."*

Winning Streak

Olympic medals: 4

2000 (Sydney)
- Gold Medal: 100 m, 4 x 100 m relay

2004 (Athens)
- Silver Medal: 4 x 100 m relay
- Bronze Medal: 100 m

Other Highlights
- Won 5 gold medals in the World Championships between 1997 and 2001, 3 of which were for 100 m, 1 for 200 m and 1 for 4 x 100 m relay
- Holds the world record for the 60 m sprint at 6.39 seconds

Michael Phelps (2000-2008)

Known as the '*Baltimore Bullet*,' this American swimmer is one of the greatest Olympians ever. He holds the Olympic record for winning the most gold medals (eight) in a single Games and the most gold medals (14) in a career. Born in 1985, Phelps started swimming at the age of seven. At 15, he became the youngest swimmer since 1932 to participate in the Olympics, although he did not win any medals at the Sydney Games. In the following year at the US Spring Nationals, Phelps became the youngest swimmer to set a world record in the 200 m butterfly. Today, he has broken more world records than any other swimmer and has won scores of medals.

Winning Streak

Olympic medals: 16

2004 (Athens)
- Gold Medal: 4 x 200 m freestyle relay, 100 m butterfly, 200 m butterfly, 200 m individual medley, 400 m individual medley, 4 x 100 m medley relay
- Bronze Medal: 200 m freestyle, 4 x 100 m freestyle relay

2008 (Beijing)
- Gold Medal: 200 m freestyle, 4 x 100 m freestyle relay, 4 x 200 m freestyle relay, 100 m butterfly, 200 m butterfly, 200 m individual medley, 400 m Individual medley, 4 x 100 m medley relay

Other Highlights
- Has won many awards and 50 gold medals in major international competitions

Venus Williams (2000-2008)

Venus Ebony Starr Williams is one of the most celebrated tennis stars of all time. Born in 1980, this American athlete is coached by her father Richard Williams, and is the older sister of tennis champion Serena.

She holds the fastest recorded serve in WTA history! One of her best years in tennis was in 2000, when she won singles titles at Wimbledon, the US Open and the Sydney Olympics, and doubles titles at Wimbledon and Sydney with Serena. Her victory at Wimbledon made her the first African American woman tennis champion since Althea Gibson in 1957 and 1958.

Winning Streak

Olympic medals: 3
2000 (Sydney)
- Gold Medal: singles, doubles

2008 (Beijing)
- Gold Medal: doubles

Other Highlights
- Won Wimbledon Grand Slam in 2000, 2001, 2005, 2007 and 2008 and the US Open in 2000 and 2001
- Holds the record for the fastest serve by a woman in the US Open, French Open and Wimbledon

Usain Bolt (2004-2008)

This Jamaican sprinter is called the '*Lightning Bolt*' for a good reason. Born in 1986 Jamaica, young Bolt showed great interest in cricket. However, his coach recognised Bolt's talent and steered him towards track and field events. There was no stopping Bolt after that. At 15, he won a gold and two silver medals at the World Junior Championship in Jamaica, making him the youngest junior gold medalist ever.

He soon accumulated a number of medals and world records. Unfortunately, a leg injury meant that he did not win any medals in the 2004 Olympics, but the determined sprinter made a comeback in 2008 in Beijing. There, on the eve of his 22nd birthday, he became the first athlete since Carl Lewis to win the double sprint (100 m and 200 m) gold. He was also the first man to break the world record for both events.

Winning Streak

Olympic medals: 3
2008 (Beijing)
- Gold Medal: 100 m, 200 m, 4 x 100 m relay

Other Highlights
- Broke the world record for 100 m, 200 m and 4 x 100 m relay
- Won 3 gold medals in the 2009 World Championships 200 m
- Became the youngest ever gold medalist (200 m) at the 2002 World Junior Championships

MEDAL TABLES

Statistics relating to the modern Olympic Games

The Olympic Games Through the Years

The Olympic Games have changed dramatically over the years — in terms of the numbers of athletes and nations participating, the number of sports and individual events contested, and in terms of the percentage of female athletes competing at the Games. The following table shows this trend.

Summer Games

Summer Games	Year	Number of Athletes	Women Athletes	Number of NOCs	Number of Events
Athens	1896	241	0	14	43
Paris	1900	997	22	24	95
St. Louis	1904	651	6	12	91
London	1908	2,008	37	22	110
Stockholm	1912	2,407	48	28	102
Antwerp	1920	2,626	65	29	154
Paris	1924	3,089	135	44	126
Amsterdam	1928	2,883	277	46	109
Los Angeles	1932	1,332	126	37	117
Berlin	1936	3963	331	49	129
London	1948	4,104	390	59	136
Helsinki	1952	4,955	519	69	149
Melbourne	1956	3,314	376	72	145
Rome	1960	5,338	611	83	150
Tokyo	1964	5,151	678	93	163
Mexico City	1968	5,516	781	112	172
Munich	1972	7,134	1,059	121	195
Montreal	1976	6,084	1,260	92	198
Moscow	1980	5,179	1,115	80	203
Los Angeles	1984	6,829	1,566	140	221
Seoul	1988	8,391	2,194	159	237
Barcelona	1992	9,356	2,704	169	257
Atlanta	1996	10,318	3,512	197	271
Sydney	2000	10,651	4,069	199	300
Athens	2004	10,625	4,329	201	301
Beijing	2008	10,942	4,637	204	302

Notes
1. People often talk about the number of countries taking part in the Games, but it would be more accurate to refer to the NOCs — or National Olympic Committees. For example, the media referred to 204 'countries' competing in the 2008 Summer Olympic Games in Beijing but some of these 'countries' are actually territories or other entities that have been permitted by the International Olympic Committee to have their own National Olympic Committee: Bermuda, the British Virgin Islands and the Cayman Islands (which are all territories of the United Kingdom); Puerto Rico, Guam, American Samoa and the US Virgin Islands (all territories of the US); Hong Kong (which is a special administrative region of China); Aruba (part of the Netherlands) and Netherlands Antilles (a territory of the Netherlands); the Cook Islands (self-governing in free association with New Zealand); and Palestine (whose official country status is disputed). There were only 3 officially recognised independent countries that did not participate in the Olympic Games in 2008. These were Brunei (which did not register its athletes on time); the new country of Kosovo (which does not yet have a NOC); and the Vatican City (which does not have a NOC).
2. Some discrepancies exist due to incomplete or inaccurate records, countries participating in Opening Ceremonies but not competing in events and, at the earliest Games, events being held at the same time that were not clearly part of the Olympic Games, or that the athletes received payment for.

Winter Games

Winter Games	Year	Number of Athletes	Women Athletes	Number of NOCs	Number of Events
Chamonix, France	1924	258	11	16	16
St. Moritz, Switzerland	1928	464	26	25	14
Lake Placid, United States	1932	252	21	17	14
Garmisch-Partenkirchen, Germany	1936	646	80	28	17
St. Moritz, Switzerland	1948	669	77	28	22
Oslo, Norway	1952	694	109	30	22
Cortina d'Ampezzo, Italy	1956	821	134	32	24
Squaw Valley, United States	1960	665	144	30	27
Innsbruck, Austria	1964	1091	199	36	34
Grenoble, France	1968	1158	211	37	35
Sapporo, Japan	1972	1006	205	35	35
Innsbruck, Austria	1976	1123	231	37	37
Lake Placid, United States	1980	1072	232	37	38
Sarajevo, Yugoslavia	1984	1272	274	49	39
Calgary, Canada	1988	1423	301	57	46
Albertville, France	1992	1801	488	64	57
Lillehammer, Norway	1994	1737	522	67	61
Nagano, Japan	1998	2176	787	72	68
Salt Lake City, United States	2002	2399	886	77	78
Turin, Italy	2006	2508	960	80	84
Vancouver, Canada	2010	2579	1,043	82	86

Medal events contested in the 2010 Winter Games

- Alpine skiing — *Men's and women's downhill, super giant slalom, giant slalom, slalom and Alpine combined*
- Biathlon — *Sprint (men: 10 km; women: 7.5 km), the individual (men: 20 km; women: 15 km), the pursuit (men: 12.5 km; women: 10 km), the relay (men: 4x7.5 km; women: 4x6 km), and the mass start (men: 15 km; women: 12.5 km)*
- Bobsled — *Four-man race, two-man race and two-woman race*
- Cross-country skiing — *Men's sprint, team sprint, 30 km pursuit, 15 km, 50 km and 4x10 km relay; women's sprint, team sprint, 15 km pursuit, 10 km, 30 km (women) and 4x5 km relay*
- Curling — *Men's and women's tournaments*
- Figure skating — *Men's and women's singles; pairs; and ice dancing*
- Freestyle skiing — *Men's and women's moguls, aerials and skicross*
- Ice hockey — *Men's and women's tournaments*
- Luge — *Men's and women's singles, men's doubles*
- Nordic combined — *Men's 10 km individual normal hill, 10 km individual large hill and team*
- Short track speed skating — *Men's and women's 500 metres, 1,000 metres, 1,500 metres; women's 3,000 metre relay; and men's 5,000 metre relay*
- Skeleton — *Men's and women's events*
- Ski jumping — *Men's individual large hill, individual small hill and team large hill*
- Snowboarding — *Men's and women's parallel giant slalom, half-pipe and snowboard cross*
- Speed skating — *Men's and women's 500 metres, 1,000 metres, 1,500 metres, 5,000 metres and team pursuit; women's 3,000 metres; men's 10,000 metres*

Medalists Through The Years

In the very first Olympic Games in 1896 in Athens there were 43 events held altogether, including swimming, road and track cycling, artistic gymnastics, Greco-Roman wrestling, athletics, fencing, shooting, tennis and weightlifting. Over the years, some of those events have continued to make an appearance, others have been in and out of favour, while others still have disappeared altogether — such as the tug-of-war which was only contested between 1896 and 1920. Some other sports that have come and gone are croquet, cricket, jeu de paume, pelota, polo, roque, rackets, lacrosse and motor boating. Indeed, only five sports have been contested at every Summer Olympic Games since 1896: athletics, cycling, fencing, gymnastics and swimming and of course, within those the individual events have often changed.

What follows is a record of all the medal winners in the events that were contested at the very first Olympiad, and are still on the programme for the latest Olympics. It is particularly interesting to note the improvements in times, heights and distances over the years. Since only men were allowed to compete in the first Olympic Games, all results are for men's competitions.

Medalists Through the Years: *100 metres Sprint*

Games	Gold	Silver	Bronze	Winning Time *secs*
1896 Athens	Tom Burke (USA)	Fritz Hoffmann (GER)	Francis Lane (USA) Alajos Szokolyi (HUN)	12
1900 Paris	Frank Jarvis (USA)	Walter Tewksbury (USA)	Stanley Rowley (AUS)	11
1904 St. Louis	Archie Hahn (USA)	Nate Cartmell (USA)	William Hogenson (USA)	11
1908 London	Reggie Walker (RSA)	James Rector (USA)	Bobby Kerr (CAN)	10.8
1912 Stockholm	Ralph Craig (USA)	Alvah Meyer (USA)	Don Lippincott (USA)	10.8
1920 Antwerp	Charlie Paddock (USA)	Morris Kirksey (USA)	Harry Edward (GBR)	10.8
1924 Paris	Harold Abrahams (GBR)	Jackson Scholz (USA)	Arthur Porritt (NZL)	10.6
1928 Amsterdam	Percy Williams (CAN)	Jack London (GBR)	Georg Lammers (GER)	10.8
1932 Los Angeles	Eddie Tolan (USA)	Ralph Metcalfe (USA)	Arthur Jonath (GER)	10.38
1936 Berlin	Jesse Owens (USA)	Ralph Metcalfe (USA)	Tinus Osendarp (NED)	10.3
1948 London	Harrison Dillard (USA)	Barney Ewell (USA)	Lloyd LaBeach (PAN)	10.3
1952 Helsinki	Lindy Remigino (USA)	Herb McKenley (JAM)	Emmanuel McDonald Bailey (GBR)	10.4
1956 Melbourne	Bobby Joe Morrow (USA)	Thane Baker (USA)	Hector Hogan (AUS)	10.5
1960 Rome	Armin Hary (EUA*)	David Sime (USA)	Peter Radford (GBR)	10.2
1964 Tokyo	Bob Hayes (USA)	Enrique Figuerola (CUB)	Harry Jerome (CAN)	10
1968 Mexico City	Jim Hines (USA)	Lennox Miller (JAM)	Charles Greene (USA)	9.95
1972 Munich	Valeri Borzov (URS)	Robert Taylor (USA)	Lennox Miller (JAM)	10.14
1976 Montreal	Hasely Crawford (TRI)	Don Quarrie (JAM)	Valeri Borzov (URS)	10.06
1980 Moscow	Allan Wells (GBR)	Silvio Leonard (CUB)	Petar Petrov (BUL)	10.25
1984 Los Angeles	Carl Lewis (USA)	Sam Graddy (USA)	Ben Johnson (CAN)	9.99
1988 Seoul	Carl Lewis (USA)	Linford Christie (GBR)	Calvin Smith (USA)	9.92
1992 Barcelona	Linford Christie (GBR)	Frankie Fredericks (NAM)	Dennis Mitchell (USA)	9.96
1996 Atlanta	Donovan Bailey (CAN)	Frankie Fredericks (NAM)	Ato Boldon (TRI)	9.84
2000 Sydney	Maurice Greene (USA)	Ato Boldon (TRI)	Obadele Thompson (BAR)	9.87
2004 Athens	Justin Gatlin (USA)	Francis Obikwelu (POR)	Maurice Greene (USA)	9.85
2008 Beijing	Usain Bolt (JAM)	Richard Thompson (TRI)	Walter Dix (USA)	9.69

n.b. Gold, silver, and bronze medals were not awarded at the early Olympic Games — at the 1896 Summer Olympics, winners received a silver medal and the second place finisher received a bronze medal. In 1900, most winners received cups or trophies instead of medals. (At the ancient Olympic Games only one winner per event was crowned with an olive wreath.) Gold, silver, and bronze medals were retroactively awarded by the International Olympic Committee to reflect the later practice of awarding such medals to 1st, 2nd, and 3rd place competitors respectively, which began at the 1904 Olympics.

* EUA was the code given to the Unified Team of Germany between 1956 and 1964

* The first final ended with Robbins finishing first, Carpenter following him, Halswelle in third, and Taylor at the back. Roscoe Badger, one of the British umpires of the event, noticed Carpenter manoeuvering so as to prevent Halswelle from passing the two leading Americans. This was legal at the time under the American rules under which Carpenter normally competed, but prohibited by the British rules that were in effect for the Olympics. Badger signalled to the judges to declare the race void. At the official inquiry later that day, the judges upheld the disqualification of Carpenter and ordered a second final to be run with Carpenter excluded. However, in the second final, the other two competitors, who were both American, refused to run, protesting the decision by the judges. Halswelle ran the 400 metres by himself, finishing in 50 seconds. His win is the one and only walkover win in Olympic track and field history.

Medalists Through the Years: *400 metres*

Games	Gold	Silver	Bronze	Winning Time secs
1896 Athens	Tom Burke (USA)	Herbert Jamison (USA)	Charles Gmelin (GBR)	54.2
1900 Paris	Maxey Long (USA)	William Holland (USA)	Ernst Schultz (DEN)	49.4
1904 St. Louis	Harry Hillman (USA)	Frank Waller (USA)	Herman Groman (USA)	49.2
1908 London	Wyndham Halswelle (GBR)*	none awarded	none awarded	50*
1912 Stockholm	Charles Reidpath (USA)	Hanns Braun (GER)	Edward Lindberg (USA)	48.2
1920 Antwerp	Bevil Rudd (RSA)	Guy Butler (GBR)	Nils Engdahl (SWE)	49.6
1924 Paris	Eric Liddell (GBR)	Horatio Fitch (USA)	Guy Butler (GBR)	47.6
1928 Amsterdam	Ray Barbuti (USA)	James Ball (CAN)	Joachim Büchner (GER)	47.8
1932 Los Angeles	Bill Carr (USA)	Ben Eastman (USA)	Alex Wilson (CAN)	46.28
1936 Berlin	Archie Williams (USA)	Godfrey Brown (GBR)	James LuValle (USA)	46.5
1948 London	Arthur Wint (JAM)	Herb McKenley (JAM)	Mal Whitfield (USA)	46.2
1952 Helsinki	George Rhoden (JAM)	Herb McKenley (JAM)	Ollie Matson (USA)	45.9
1956 Melbourne	Charlie Jenkins (USA)	Karl-Friedrich Haas (EUA)	Voitto Hellstén (FIN)	46.7
			Ardalion Ignatyev (URS)	
1960 Rome	Otis Davis (USA)	Carl Kaufmann (EUA)	Malcolm Spence (RSA)	44.9
1964 Tokyo	Michael Larrabee (USA)	Wendell Mottley (TRI)	Andrzej Badewski (POL)	45.1
1968 Mexico City	Lee Evans (USA)	Larry James (USA)	Ron Freeman (USA)	43.8
1972 Munich	Vincent Matthews (USA)	Wayne Collett (USA)	Julius Sang (KEN)	44.66
1976 Montreal	Alberto Juantorena (CUB)	Fred Newhouse (USA)	Herman Frazier (USA)	44.26
1980 Moscow	Viktor Markin (URS)	Rick Mitchell (AUS)	Frank Schaffer (GDR)	44.6
1984 Los Angeles	Alonzo Babers (USA)	Gabriel Tiacoh (CIV)	Antonio McKay (USA)	44.29
1988 Seoul	Steve Lewis (USA)	Butch Reynolds (USA)	Danny Everett (USA)	43.87
1992 Barcelona	Quincy Watts (USA)	Steve Lewis (USA)	Samson Kitur (KEN)	43.5
1996 Atlanta	Michael Johnson (USA)	Roger Black (GBR)	Davis Kamoga (UGA)	43.49
2000 Sydney	Michael Johnson (USA)	Alvin Harrison (USA)	Greg Haughton (JAM)	43.84
2004 Athens	Jeremy Wariner (USA)	Otis Harris (USA)	Derrick Brew (USA)	44
2008 Beijing	LaShawn Merritt (USA)	Jeremy Wariner (USA)	David Neville (USA)	43.75

Medalists Through the Years: *800 metres*

Games	Gold	Silver	Bronze	Winning Time
1896 Athens	Edwin Flack (AUS)	Nándor Dáni (HUN)	Dimitrios Golemis (GRE)	2:11.0
1900 Paris	Alfred Tysoe (GBR)	John Cregan (USA)	David Hall (USA)	2:.01.2
1904 St. Louis	Jim Lightbody (USA)	Howard Valentine (USA)	Emil Breitkreutz (USA)	1:56.0
1908 London	Mel Sheppard (USA)	Emilio Lunghi (ITA)	Hanns Braun (GER)	1:52.8
1912 Stockholm	Ted Meredith (USA)	Mel Sheppard (USA)	Ira Davenport (USA)	1:51.9
1920 Antwerp	Albert Hill (GBR)	Earl Eby (USA)	Bevil Rudd (RSA)	1:53.4
1924 Paris	Douglas Lowe (GBR)	Paul Martin (SUI)	Schuyler Enck (USA)	1:52.4
1928 Amsterdam	Douglas Lowe (GBR)	Erik Byléhn (SWE)	Hermann Engelhard (GER)	1:51.8
1932 Los Angeles	Thomas Hampson (GBR)	Alex Wilson (CAN)	Phil Edwards (CAN)	1:49.7
1936 Berlin	John Woodruff (USA)	Mario Lanzi (ITA)	Phil Edwards (CAN)	1:52.9
1948 London	Mal Whitfield (USA)	Arthur Wint (JAM)	Marcel Hansenne (FRA)	1:49.2
1952 Helsinki	Mal Whitfield (USA)	Arthur Wint (JAM)	Heinz Ulzheimer (GER)	1:49.2
1956 Melbourne	Tom Courtney (USA)	Derek Johnson (GBR)	Audun Boysen (NOR)	1:47.7
1960 Rome	Peter Snell (NZL)	Roger Moens (BEL)	George Kerr (BWI)	1:46.3
1964 Tokyo	Peter Snell (NZL)	Bill Crothers (CAN)	Wilson Kiprugut (KEN)	1:45.1
1968 Mexico City	Ralph Doubell (AUS)	Wilson Kiprugut (KEN)	Tom Farrell (USA)	1:44.3
1972 Munich	Dave Wottle (USA)	Yevgeniy Arzhanov (URS)	Mike Boit (KEN)	1:45.9
1976 Montreal	Alberto Juantorena (CUB)	Ivo Van Damme (BEL)	Rick Wohlhuter (USA)	1:43.50
1980 Moscow	Steve Ovett (GBR)	Sebastian Coe (GBR)	Nikolay Kirov (URS)	1:45.40
1984 Los Angeles	Joaquim Cruz (BRA)	Sebastian Coe (GBR)	Earl Jones (USA)	1:43.00
1988 Seoul	Paul Ereng (KEN)	Joaquim Cruz (BRA)	Saïd Aouita (MAR)	1:43.45
1992 Barcelona	William Tanui (KEN)	Nixon Kiprotich (KEN)	Johnny Gray (USA)	1:43.66
1996 Atlanta	Vebjørn Rodal (NOR)	Hezekiél Sepeng (RSA)	Fred Onyancha (KEN)	1:42.58
2000 Sydney	Nils Schumann (GER)	Wilson Kipketer (DEN)	Djabir Saïd-Guerni (ALG)	1:45.08
2004 Athens	Yuriy Borzakovskiy (RUS)	Mbulaeni Mulaudzi (RSA)	Wilson Kipketer (DEN)	1:44.45
2008 Beijing	Wilfred Bungei (KEN)	Ismail Ahmed Ismail (SUD)	Alfred Kirwa Yego (KEN)	1:44.65

Medalists Through the Years: *1,500 metres*

Games	Gold	Silver	Bronze	Winning Time
1896 Athens	Edwin Flack (AUS)	Arthur Blake (USA)	Albin Lermusiaux (FRA)	4:33.2
1900 Paris	Charles Bennett (GBR)	Henri Deloge (FRA)	John Bray (USA)	4:06.2
1904 St. Louis	Jim Lightbody (USA)	William Verner (USA)	Lacey Hearn (USA)	4:05.4
1908 London	Mel Sheppard (USA)	Harold Wilson (GBR)	Norman Hallows (GBR)	4:03.4
1912 Stockholm	Arnold Jackson (GBR)	Abel Kiviat (USA)	Norman Taber (USA)	3:56.8
1920 Antwerp	Albert Hill (GBR)	Philip Baker (GBR)	Lawrence Shields (USA)	4:01.8
1924 Paris	Paavo Nurmi (FIN)	Willy Schärer (SUI)	Henry Stallard (GBR)	3:53.6
1928 Amsterdam	Harry Larva (FIN)	Jules Ladoumègue (FRA)	Eino Purje (FIN)	3:53.2
1932 Los Angeles	Luigi Beccali (ITA)	Jerry Cornes (GBR)	Phil Edwards (CAN)	3:51.2
1936 Berlin	Jack Lovelock (NZL)	Glenn Cunningham (USA)	Luigi Beccali (ITA)	3:47.8
1948 London	Henry Eriksson (SWE)	Lennart Strand (SWE)	Wim Slijkhuis (NED)	3:49.8
1952 Helsinki	Josy Barthel (LUX)	Bob McMillen (USA)	Werner Lueg (GER)	3:45.1
1956 Melbourne	Ron Delany (IRL)	Klaus Richtzenhain (EUA)	John Landy (AUS)	3:41.2
1960 Rome	Herb Elliott (AUS)	Michel Jazy (FRA)	István Rózsavölgyi (HUN)	3:35.6
1964 Tokyo	Peter Snell (NZL)	Josef Odlozil (TCH)	John Davies (NZL)	3:38.1
1968 Mexico City	Kipchoge Keino (KEN)	Jim Ryun (USA)	Bodo Tümmler (FRG)	3:34.9
1972 Munich	Pekka Vasala (FIN)	Kipchoge Keino (KEN)	Rod Dixon (NZL)	3:36.3
1976 Montreal	John Walker (NZL)	Ivo van Damme (BEL)	Paul-Heinz Wellmann (FRG)	3:39.17
1980 Moscow	Sebastian Coe (GBR)	Jürgen Straub (GDR)	Steve Ovett (GBR)	3:38.4
1984 Los Angeles	Sebastian Coe (GBR)	Steve Cram (GBR)	José Manuel Abascal (ESP)	3:32.53
1988 Seoul	Peter Rono (KEN)	Peter Elliott (GBR)	Jens-Peter Herold (GDR)	3:35.96
1992 Barcelona	Fermín Cacho (ESP)	Rachid El Basir (MAR)	Mohammed Suleiman (QAT)	3:40.12
1996 Atlanta	Noureddine Morceli (ALG)	Fermín Cacho (ESP)	Stephen Kipkorir (KEN)	3:35.78
2000 Sydney	Noah Ngeny (KEN)	Hicham El Guerrouj (MAR)	Bernard Lagat (KEN)	3:32.07
2004 Athens	Hicham El Guerrouj (MAR)	Bernard Lagat (KEN)	Rui Silva (POR)	3:34.18
2008 Beijing	Asbel Kiprop (KEN)	Nick Willis (NZL)	Mehdi Baala (FRA)	3:32.94

Medalists Through the Years: *Marathon*

Games	Gold	Silver	Bronze	Winning Time
1896 Athens	Spiridon Louis (GRE)	Kharilaos Vasilakos (GRE)	Gyula Kellner (HUN)	2:58:50
1900 Paris	Michel Théato (FRA)	Émile Champion (FRA)	Ernst Fast (SWE)	2:59:45
1904 St. Louis	Thomas J. Hicks (USA)	Albert Coray (USA)	Arthur Newton (USA)	3:28:53
1908 London	Johnny Hayes (USA)	Charles Hefferon (RSA)	Joseph Forshaw (USA)	2:55:18.4
1912 Stockholm	Kenneth McArthur (RSA)	Christian Gitsham (RSA)	Gaston Strobino (USA)	2:36:54.8
1920 Antwerp	Hannes Kolehmainen (FIN)	Jüri Lossmann (EST)	Valerio Arri (ITA)	2:32:35.8
1924 Paris	Albin Stenroos (FIN)	Romeo Bertini (ITA)	Clarence DeMar (USA)	2:41:22.6
1928 Amsterdam	Boughera El Ouafi (FRA)	Manuel Plaza Reyes (CHI)	Martti Marttelin (FIN)	2:32:57.0
1932 Los Angeles	Juan Carlos Zabala (ARG)	Samuel Ferris (GBR)	Armas Toivonen (FIN)	2:31:36.0
1936 Berlin	Sohn Kee-chung [Korean] (JPN)	Ernest Harper (GBR)	Nan Shoryu [Korean] (JPN)	2:29:19.2
1948 London	Delfo Cabrera (ARG)	Thomas Richards (GBR)	Etienne Gailly (BEL)	2:34:51.6
1952 Helsinki	Emil Zátopek (TCH)	Reinaldo Gorno (ARG)	Gustaf Jansson (SWE)	2:23:03.2
1956 Melbourne	Alain Mimoun (FRA)	Franjo Mihalic (YUG)	Veikko Karvonen (FIN)	2:25:00.0
1960 Rome	Abebe Bikila (ETH)	Rhadi Ben Abdesselam (MAR)	Barry Magee (NZL)	2:15:16.2
1964 Tokyo	Abebe Bikila (ETH)	Basil Heatley (GBR)	Kokichi Tsuburaya (JPN)	2:12:11.2
1968 Mexico City	Mamo Wolde (ETH)	Kenji Kimihara (JPN)	Mike Ryan (NZL)	2:20:26.4
1972 Munich	Frank Shorter (USA)	Karel Lismont (BEL)	Mamo Wolde (ETH)	2:12:19.8
1976 Montreal	Waldemar Cierpinski (GDR)	Frank Shorter (USA)	Karel Lismont (BEL)	2:09:55
1980 Moscow	Waldemar Cierpinski (GDR)	Gerard Nijboer (NED)	Satymkul Dzhumanazarov (URS)	2:11:03
1984 Los Angeles	Carlos Lopes (POR)	John Treacy (IRL)	Charlie Spedding (GBR)	2:09:21
1988 Seoul	Gelindo Bordin (ITA)	Douglas Wakiihuri (KEN)	Ahmed Salah (DJI)	2:10:32
1992 Barcelona	Hwang Young-Cho (KOR)	Koichi Morishita (JPN)	Stephan Freigang (GER)	2:13:23
1996 Atlanta	Josia Thugwane (RSA)	Lee Bong-Ju (KOR)	Erick Wainaina (KEN)	2:12:36
2000 Sydney	Gezahegne Abera (ETH)	Erick Wainaina (KEN)	Tesfaye Tola (ETH)	2:10:11
2004 Athens	Stefano Baldini (ITA)	Mebrahtom Keflezighi (USA)	Vanderlei de Lima (BRA)	2:10:55
2008 Beijing	Samuel Wanjiru (KEN)	Jaouad Gharib (MAR)	Tsegay Kebede (ETH)	2:06:32

The distance of the marathon (created for the 1896 Olympics, and contested at all Olympics since) varied in the early years, before being standardised at 42,195 m (26 miles 385 yards) in 1924, the distance run at the 1908 Olympics. In other years, the distances have been as follows: 1896 — 40,000 m (approximately); 1900 — 40,260 m; 1904 — 40,000 m; 1912 — 40,200 m; 1920 — 40,750 m

Medalists Through the Years: *110 m Hurdles*

Games	Gold	Silver	Bronze	Winning Time
1896 Athens	Thomas Curtis (USA)	Grantley Goulding (GBR)	none awarded	17.6
1900 Paris	Alvin Kraenzlein (USA)	John McLean (USA)	Fred Moloney (USA)	15.4
1904 St. Louis	Frederick Schule (USA)	Thaddeus Shideler (USA)	Lesley Ashburner (USA)	16.0
1908 London	Forrest Smithson (USA)	John Garrels (USA)	Arthur Shaw (USA)	15.0
1912 Stockholm	Frederick Kelly (USA)	James Wendell (USA)	Martin Hawkins (USA)	15.1
1920 Antwerp	Earl Thomson (CAN)	Harold Barron (USA)	Frederick Murray (USA)	14.8
1924 Paris	Daniel Kinsey (USA)	Sydney Atkinson (RSA)	Sten Pettersson (SWE)	15.0
1928 Amsterdam	Sidney Atkinson (RSA)	Steve Anderson (USA)	John Collier (USA)	14.8
1932 Los Angeles	George Saling (USA)	Percy Beard (USA)	Donald Finlay (GBR)	14.6
1936 Berlin	Forrest Towns (USA)	Donald Finlay (GBR)	Frederick Pollard, Jr. (USA)	14.2
1948 London	William Porter (USA)	Clyde Scott (USA)	Craig Dixon (USA)	13.9
1952 Helsinki	Harrison Dillard (USA)	Jack Davis (USA)	Arthur Barnard (USA)	13.7
1956 Melbourne	Lee Calhoun (USA)	Jack Davis (USA)	Joel Shankle (USA)	13.5
1960 Rome	Lee Calhoun (USA)	Willie May (USA)	Hayes Jones (USA)	13.8
1964 Tokyo	Hayes Jones (USA)	Blaine Lindgren (USA)	Anatoly Mikhailov (URS)	13.6
1968 Mexico City	Willie Davenport (USA)	Ervin Hall (USA)	Eddy Ottoz (ITA)	13.3
1972 Munich	Rod Milburn (USA)	Guy Drut (FRA)	Thomas Hill (USA)	13.24
1976 Montreal	Guy Drut (FRA)	Alejandro Casañas (CUB)	Willie Davenport (USA)	13.30
1980 Moscow	Thomas Munkelt (GDR)	Alejandro Casañas (CUB)	Aleksandr Puchkov (URS)	13.39
1984 Los Angeles	Roger Kingdom (USA)	Greg Foster (USA)	Arto Bryggare (FIN)	13.20
1988 Seoul	Roger Kingdom (USA)	Colin Jackson (GBR)	Tonie Campbell (USA)	12.98
1992 Barcelona	Mark McKoy (CAN)	Tony Dees (USA)	Jack Pierce (USA)	13.12
1996 Atlanta	Allen Johnson (USA)	Mark Crear (USA)	Florian Schwarthoff (GER)	12.95
2000 Sydney	Anier García (CUB)	Terrence Trammell (USA)	Mark Crear (USA)	13.00
2004 Athens	Liu Xiang (CHN)	Terrence Trammell (USA)	Anier García (CUB)	12.91
2008 Beijing	Dayron Robles (CUB)	David Payne (USA)	David Oliver (USA)	12.93

Medalists Through the Years: *High Jump*

Games	Gold	Silver	Bronze	Height (m)
1896 Athens	Ellery Clark (USA)	James Connolly (USA)	none awarded	1.81
		Robert Garrett (USA)		
1900 Paris	Irving Baxter (USA)	Patrick Leahy (GBR)	Lajos Gönczy (HUN)	1.90
1904 St. Louis	Samuel Jones (USA)	Garrett Serviss (USA)	Paul Weinstein (GER)	1.80
1908 London	Harry Porter (USA)	Georges André (FRA), Cornelius Leahy (GBR), István Somodi (HUN)	none awarded	1.905
1912 Stockholm	Alma Richards (USA)	Hans Liesche (GER)	George Horine (USA)	1.93
1920 Antwerp	Richmond Landon (USA)	Harold Muller (USA)	Bo Ekelund (SWE)	1.935
1924 Paris	Harold Osborn (USA)	Leroy Brown (USA)	Pierre Lewden (FRA)	1.98
1928 Amsterdam	Robert Wade King (USA)	Benjamin Hedges (USA)	Claude Ménard (FRA)	1.94
1932 Los Angeles	Duncan McNaughton (CAN)	Robert van Osdel (USA)	Simeon Toribio (PHI)	1.97
1936 Berlin	Cornelius Johnson (USA)	Dave Albritton (USA)	Delos Thurber (USA)	2.03
1948 London	John Winter (AUS)	Bjørn Paulson (NOR)	George Stanich (USA)	1.98
1952 Helsinki	Walter Davis (USA)	Kenneth Wiesner (USA)	José da Conceição (BRA)	2.04
1956 Melbourne	Charles Dumas (USA)	Charles Porter (AUS)	Igor Kashkarov (URS)	2.12
1960 Rome	Robert Shavlakadze (URS)	Valeriy Brumel (URS)	John Thomas (USA)	2.16
1964 Tokyo	Valeriy Brumel (URS)	John Thomas (USA)	John Rambo (USA)	2.18
1968 Mexico City	Dick Fosbury (USA)	Ed Caruthers (USA)	Valentin Gavrilov (URS)	2.24
1972 Munich	Jüri Tarmak (URS)	Stefan Junge (GDR)	Dwight Stones (USA)	2.23
1976 Montreal	Jacek Wszola (POL)	Greg Joy (CAN)	Dwight Stones (USA)	2.25
1980 Moscow	Gerd Wessig (GDR)	Jacek Wszola (POL)	Jörg Freimuth (GDR)	2.36
1984 Los Angeles	Dietmar Mögenburg (FRG)	Patrik Sjöberg (SWE)	Zhu Jianhua (CHN)	2.35
1988 Seoul	Hennadiy Avdeyenko (URS)	Hollis Conway (USA)	Rudolf Povarnitsyn (URS), Patrik Sjöberg (SWE)	2.38
1992 Barcelona	Javier Sotomayor (CUB)	Patrik Sjöberg (SWE)	Hollis Conway (USA), Tim Forsyth (AUS), Artur Partyka (POL)	2.34
1996 Atlanta	Charles Austin (USA)	Artur Partyka (POL)	Steve Smith (GBR)	2.39
2000 Sydney	Sergey Klyugin (RUS)	Javier Sotomayor (CUB)	Abderrahmane Hammad (ALG)	2.35
2004 Athens	Stefan Holm (SWE)	Matt Hemingway (USA)	Jaroslav Bába (CZE)	2.36
2008 Beijing	Andrey Silnov (RUS)	Germaine Mason (GBR)	Yaroslav Rybakov (RUS)	2.36

Medalists Through the Years: *Pole Vault*

Games	Gold	Silver	Bronze	Height (m)
1896 Athens	Welles Hoyt (USA)	Albert Tyler (USA)	Evangelos Damaskos (GRE), Ioannis Theodoropoulos (GRE)	3.30
1900 Paris	Irving Baxter (USA)	Meredith Colket (USA)	Carl-Albert Andersen (NOR)	3.30
1904 St. Louis	Charles Dvorak (USA)	LeRoy Samse (USA)	Louis Wilkins (USA)	3.50
1908 London	Edward Cook (USA), Alfred Gilbert (USA)	none awarded	Edward Archibald (CAN), Charles Jacobs (USA), Bruno Söderström (SWE)	3.71
1912 Stockholm	Harry Babcock (USA)	Frank Nelson (USA), Marc Wright (USA)	William Halpenny (CAN), Frank Murphy (USA), Bertil Uggla (SWE)	3.95
1920 Antwerp	Frank Foss (USA)	Henry Petersen (DEN)	Edwin Myers (USA)	4.09
1924 Paris	Lee Barnes (USA)	Glen Graham (USA)	James Brooker (USA)	3.95
1928 Amsterdam	Sabin Carr (USA)	William Droegemuller (USA)	Charles McGinnis (USA)	4.20
1932 Los Angeles	William Miller (USA)	Shuhei Nishida (JPN)	George Jefferson (USA)	4.31
1936 Berlin	Earle Meadows (USA)	Shuhei Nishida (JPN)	Sueo Oe (JPN)	4.35
1948 London	Guinn Smith (USA)	Erkki Kataja (FIN)	Bob Richards (USA)	4.30
1952 Helsinki	Bob Richards (USA)	Donald Laz (USA)	Ragnar Lundberg (SWE)	4.55
1956 Melbourne	Bob Richards (USA)	Bob Gutowski (USA)	Georgios Roubanis (GRE)	4.56
1960 Rome	Don Bragg (USA)	Ron Morris (USA)	Eeles Landström (FIN)	4.70
1964 Tokyo	Fred Hansen (USA)	Wolfgang Reinhardt (EUA)	Klaus Lehnertz (EUA)	5.10
1968 Mexico City	Bob Seagren (USA)	Claus Schiprowski (FRG)	Wolfgang Nordwig (GDR)	5.40
1972 Munich	Wolfgang Nordwig (GDR)	Bob Seagren (USA)	Jan Johnson (USA)	5.50
1976 Montreal	Tadeusz Slusarski (POL)	Antti Kalliomäki (FIN)	Dave Roberts (USA)	5.50
1980 Moscow	Wladyslaw Kozakiewicz (POL)	Tadeusz Slusarski (POL), Konstantin Volkov (URS)	none awarded	5.78
1984 Los Angeles	Pierre Quinon (FRA)	Mike Tully (USA)	Earl Bell (USA), Thierry Vigneron (FRA)	5.75
1988 Seoul	Sergey Bubka (URS)	Rodion Gataullin (URS)	Grigoriy Yegorov (URS)	5.90
1992 Barcelona	Maksim Tarasov (EUN)	Igor Trandenkov (EUN)	Javier García Chico (ESP)	5.80
1996 Atlanta	Jean Galfione (FRA)	Igor Trandenkov (RUS)	Andrei Tivontchik (GER)	5.92
2000 Sydney	Nick Hysong (USA)	Lawrence Johnson (USA)	Maksim Tarasov (RUS)	5.90
2004 Athens	Timothy Mack (USA)	Toby Stevenson (USA)	Giuseppe Gibilisco (ITA)	5.95
2008 Beijing	Steven Hooker (AUS)	Yevgeny Lukyanenko (RUS)	Denys Yurchenko (UKR)	5.96

Medalists Through the Years: *Long Jump*

Games	Gold	Silver	Bronze	Length (m)
1896 Athens	Ellery Clark (USA)	Robert Garrett (USA)	James Connolly (USA)	6.35
1900 Paris	Alvin Kraenzlein (USA)	Myer Prinstein (USA)	Patrick Leahy (GBR)	7.185
1904 St. Louis	Myer Prinstein (USA)	Daniel Frank (USA)	Robert Stangland (USA)	7.34
1908 London	Frank Irons (USA)	Daniel Kelly (USA)	Calvin Bricker (CAN)	7.48
1912 Stockholm	Albert Gutterson (USA)	Calvin Bricker (CAN)	Georg Åberg (SWE)	7.60
1920 Antwerp	William Petersson (SWE)	Carl Johnson (USA)	Erik Abrahamsson (SWE)	7.15
1924 Paris	William DeHart Hubbard (USA)	Edward Gourdin (USA)	Sverre Hansen (NOR)	7.44
1928 Amsterdam	Ed Hamm (USA)	Silvio Cator (HAI)	Alfred Bates (USA)	7.73
1932 Los Angeles	Ed Gordon (USA)	Lambert Redd (USA)	Chuhei Nambu (JPN)	7.64
1936 Berlin	Jesse Owens (USA)	Lutz Long (GER)	Naoto Tajima (JPN)	8.06
1948 London	Willie Steele (USA)	Theo Bruce (AUS)	Herb Douglas (USA)	7.825
1952 Helsinki	Jerome Biffle (USA)	Meredith Gourdine (USA)	Ödön Földessy (HUN)	7.57
1956 Melbourne	Gregory Bell (USA)	John Bennett (USA)	Jorma Valkama (FIN)	7.83
1960 Rome	Ralph Boston (USA)	Irvin Roberson (USA)	Igor Ter-Ovanesyan (URS)	8.12
1964 Tokyo	Lynn Davies (GBR)	Ralph Boston (USA)	Igor Ter-Ovanesyan (URS)	8.07
1968 Mexico City	Bob Beamon (USA)	Klaus Beer (GDR)	Ralph Boston (USA)	8.90
1972 Munich	Randy Williams (USA)	Hans Baumgartner (FRG)	Arnie Robinson (USA)	8.24
1976 Montreal	Arnie Robinson (USA)	Randy Williams (USA)	Frank Wartenberg (GDR)	8.35
1980 Moscow	Lutz Dombrowski (GDR)	Frank Paschek (GDR)	Valeriy Podluzhniy (URS)	8.54
1984 Los Angeles	Carl Lewis (USA)	Gary Honey (AUS)	Giovanni Evangelisti (ITA)	8.54
1988 Seoul	Carl Lewis (USA)	Mike Powell (USA)	Larry Myricks (USA)	8.72
1992 Barcelona	Carl Lewis (USA)	Mike Powell (USA)	Joe Greene (USA)	8.67
1996 Atlanta	Carl Lewis (USA)	James Beckford (JAM)	Joe Greene (USA)	8.50
2000 Sydney	Iván Pedroso (CUB)	Jai Taurima (AUS)	Roman Shchurenko (UKR)	8.55
2004 Athens	Dwight Phillips (USA)	John Moffitt (USA)	Joan Lino Martínez (ESP)	8.59
2008 Beijing	Irving Saladino (PAN)	Khotso Mokoena (RSA)	Ibrahim Camejo (CUB)	8.34

Medalists Through the Years: *Triple Jump*

Games	Gold	Silver	Bronze	Length (m)
1896 Athens	James Connolly (USA)	Alexandre Tufféri (FRA)	Ioannis Persakis (GRE)	13.71
1900 Paris	Myer Prinstein (USA)	James Connolly (USA)	Lewis Sheldon (USA)	14.47
1904 St. Louis	Myer Prinstein (USA)	Frederick Engelhardt (USA)	Robert Stangland (USA)	14.325
1908 London	Tim Ahearne (GBR)	Garfield MacDonald (CAN)	Edvard Larsen (NOR)	14.92
1912 Stockholm	Gustaf Lindblom (SWE)	Georg Åberg (SWE)	Erik Almlöf (SWE)	14.76
1920 Antwerp	Vilho Tuulos (FIN)	Folke Jansson (SWE)	Erik Almlöf (SWE)	14.505
1924 Paris	Nick Winter (AUS)	Luis Brunetto (ARG)	Vilho Tuulos (FIN)	15.525
1928 Amsterdam	Mikio Oda (JPN)	Levi Casey (USA)	Vilho Tuulos (FIN)	15.21
1932 Los Angeles	Chuhei Nambu (JPN)	Erik Svensson (SWE)	Kenkichi Oshima (JPN)	15.72
1936 Berlin	Naoto Tajima (JPN)	Masao Harada (JPN)	Jack Metcalfe (AUS)	16.00
1948 London	Arne Åhman (SWE)	George Avery (AUS)	Ruhi Sarialp (TUR)	15.40
1952 Helsinki	Adhemar da Silva (BRA)	Leonid Shcherbakov (URS)	Arnoldo Devonish (VEN)	16.22
1956 Melbourne	Adhemar da Silva (BRA)	Vilhjálmur Einarsson (ISL)	Vitold Kreyer (URS)	16.35
1960 Rome	Józef Szmidt (POL)	Vladimir Goryaev (URS)	Vitold Kreyer (URS)	16.81
1964 Tokyo	Józef Szmidt (POL)	Oleg Fedoseyev (URS)	Viktor Kravchenko (URS)	16.85
1968 Mexico City	Viktor Saneyev (URS)	Nelson Prudencio (BRA)	Giuseppe Gentile (ITA)	17.39
1972 Munich	Viktor Saneyev (URS)	Jörg Drehmel (GDR)	Nelson Prudencio (BRA)	17.35
1976 Montreal	Viktor Saneyev (URS)	James Butts (USA)	João Carlos de Oliveira (BRA)	17.29
1980 Moscow	Jaak Uudmäe (URS)	Viktor Saneyev (URS)	João Carlos de Oliveira (BRA)	17.35
1984 Los Angeles	Al Joyner (USA)	Mike Conley, Sr. (USA)	Keith Connor (GBR)	17.26
1988 Seoul	Hristo Markov (BUL)	Igor Lapshin (URS)	Aleksandr Kovalenko (URS)	17.61
1992 Barcelona	Mike Conley, Sr. (USA)	Charles Simpkins (USA)	Frank Rutherford (BAH)	18.17
1996 Atlanta	Kenny Harrison (USA)	Jonathan Edwards (GBR)	Yoelbi Quesada (CUB)	18.09
2000 Sydney	Jonathan Edwards (GBR)	Yoel García (CUB)	Denis Kapustin (RUS)	17.71
2004 Athens	Christian Olsson (SWE)	Marian Oprea (ROU)	Danil Burkenya (RUS)	17.79
2008 Beijing	Nelson Évora (POR)	Phillips Idowu (GBR)	Leevan Sands (BAH)	17.67

Medalists Through the Years: *Shot Put*

Games	Gold	Silver	Bronze	Length (m)
1896 Athens	Robert Garrett (USA)	Miltiades Gouskos (GRE)	Georgios Papasideris (GRE)	11.22
1900 Paris	Richard Sheldon (USA)	Josiah McCracken (USA)	Robert Garrett (USA)	14.10
1904 St. Louis	Ralph Rose (USA)	Wesley Coe (USA)	Leon Feuerbach (USA)	14.81
1908 London	Ralph Rose (USA)	Denis Horgan (GBR)	John Garrels (USA)	14.21
1912 Stockholm	Patrick McDonald (USA)	Ralph Rose (USA)	Lawrence Whitney (USA)	15.34
1920 Antwerp	Ville Pörhölä (FIN)	Elmer Niklander (FIN)	Harry Liversedge (USA)	14.81
1924 Paris	Clarence Houser (USA)	Glenn Hartranft (USA)	Ralph Hills (USA)	14.995
1928 Amsterdam	John Kuck (USA)	Herman Brix (USA)	Emil Hirschfeld (GER)	15.87
1932 Los Angeles	Leo Sexton (USA)	Harlow Rothert (USA)	Frantisek Douda (TCH)	16.005
1936 Berlin	Hans Woellke (GER)	Sulo Bärlund (FIN)	Gerhard Stöck (GER)	16.20
1948 London	Wilbur Thompson (USA)	Jim Delaney (USA)	Jim Fuchs (USA)	17.12
1952 Helsinki	Parry O'Brien (USA)	Darrow Hooper (USA)	Jim Fuchs (USA)	17.41
1956 Melbourne	Parry O'Brien (USA)	Bill Nieder (USA)	Jirí Skobla (TCH)	18.57
1960 Rome	Bill Nieder (USA)	Parry O'Brien (USA)	Dallas Long (USA)	19.68
1964 Tokyo	Dallas Long (USA)	Randy Matson (USA)	Vilmos Varjú (HUN)	20.33
1968 Mexico City	Randy Matson (USA)	George Woods (USA)	Eduard Gushchin (URS)	20.54
1972 Munich	Wladyslaw Komar (POL)	George Woods (USA)	Hartmut Briesenick (GDR)	21.18
1976 Montreal	Udo Beyer (GDR)	Yevgeny Mironov (URS)	Aleksandr Baryshnikov (URS)	21.05
1980 Moscow	Vladimir Kiselyov (URS)	Aleksandr Baryshnikov (URS)	Udo Beyer (GDR)	21.35
1984 Los Angeles	Alessandro Andrei (ITA)	Mike Carter (USA)	Dave Laut (USA)	21.16
1988 Seoul	Ulf Timmermann (GDR)	Randy Barnes (USA)	Werner Günthör (SUI)	22.47
1992 Barcelona	Mike Stulce (USA)	Jim Doehring (USA)	Vyacheslav Lykho (EUN)	21.70
1996 Atlanta	Randy Barnes (USA)	John Godina (USA)	Oleksandr Bagach (UKR)	21.62
2000 Sydney	Arsi Harju (FIN)	Adam Nelson (USA)	John Godina (USA)	21.29
2004 Athens	Yuriy Bilonoh (UKR)	Adam Nelson (USA)	Joachim Olsen (DEN)	21.16
2008 Beijing	Tomasz Majewski (POL)	Christian Cantwell (USA)	Andrei Mikhnevich (BLR)	21.51

Medalists Through the Years: *Discus Throw*

Games	Gold	Silver	Bronze	Length (m)
1896 Athens	Robert Garrett (USA)	Panagiotis Paraskevopoulos (GRE)	Sotirios Versis (GRE)	29.15
1900 Paris	Rudolf Bauer (HUN)	Frantisek Janda-Suk (BOH)	Richard Sheldon (USA)	36.04
1904 St. Louis	Martin Sheridan (USA)	Ralph Rose (USA)	Nikolaos Georgantas (GRE)	39.28
1908 London	Martin Sheridan (USA)	Merritt Giffin (USA)	Marquis Horr (USA)	40.89
1912 Stockholm	Armas Taipale (FIN)	Richard Byrd (USA)	James Duncan (USA)	45.21
1920 Antwerp	Elmer Niklander (FIN)	Armas Taipale (FIN)	Gus Pope (USA)	44.685
1924 Paris	Clarence Houser (USA)	Vilho Niittymaa (FIN)	Thomas Lieb (USA)	46.155
1928 Amsterdam	Clarence Houser (USA)	Antero Kivi (FIN)	James Corson (USA)	47.32
1932 Los Angeles	John Anderson (USA)	Henri LaBorde (USA)	Paul Winter (FRA)	49.49
1936 Berlin	Ken Carpenter (USA)	Gordon Dunn (USA)	Giorgio Oberweger (ITA)	50.48
1948 London	Adolfo Consolini (ITA)	Giuseppe Tosi (ITA)	Fortune Gordien (USA)	52.78
1952 Helsinki	Sim Iness (USA)	Adolfo Consolini (ITA)	James Dillion (USA)	55.03
1956 Melbourne	Al Oerter (USA)	Fortune Gordien (USA)	Des Koch (USA)	56.36
1960 Rome	Al Oerter (USA)	Rink Babka (USA)	Dick Cochran (USA)	59.18
1964 Tokyo	Al Oerter (USA)	Ludvík Danek (TCH)	Dave Weill (USA)	61.00
1968 Mexico City	Al Oerter (USA)	Lothar Milde (GDR)	Ludvík Danek (TCH)	64.78
1972 Munich	Ludvík Danek (TCH)	Jay Silvester (USA)	Ricky Bruch (SWE)	64.40
1976 Montreal	Mac Wilkins (USA)	Wolfgang Schmidt (GDR)	John Powell (USA)	67.50
1980 Moscow	Viktor Rashchupkin (URS)	Imrich Bugár (TCH)	Luis Delís (CUB)	66.64
1984 Los Angeles	Rolf Danneberg (FRG)	Mac Wilkins (USA)	John Powell (USA)	66.60
1988 Seoul	Jürgen Schult (GDR)	Romas Ubartas (URS)	Rolf Danneberg (FRG)	68.82
1992 Barcelona	Romas Ubartas (LTU)	Jürgen Schult (GER)	Roberto Moya (CUB)	65.12
1996 Atlanta	Lars Riedel (GER)	Vladimir Dubrovshchik (BLR)	Vasiliy Kaptyukh (BLR)	69.40
2000 Sydney	Virgilijus Alekna (LTU)	Lars Riedel (GER)	Frantz Kruger (RSA)	69.30
2004 Athens	Virgilijus Alekna (LTU)	Zoltán Kovágó (HUN)	Aleksander Tammert (EST)	69.89
2008 Beijing	Gerd Kanter (EST)	Piotr Malachowski (POL)	Virgilijus Alekna (LTU)	68.82

Medalists Through the Years: *Swimming 100 m freestyle*

Games	Gold	Silver	Bronze	Winning Time
1896 Athens	Alfréd Hajós (HUN)	Otto Herschmann (AUT)	none awarded	1:22.2
1900—1904	not included in the Olympic program			
1908 London	Charles Daniels (USA)	Zoltán Halmay (HUN)	Harald Julin (SWE)	1:05.6
1912 Stockholm	Duke Kahanamoku (USA)	Cecil Healy (ANZ)	Kenneth Huszagh (USA)	1:03.4
1920 Antwerp	Duke Kahanamoku (USA)	Pua Kealoha (USA)	William Harris (USA)	1:.00.4
1924 Paris	Johnny Weissmuller (USA)	Duke Kahanamoku (USA)	Samuel Kahanamoku (USA)	59.0
1928 Amsterdam	Johnny Weissmuller (USA)	István Bárány (HUN)	Katsuo Takaishi (JPN)	58.6
1932 Los Angeles	Yasuji Miyazaki (JPN)	Tatsugo Kawaishi (JPN)	Albert Schwartz (USA)	58.2
1936 Berlin	Ferenc Csik (HUN)	Masanori Yusa (JPN)	Shigeo Arai (JPN)	57.6
1948 London	Walter Ris (USA)	Alan Ford (USA)	Géza Kádas (HUN)	57.3
1952 Helsinki	Clarke Scholes (USA)	Hiroshi Suzuki (JPN)	Göran Larsson (SWE)	57.4
1956 Melbourne	Jon Henricks (AUS)	John Devitt (AUS)	Gary Chapman (AUS)	55.4
1960 Rome	John Devitt (AUS)	Lance Larson (USA)	Manuel dos Santos (BRA)	55.2
1964 Tokyo	Don Schollander (USA)	Robert McGregor (GBR)	Hans-Joachim Klein (EUA)	53.4
1968 Mexico City	Mike Wenden (AUS)	Kenneth Walsh (USA)	Mark Spitz (USA)	52.2
1972 Munich	Mark Spitz (USA)	Jerry Heidenreich (USA)	Vladimir Bure (URS)	51.22
1976 Montreal	Jim Montgomery (USA)	Jack Babashoff (USA)	Peter Nocke (FRG)	49.99
1980 Moscow	Jörg Woithe (GDR)	Per Holmertz (SWE)	Per Johansson (SWE)	50.40
1984 Los Angeles	Rowdy Gaines (USA)	Mark Stockwell (AUS)	Per Johansson (SWE)	49.80
1988 Seoul	Matt Biondi (USA)	Chris Jacobs (USA)	Stéphan Caron (FRA)	48.63
1992 Barcelona	Alexander Popov (EUN)	Gustavo Borges (BRA)	Stéphan Caron (FRA)	49.02
1996 Atlanta	Alexander Popov (RUS)	Gary Hall, Jr. (USA)	Gustavo Borges (BRA)	48.74
2000 Sydney	Pieter van den Hoogenband (NED)	Alexander Popov (RUS)	Gary Hall, Jr. (USA)	48.30
2004 Athens	Pieter van den Hoogenband (NED)	Roland Mark Schoeman (RSA)	Ian Thorpe (AUS)	48.17
2008 Beijing	Alain Bernard (FRA)	Eamon Sullivan (AUS)	César Cielo Filho (BRA), Jason Lezak (USA)	47.21

Medalists Through the Years: *Cycling Road Race, Individual*

Games	Gold	Silver	Bronze	Winning Time
1896 Athens	Aristidis Konstantinidis (GRE)	August von Gödrich (GER)	Edward Battell (GBR)	3:21:10
1900–1908	not included in the Olympic program			
1912 Stockholm	Rudolph Lewis (RSA)	Frederick Grubb (GBR)	Carl Schutte (USA)	10:42:39.0
1920 Antwerp	Harry Stenqvist (SWE)	Henry Kaltenbrun (RSA)	Fernand Canteloube (FRA)	4:40:01.8
1924 Paris	Armand Blanchonnet (FRA)	Henri Hoevenaers (BEL)	René Hamel (FRA)	6:20:48.0
1928 Amsterdam	Henry Hansen (DEN)	Frank Southall (GBR)	Gösta Carlsson (SWE)	4:47:18
1932 Los Angeles	Attilio Pavesi (ITA)	Guglielmo Segato (ITA)	Bernhard Britz (SWE)	2:28:05.6
1936 Berlin	Robert Charpentier (FRA)	Guy Lapébie (FRA)	Ernst Nievergelt (SUI)	2:33:05.0
1948 London	José Beyaert (FRA)	Gerrit Voorting (NED)	Lode Wouters (BEL)	5:18:12.6
1952 Helsinki	André Noyelle (BEL)	Robert Grondelaers (BEL)	Edi Ziegler (GER)	5:06:03.4
1956 Melbourne	Ercole Baldini (ITA)	Arnaud Geyre (FRA)	Alan Jackson (GBR)	5:21:17
1960 Rome	Viktor Kapitonov (URS)	Livio Trapè (ITA)	Willy van den Berghen (BEL)	4:20:37
1964 Tokyo	Mario Zanin (ITA)	Kjell Rodian (DEN)	Walter Godefroot (BEL)	4:39:51.63
1968 Mexico City	Pierfranco Vianelli (ITA)	Leif Mortensen (DEN)	Gösta Pettersson (SWE)	4:41:25.24
1972 Munich	Hennie Kuiper (NED)	Clyde Sefton (AUS)	none awarded	4:14:37
1976 Montreal	Bernt Johansson (SWE)	Giuseppe Martinelli (ITA)	Mieczyslaw Nowicki (POL)	4:46:52
1980 Moscow	Sergei Sukhoruchenkov (URS)	Czeslaw Lang (POL)	Yuri Barinov (URS)	4:48:28.9
1984 Los Angeles	Alexi Grewal (USA)	Steve Bauer (CAN)	Dag Otto Lauritzen (NOR)	4:59:57
1988 Seoul	Olaf Ludwig (GDR)	Bernd Gröne (FRG)	Christian Henn (FRG)	4:32:22
1992 Barcelona	Fabio Casartelli (ITA)	Erik Dekker (NED)	Dainis Ozols (LAT)	4:35:21
1996 Atlanta	Pascal Richard (SUI)	Rolf Sørensen (DEN)	Max Sciandri (GBR)	4:53:56
2000 Sydney	Jan Ullrich (GER)	Alexander Vinokourov (KAZ)	Andreas Klöden (GER)	5:29:08
2004 Athens	Paolo Bettini (ITA)	Sérgio Paulinho (POR)	Axel Merckx (BEL)	5:41:44
2008 Beijing	Samuel Sánchez (ESP)	Fabian Cancellara (SUI)	Alexandr Kolobnev (RUS)	6:23:49

The Road Race is approximately 240km (150 miles) for men and 130km (80 miles) for women. The competitors all start together and the first past the line is the winner. At 245.4km, the distance for Men's Cycling Road Race in Beijing was the longest in recent Olympic history.

Medalists Through the Years: *Cycling Sprint, Individual*

Games	Gold	Silver	Bronze
1896 Athens	Paul Masson (FRA)	Stamatios Nikolopoulos (GRE)	Léon Flameng (FRA)
1900 Paris	Georges Taillandier (FRA)	Fernand Sanz (FRA)	John Henry Lake (USA)
1904 St. Louis	not included in the Olympic program		
1908 London	No medalists - race declared void as time limit was exceeded in final		
1912 Stockholm	not included in the Olympic program		
1920 Antwerp	Maurice Peeters (NED)	Horace Johnson (GBR)	Harry Ryan (GBR)
1924 Paris	Lucien Michard (FRA)	Jacob Meijer (NED)	Jean Cugnot (FRA)
1928 Amsterdam	Roger Beaufrand (FRA)	Antoine Mazairac (NED)	Willy Hansen (DEN)
1932 Los Angeles	Jacobus van Egmond (NED)	Louis Chaillot (FRA)	Bruno Pellizzari (ITA)
1936 Berlin	Toni Merkens (GER)	Arie van Vliet (NED)	Louis Chaillot (FRA)
1948 London	Mario Ghella (ITA)	Reginald Harris (GBR)	Axel Schandorff (DEN)
1952 Helsinki	Enzo Sacchi (ITA)	Lionel Cox (AUS)	Werner Potzernheim (GER)
1956 Melbourne	Michel Rousseau (FRA)	Guglielmo Presenti (ITA)	Dick Ploog (AUS)
1960 Rome	Sante Gaiardoni (ITA)	Leo Sterckx (BEL)	Valentino Gasparella (ITA)
1964 Tokyo	Giovanni Pettenella (ITA)	Sergio Bianchetto (ITA)	Daniel Morelon (FRA)
1968 Mexico City	Daniel Morelon (FRA)	Giordano Turrini (ITA)	Pierre Trentin (FRA)
1972 Munich	Daniel Morelon (FRA)	John Nicholson (AUS)	Omar Pkhakadze (URS)
1976 Montreal	Anton Tkac (TCH)	Daniel Morelon (FRA)	Hans-Jurgen Geschke (GDR)
1980 Moscow	Lutz Heßlich (GDR)	Yave Cahard (FRA)	Sergei Kopylov (URS)
1984 Los Angeles	Mark Gorski (USA)	Nelson Vails (USA)	Tsutomu Sakamoto (JPN)
1988 Seoul	Lutz Heßlich (GDR)	Nikolai Kovsh (URS)	Gary Neiwand (AUS)
1992 Barcelona	Jens Fiedler (GER)	Gary Neiwand (AUS)	Curt Harnett (CAN)
1996 Atlanta	Jens Fiedler (GER)	Marty Nothstein (USA)	Curt Harnett (CAN)
2000 Sydney	Marty Nothstein (USA)	Florian Rousseau (FRA)	Jens Fiedler (GER)
2004 Athens	Ryan Bayley (AUS)	Theo Bos (NED)	René Wolff (GER)
2008 Beijing	Chris Hoy (GBR)	Jason Kenny (GBR)	Mickaël Bourgain (FRA)

Medalists Through the Years: *Fencing Foil, Individual*

Games	Gold	Silver	Bronze
1896 Athens	Eugène-Henri Gravelotte (FRA)	Henri Callot (FRA)	Perikles Pierrakos-Mavromichalis (GRE)
1900 Paris	Émile Coste (FRA)	Henri Masson (FRA)	Marcel Jacques Boulenger (FRA)
1904 St. Louis	Ramón Fonst (CUB)	Albertson Van Zo Post (CUB)	Charles Tatham (CUB)
1908 London	not included in the Olympic program		
1912 Stockholm	Nedo Nadi (ITA)	Pietro Speciale (ITA)	Richard Verderber (AUT)
1920 Antwerp	Nedo Nadi (ITA)	Philippe Cattiau (FRA)	Roger Ducret (FRA)
1924 Paris	Roger Ducret (FRA)	Philippe Cattiau (FRA)	Maurice E. van Damme (BEL)
1928 Amsterdam	Lucien Gaudin (FRA)	Erwin Casmir (GER)	Giulio Gaudini (ITA)
1932 Los Angeles	Gustavo Marzi (ITA)	Joseph L. Levis (USA)	Giulio Gaudini (ITA)
1936 Berlin	Giulio Gaudini (ITA)	Edward Gardère (FRA)	Giorgio Bocchino (ITA)
1948 London	Jehan Buhan (FRA)	Christian d'Oriola (FRA)	Lajos Maszlay (HUN)
1952 Helsinki	Christian d'Oriola (FRA)	Edoardo Mangiarotti (ITA)	Manlio Di Rosa (ITA)
1956 Melbourne	Christian d'Oriola (FRA)	Giancarlo Bergamini (ITA)	Antonio Spallino (ITA)
1960 Rome	Viktor Zhdanovich (URS)	Yuri Sisikin (URS)	Albert Axelrod (USA)
1964 Tokyo	Egon Franke (POL)	Jean Claude Magnan (FRA)	Daniel Revenu (FRA)
1968 Mexico City	Ion Drîmba (ROU)	Jeno Kamuti (HUN)	Daniel Revenu (FRA)
1972 Munich	Witold Woyda (POL)	Jeno Kamuti (HUN)	Christian Noël (FRA)
1976 Montreal	Fabio dal Zotto (ITA)	Alexandr Romankov (URS)	Bernard Talvard (FRA)
1980 Moscow	Vladimir Smirnov (URS)	Pascal Jolyot (FRA)	Alexandr Romankov (URS)
1984 Los Angeles	Mauro Numa (ITA)	Matthias Behr (FRG)	Stefano Cerioni (ITA)
1988 Seoul	Stefano Cerioni (ITA)	Udo Wagner (GDR)	Alexandr Romankov (URS)
1992 Barcelona	Philippe Omnes (FRA)	Sergei Golubitsky (EUN)	Elvis Gregory (CUB)
1996 Atlanta	Alessandro Puccini (ITA)	Lionel Plumenail (FRA)	Franck Boidin (FRA)
2000 Sydney	Kim Young-Ho (KOR)	Ralf Bissdorf (GER)	Dmitriy Shevchenko (RUS)
2004 Athens	Brice Guyart (FRA)	Salvatore Sanzo (ITA)	Andrea Cassara (ITA)
2008 Beijing	Benjamin Kleibrink (GER)	Yuki Ota (JPN)	Salvatore Sanzo (ITA)

Medalists Through the Years: *Fencing Sabre, Individual*

Games	Gold	Silver	Bronze
1896 Athens	Ioannis Georgiadis (GRE)	Telemachos Karakalos (GRE)	Holger Nielsen (DEN)
1900 Paris	Louis Venant Gabriel de la Falaise (FRA)	Léon Thiébaut (FRA)	Siegfried Flesch (AUT)
1904 St. Louis	Manuel Díaz (CUB)	William Grebe (USA)	Albertson Van Zo Post (CUB)
1908 London	Jeno Fuchs (HUN)	Béla Zulawsky (HUN)	Vilém Goppold von Lobsdorf (BOH)
1912 Stockholm	Jeno Fuchs (HUN)	Béla Békéssy (HUN)	Ervin Mészáros (HUN)
1920 Antwerp	Nedo Nadi (ITA)	Aldo Nadi (ITA)	Adrianus de Jong (NED)
1924 Paris	Sándor Pósta (HUN)	Roger Ducret (FRA)	János Garay (HUN)
1928 Amsterdam	Odön Tersztyánszky (HUN)	Attila Petschauer (HUN)	Bino Bini (ITA)
1932 Los Angeles	György Piller (HUN)	Giulio Gaudini (ITA)	Endre Kabos (HUN)
1936 Berlin	Endre Kabos (HUN)	Gustavo Marzi (ITA)	Aladár Gerevich (HUN)
1948 London	Aladár Gerevich (HUN)	Vincenzo Pinton (ITA)	Pál Kovács (HUN)
1952 Helsinki	Pál Kovács (HUN)	Aladár Gerevich (HUN)	Tibor Berczelly (HUN)
1956 Melbourne	Rudolf Kárpáti (HUN)	Jerzy Pawlowski (POL)	Lev Kuznetsov (URS)
1960 Rome	Rudolf Kárpáti (HUN)	Zoltán Horváth (HUN)	Wladimiro Calarese (ITA)
1964 Tokyo	Tibor Pézsa (HUN)	Claude Arabo (FRA)	Umar Mavlikhanov (URS)
1968 Mexico City	Jerzy Pawlowski (POL)	Mark Rakita (URS)	Tibor Pézsa (HUN)
1972 Munich	Viktor Sidyak (URS)	Péter Maróth (HUN)	Vladimir Nazlymov (URS)
1976 Montreal	Viktor Krovopuskov (URS)	Vladimir Nazlymov (URS)	Viktor Sidyak (URS)
1980 Moscow	Viktor Krovopuskov (URS)	Mikhail Burtsev (URS)	Imre Gedovári (HUN)
1984 Los Angeles	Jean-François Lamour (FRA)	Marco Marin (ITA)	Peter Westbrook (USA)
1988 Seoul	Jean-François Lamour (FRA)	Janusz Olech (POL)	Giovanni Scalzo (ITA)
1992 Barcelona	Bence Szabó (HUN)	Marco Marin (ITA)	Jean-François Lamour (FRA)
1996 Atlanta	Stanislav Pozdniakov (RUS)	Sergey Sharikov (RUS)	Damien Touya (FRA)
2000 Sydney	Mihai Claudiu Covaliu (ROU)	Mathieu Gourdain (FRA)	Wiradech Kothny (GER)
2004 Athens	Aldo Montano (ITA)	Zsolt Nemcsik (HUN)	Vladislav Tretiak (UKR)
2008 Beijing	Zhong Man (CHN)	Nicolas Lopez (FRA)	Mihai Claudiu Covaliu (ROU)

Medalists Through the Years: *Shooting 50 m Pistol*

Games	Gold	Silver	Bronze
1896 Athens	Sumner Paine (USA)	Holger Nielsen (DEN)	Joannis Phrangoudis (GRE)
1900 Paris	Karl Röderer (SUI)	Achille Paroche (FRA)	Konrad Stäheli (SUI)
1904 St. Louis	not included in the Olympic program		
1908 London	Paul Van Asbroeck (BEL)	Réginald Storms (BEL)	James Gorman (USA)
1912 Stockholm	Alfred Lane (USA)	Peter Dolfen (USA)	Charles Stewart (GBR)
1920 Antwerp	Karl Frederick (USA)	Afrânio da Costa (BRA)	Alfred Lane (USA)
1924—1932	not included in the Olympic program		
1936 Berlin	Torsten Ullman (SWE)	Erich Krempel (GER)	Charles des Jammonières (FRA)
1948 London	Edwin Vasquez Cam (PER)	Rudolf Schnyder (SUI)	Torsten Ullman (SWE)
1952 Helsinki	Huelet Benner (USA)	Angel Leon de Gozalo (ESP)	Ambrus Balogh (HUN)
1956 Melbourne	Pentti Linnosvuo (FIN)	Makhmud Umarov (URS)	Offutt Pinion (USA)
1960 Rome	Aleksey Gushchin (URS)	Makhmud Umarov (URS)	Yoshihisa Yoshikawa (JPN)
1964 Tokyo	Väinö Markkanen (FIN)	Franklin Green (USA)	Yoshihisa Yoshikawa (JPN)
1968 Mexico City	Grigori Kosych (URS)	Heinz Mertel (FRG)	Harald Vollmar (GDR)
1972 Munich	Ragnar Skanåker (SWE)	Daniel Iuga (ROU)	Rudolf Dollinger (AUT)
1976 Montreal	Uwe Potteck (GDR)	Harald Vollmar (GDR)	Rudolf Dollinger (AUT)
1980 Moscow	Aleksandr Melentiev (URS)	Harald Vollmar (GDR)	Lubtcho Diakov (BUL)
1984 Los Angeles	Xu Haifeng (CHN)	Ragnar Skanåker (SWE)	Wang Yifu (CHN)
1988 Seoul	Sorin Babii (ROU)	Ragnar Skanåker (SWE)	Igor Basinski (URS)
1992 Barcelona	Kanstantsin Lukashyk (EUN)	Wang Yifu (CHN)	Ragnar Skanåker (SWE)
1996 Atlanta	Boris Kokorev (RUS)	Igor Basinski (BLR)	Roberto Di Donna (ITA)
2000 Sydney	Tanyu Kiryakov (BUL)	Igor Basinski (BLR)	Martin Tenk (CZE)
2004 Athens	Mikhail Nestruyev (RUS)	Jin Jong-oh (KOR)	Kim Jong-su (PRK)
2008 Beijing	Jin Jong-oh (KOR)	Tan Zongliang (CHN)	Vladimir Isakov (RUS)

This event has also been known as Free Pistol. From 1972 to 1980, this event was mixed (open to both men and women shooters), although all medals were won by men at these Games, except for in 1976 when Margaret Murdock of the US won the silver medal.

Medalists Through the Years: *Shooting 25 m Rapid Fire Pistol*

Games	Gold	Silver	Bronze
1896 Athens	Ioannis Frangoudis (GRE)	Georgios Orfanidis (GRE)	Holger Nielsen (DEN)
1900 Paris	Maurice Larrouy (FRA)	Léon Moreaux (FRA)	Eugène Balme (FRA)
1904—1908	not included in the Olympic program		
1912 Stockholm	Alfred Lane (USA)	Paul Palén (SWE)	Johan Hübner von Holst (SWE)
1920 Antwerp	Guilherme Paraense (BRA)	Raymond Bracken (USA)	Fritz Zulauf (SUI)
1924 Paris	Henry Bailey (USA)	Vilhelm Carlberg (SWE)	Lennart Hannelius (FIN)
1928 Amsterdam	not included in the Olympic program		
1932 Los Angeles	Renzo Morigi (ITA)	Heinz Hax (GER)	Domenico Matteucci (ITA)
1936 Berlin	Cornelius van Oyen (GER)	Heinz Hax (GER)	Torsten Ullman (SWE)
1948 London	Károly Takács (HUN)	Carlos Diaz Sáenz (ARG)	Sven Lundquist (SWE)
1952 Helsinki	Károly Takács (HUN)	Szilárd Kun (HUN)	Gheorghe Lichiardopol (ROU)
1956 Melbourne	Stefan Petrescu (ROU)	Yevgeni Cherkasov (URS)	Gheorghe Lichiardopol (ROU)
1960 Rome	William McMillan (USA)	Pentti Linnosvuo (FIN)	Aleksandr Zabelin (URS)
1964 Tokyo	Pentti Linnosvuo (FIN)	Ion Tripsa (ROU)	Lubomír Nácovsky (TCH)
1968 Mexico City	Józef Zapedzki (POL)	Marcel Rosca (ROU)	Renart Suleymanov (URS)
1972 Munich	Józef Zapedzki (POL)	Ladislav Falta (TCH)	Viktor Torshin (URS)
1976 Montreal	Norbert Klaar (GDR)	Jürgen Wiefel (GDR)	Roberto Ferraris (ITA)
1980 Moscow	Corneliu Ion (ROU)	Jürgen Wiefel (GDR)	Gerhard Petritsch (AUT)
1984 Los Angeles	Takeo Kamachi (JPN)	Corneliu Ion (ROU)	Rauno Bies (FIN)
1988 Seoul	Afanasijs Kuzmins (URS)	Ralf Schumann (GDR)	Zoltán Kovács (HUN)
1992 Barcelona	Ralf Schumann (GER)	Afanasijs Kuzmins (LAT)	Vladimir Vokhmyanin (EUN)
1996 Atlanta	Ralf Schumann (GER)	Emil Milev (BUL)	Vladimir Vokhmyanin (KAZ)
2000 Sydney	Sergei Alifirenko (RUS)	Michel Ansermet (SUI)	Iulian Raicea (ROU)
2004 Athens	Ralf Schumann (GER)	Sergei Polyakov (RUS)	Sergei Alifirenko (RUS)
2008 Beijing	Oleksandr Petriv (UKR)	Ralf Schumann (GER)	Christian Reitz (GER)

Medalists Through the Years: *Tennis Singles*

Games	Gold	Silver	Bronze
1896 Athens	John Pius Boland (GBR)	Dionysios Kasdaglis (GRE)	Momcsilló Tapavicza (HUN)
			Konstantinos Paspatis (GRE)
1900 Paris	Lawrence Doherty (GBR)	Harold Mahoney (GBR)	Reginald Doherty (GBR)
			Arthur Norris (GBR)
1904 St. Louis	Beals Wright (USA)	Robert LeRoy (USA)	Alphonzo Bell (USA)
			Edgar Leonard (USA)
1908 London	Josiah Ritchie (GBR)	Otto Froitzheim (GER)	Wilberforce Eaves (GBR)
1912 Stockholm	Charles Winslow (RSA)	Harold Kitson (RSA)	Oscar Kreuzer (GER)
1920 Antwerp	Louis Raymond (RSA)	Ichiya Kumagae (JPN)	Charles Winslow (RSA)
1924 Paris	Vincent Richards (USA)	Henri Cochet (FRA)	Umberto De Morpurgo (ITA)
1928—1984	not included in the Olympic program		
1988 Seoul	Miloslav Mecír (TCH)	Tim Mayotte (USA)	Stefan Edberg (SWE)
			Brad Gilbert (USA)
1992 Barcelona	Marc Rosset (SUI)	Jordi Arrese (ESP)	Andrei Cherkasov (EUN)
			Goran Ivanisevic (CRO)
1996 Atlanta	Andre Agassi (USA)	Sergi Bruguera (ESP)	Leander Paes (IND)
2000 Sydney	Yevgeny Kafelnikov (RUS)	Tommy Haas (GER)	Arnaud di Pasquale (FRA)
2004 Athens	Nicolás Massú (CHI)	Mardy Fish (USA)	Fernando González (CHI)
2008 Beijing	Rafael Nadal (ESP)	Fernando González (CHI)	Novak Djokovic (SRB)

Medalists Through the Years: *Tennis Doubles*

Games	Gold	Silver	Bronze
1896 Athens	John Pius Boland (GBR) and Friedrich Traun (GER)	Demetrios Petrokokkinos and Dionysios Kasdaglis (GRE)	Edwin Flack (AUS) and George S. Robertson (GBR)
1900 Paris	Lawrence Doherty and Reginald Doherty (GBR)	Max Décugis (FRA) and Basil Spalding de Garmendia (USA)	Georges de la Chapelle and André Prévost (FRA)
			Harold Mahoney and Arthur Norris (GBR)
1904 St. Louis	Edgar Leonard and Beals Wright (USA)	Alphonzo Bell and Robert LeRoy (USA)	Joseph Wear and Allen West (USA)
			Clarence Gamble and Arthur Wear (USA)
1908 London	George Hillyard and Reginald Doherty (GBR)	Major Josiah Ritchie and James Parke (GBR)	Clement Cazalet and Charles Dixon (GBR)
1912 Stockholm	Harry Kitson and Charles Winslow (RSA)	Arthur Zborzil and Fritz Pipes (AUT)	Albert Canet and Edouard Mény de Marangue (FRA)
1920 Antwerp	Oswald Turnbull and Maxwell Woosnam (GBR)	Ichiya Kumagae and Seiichiro Kashio (JPN)	Max Décugis and Pierre Albarran (FRA)
1924 Paris	Vincent Richards and Francis Hunter (USA)	Jacques Brugnon and Henri Cochet (FRA)	Jean Borotra and René Lacoste (FRA)
1928—1984	not included in the Olympic program		
1988 Seoul	Ken Flach and Robert Seguso (USA)	Emilio Sánchez and Sergio Casal (ESP)	Miloslav Mecír and Milan Srejber (TCH)
			Stefan Edberg and Anders Jærryd (SWE)
1992 Barcelona	Boris Becker and Michael Stich (GER)	Wayne Ferreira and Piet Norval (RSA)	Javier Frana and Christian Miniussi (ARG)
			Goran Ivanisevic and Goran Prpic (CRO)
1996 Atlanta	Todd Woodbridge and Mark Woodforde (AUS)	Neil Broad and Tim Henman (GBR)	Marc-Kevin Goellner and David Prinosil (GER)
2000 Sydney	Sébastien Lareau and Daniel Nestor (CAN)	Todd Woodbridge and Mark Woodforde (AUS)	Àlex Corretja and Albert Costa (ESP)
2004 Athens	Fernando González and Nicolás Massú (CHI)	Nicolas Kiefer and Rainer Schüttler (GER)	Mario Ancic and Ivan Ljubicic (CRO)
2008 Beijing	Roger Federer and Stanislas Wawrinka (SUI)	Simon Aspelin and Thomas Johansson (SWE)	Bob Bryan and Mike Bryan (USA)

Medalists Through the Years: *Greco-Roman Wrestling, Heavyweight*

Games	Gold	Silver	Bronze
1896 Athens	Carl Schuhmann (GER)	Georgios Tsitas (GRE)	Stephanos Christopoulos (GRE)
1900 Paris	not included in the Olympic program		
1904 St. Louis	only freestyle wrestling was contested		
1908 London*	Verner Weckman (FIN) (Light Heavyweight)	Yrjö Saarela (FIN) (Light Heavyweight)	Carl Jensen (DEN) (Light Heavyweight)
	Richárd Weisz (HUN) (Super Heavyweight)	Aleksandr Petrov (RUS) (Super Heavyweight)	Søren Marinus Jensen (DEN) (Super Heavyweight)
1912 Stockholm	Yrjö Saarela (FIN)	Johan Olin (FIN)	Søren Marinus Jensen (DEN)
1920 Antwerp	Adolf Lindfors (FIN)	Poul Hansen (DEN)	Martti Nieminen (FIN)
1924 Paris	Henri Deglane (FRA)	Edil Rosenqvist (FIN)	Rajmund Badó (HUN)
1928 Amsterdam	Rudolf Svensson (SWE)	Hjalmar Nyström (FIN)	Georg Gehring (GER)
1932 Los Angeles	Carl Westergren (SWE)	Josef Urban (TCH)	Nikolaus Hirschl (AUT)
1936 Berlin	Kristjan Palusalu (EST)	John Nyman (SWE)	Kurt Hornfischer (GER)
1948 London	Ahmet Kireççi (TUR)	Tor Nilsson (SWE)	Guido Fantoni (ITA)
1952 Helsinki	Johannes Kotkas (URS)	Josef Ruzicka (TCH)	Tauno Kovanen (FIN)
1956 Melbourne	Anatoly Parfyonov (URS)	Wilfried Dietrich (EUA)	Adelmo Bulgarelli (ITA)
1960 Rome	Ivan Bogdan (URS)	Wilfried Dietrich (EUA)	Bohumil Kubát (TCH)
1964 Tokyo	István Kozma (HUN)	Anatoly Roshchin (URS)	Wilfried Dietrich (EUA)
1968 Mexico City	István Kozma (HUN)	Anatoly Roshchin (URS)	Petr Kment (TCH)
1972 Munich	Nicolae Martinescu (ROU)	Nikolai Yakovenko (URS)	Ferenc Kiss (HUN)
1976 Montreal	Nikolai Balboshin (URS)	Kamen Goranov (BUL)	Andrzej Skrzydlewski (POL)
1980 Moscow	Georgi Raikov (BUL)	Roman Bierla (POL)	Vasile Andrei (ROU)
1984 Los Angeles	Vasile Andrei (ROU)	Greg Gibson (USA)	Jozef Tertei (YUG)
1988 Seoul	Andrzej Wronski (POL)	Gerhard Himmel (FRG)	Dennis Koslowski (USA)
1992 Barcelona	Héctor Milián (CUB)	Dennis Koslowski (USA)	Sergei Demyashkevich (EUN)
1996 Atlanta	Andrzej Wronski (POL)	Sergey Lishtvan (BLR)	Mikael Ljungberg (SWE)
2000 Sydney	Mikael Ljungberg (SWE)	Davyd Saldadze (UKR)	Garrett Lowney (USA)
2004 Athens	Karam Gaber (EGY)	Ramaz Nozadze (GEO)	Mehmet Özal (TUR)
2008 Beijing	Aslanbek Khushtov (RUS)	Mirko Englich (GER)	Adam Wheeler (USA), Asset Mambetov (KAZ)

In 1896 there was no limit, +82.5 kg (1912—1928), +87 kg (1932—1960), +97 kg (1964—1968), -100 kg (1972—1996), -97 kg (2000), -96 kg (2004—Present)
* In 1908 there were 2 Heavyweight Greco-Roman Wrestling categories: Light Heavyweight was -93 kg and Super Heavyweight was +93 kg

Medalists Through the Years: *Gymnastics Horizontal Bar*

Games	Gold	Silver	Bronze
1896 Athens	Hermann Weingärtner (GER)	Alfred Flatow (GER)	none awarded
1900 Paris	not included in the Olympic program		
1904 St. Louis	Anton Heida (USA), Edward Hennig (USA)	none awarded	George Eyser (USA)
1908—1920	not included in the Olympic program		
1924 Paris	Leon Stukelj (YUG)	Jean Gutweninger (SUI)	André Higelin (FRA)
1928 Amsterdam	Georges Miez (SUI)	Romeo Neri (ITA)	Eugen Mack (SUI)
1932 Los Angeles	Dallas Bixler (USA)	Heikki Savolainen (FIN)	Einari Teräsvirta (FIN)
1936 Berlin	Aleksanteri Saarvala (FIN)	Konrad Frey (GER)	Alfred Schwarzmann (GER)
1948 London	Josef Stalder (SUI)	Walter Lehmann (SUI)	Veikko Huhtanen (FIN)
1952 Helsinki	Jack Günthard (SUI)	Alfred Schwarzmann (GER), Josef Stalder (SUI)	none awarded
1956 Melbourne	Takashi Ono (JPN)	Yuri Titov (URS)	Masao Takemoto (JPN)
1960 Rome	Takashi Ono (JPN)	Masao Takemoto (JPN)	Boris Shakhlin (URS)
1964 Tokyo	Boris Shakhlin (URS)	Yuri Titov (URS)	Miroslav Cerar (YUG)
1968 Mexico City	Akinori Nakayama (JPN), Mikhail Voronin (URS)	none awarded	Eizo Kenmotsu (JPN)
1972 Munich	Mitsuo Tsukahara (JPN)	Sawao Kato (JPN)	Shigeru Kasamatsu (JPN)
1976 Montreal	Mitsuo Tsukahara (JPN)	Eizo Kenmotsu (JPN)	Eberhard Gienger (FRG)
1980 Moscow	Stoyan Deltchev (BUL)	Alexander Dityatin (URS)	Nikolai Andrianov (URS)
1984 Los Angeles	Shinji Morisue (JPN)	Tong Fei (CHN)	Koji Gushiken (JPN)
1988 Seoul	Vladimir Artemov (URS), Valeri Liukin (URS)	none awarded	Holger Behrendt (GDR), Marius Gherman (ROU)
1992 Barcelona	Trent Dimas (USA)	Grigory Misutin (EUN), Andreas Wecker (GER)	none awarded
1996 Atlanta	Andreas Wecker (GER)	Krassimir Dounev (BUL)	Fan Bin (CHN), Alexei Nemov (RUS), Vitaly Scherbo (BLR)
2000 Sydney	Alexei Nemov (RUS)	Benjamin Varonian (FRA)	Lee Joo-Hyung (KOR)
2004 Athens	Igor Cassina (ITA)	Paul Hamm (USA)	Isao Yoneda (JPN)
2008 Beijing	Zou Kai (CHN)	Jonathan Horton (USA)	Fabian Hambuechen (GER)

Medalists Through the Years: *Gymnastics Parallel Bars*

Games	Gold	Silver	Bronze
1896 Athens	Alfred Flatow (GER)	Louis Zutter (SUI)	none
1900 Paris	not included in the Olympic program		
1904 St. Louis	George Eyser (USA)	Anton Heida (USA)	John Duha (USA)
1908—1920	not included in the Olympic program		
1924 Paris	August Güttinger (SUI)	Robert Prazák (TCH)	Giorgio Zampori (ITA)
1928 Amsterdam	Ladislav Vácha (TCH)	Josip Primozic (YUG)	Hermann Hänggi (SUI)
1932 Los Angeles	Romeo Neri (ITA)	István Pelle (HUN)	Heikki Savolainen (FIN)
1936 Berlin	Konrad Frey (GER)	Michael Reusch (SUI)	Alfred Schwarzmann (GER)
1948 London	Michael Reusch (SUI)	Veikko Huhtanen (FIN)	Christian Kipfer (SUI), Josef Stalder (SUI)
1952 Helsinki	Hans Eugster (SUI)	Viktor Chukarin (URS)	Josef Stalder (SUI)
1956 Melbourne	Viktor Chukarin (URS)	Masami Kubota (JPN)	Takashi Ono (JPN), Masao Takemoto (JPN)
1960 Rome	Boris Shakhlin (URS)	Giovanni Carminucci (ITA)	Takashi Ono (JPN)
1964 Tokyo	Yukio Endo (JPN)	Shuji Tsurumi (JPN)	Franco Menichelli (ITA)
1968 Mexico City	Akinori Nakayama (JPN)	Mikhail Voronin (URS)	Viktor Klimenko (URS)
1972 Munich	Sawao Kato (JPN)	Shigeru Kasamatsu (JPN)	Eizo Kenmotsu (JPN)
1976 Montreal	Sawao Kato (JPN)	Nikolai Andrianov (URS)	Mitsuo Tsukahara (JPN)
1980 Moscow	Alexander Tkachyov (URS)	Alexander Dityatin (URS)	Roland Brückner (GDR)
1984 Los Angeles	Bart Conner (USA)	Nobuyuki Kajitani (JPN)	Mitch Gaylord (USA)
1988 Seoul	Vladimir Artemov (URS)	Valeri Liukin (URS)	Sven Tippelt (GDR)
1992 Barcelona	Vitaly Scherbo (EUN)	Li Jing (CHN)	Igor Korobchinsky (EUN), Guo Linyao (CHN), Masayuki Matsunaga (JPN)
1996 Atlanta	Rustam Sharipov (UKR)	Jair Lynch (USA)	Vitaly Scherbo (BLR)
2000 Sydney	Li Xiaopeng (CHN)	Lee Joo-Hyung (KOR)	Alexei Nemov (RUS)
2004 Athens	Valeri Goncharov (UKR)	Hiroyuki Tomita (JPN)	Li Xiaopeng (CHN)
2008 Beijing	Li Xiaopeng (CHN)	Yoo Won-Chul (KOR)	Anton Fokin (UZB)

Medalists Through the Years: *Gymnastics Pommel Horse*

Games	Gold	Silver	Bronze
1896 Athens	Louis Zutter (SUI)	Hermann Weingärtner (GER)	none awarded
1900 Paris	not included in the Olympic program		
1904 St. Louis	Anton Heida (USA)	George Eyser (USA)	William Merz (USA)
1908—1920	not included in the Olympic program		
1924 Paris	Josef Wilhelm (SUI)	Jean Gutweninger (SUI)	Antoine Rebetez (SUI)
1928 Amsterdam	Hermann Hänggi (SUI)	Georges Miez (SUI)	Heikki Savolainen (FIN)
1932 Los Angeles	István Pelle (HUN)	Omero Bonoli (ITA)	Frank Haubold (USA)
1936 Berlin	Konrad Frey (GER)	Eugen Mack (SUI)	Albert Bachmann (SUI)
1948 London	Paavo Aaltonen (FIN), Veikko Huhtanen (FIN), Heikki Savolainen (FIN)	none awarded	none awarded
1952 Helsinki	Viktor Chukarin (URS)	Yevgeni Korolkov (URS), Grant Shaginyan (URS)	none awarded
1956 Melbourne	Boris Shakhlin (URS)	Takashi Ono (JPN)	Viktor Chukarin (URS)
1960 Rome	Eugen Ekman (FIN), Boris Shakhlin (URS)	none awarded	Shuji Tsurumi (JPN)
1964 Tokyo	Miroslav Cerar (YUG)	Shuji Tsurumi (JPN)	Yuri Tsapenko (URS)
1968 Mexico City	Miroslav Cerar (YUG)	Olli Laiho (FIN)	Mikhail Voronin (URS)
1972 Munich	Viktor Klimenko (URS)	Sawao Kato (JPN)	Eizo Kenmotsu (JPN)
1976 Montreal	Zoltán Magyar (HUN)	Eizo Kenmotsu (JPN)	Nikolai Andrianov (URS), Michael Nikolay (GDR)
1980 Moscow	Zoltán Magyar (HUN)	Alexander Dityatin (URS)	Michael Nikolay (GDR)
1984 Los Angeles	Li Ning (CHN), Peter Vidmar (USA)	none awarded	Timothy Daggett (USA)
1988 Seoul	Dmitry Bilozerchev (URS), Zsolt Borkai (HUN), Lubomir Geraskov (BUL)	none awarded	none awarded
1992 Barcelona	Pae Gil-Su (PRK) Vitaly Scherbo (EUN)	none awarded	Andreas Wecker (GER)
1996 Atlanta	Donghua Li (SUI)	Marius Urzica (ROU)	Alexei Nemov (RUS)
2000 Sydney	Marius Urzica (ROU)	Eric Poujade (FRA)	Alexei Nemov (RUS)
2004 Athens	Teng Haibin (CHN)	Marius Urzica (ROU)	Takehiro Kashima (JPN)
2008 Beijing	Xiao Qin (CHN)	Filip Ude (CRO)	Louis Smith (GBR)

Medalists Through the Years: *Gymnastics Rings*

Games	Gold	Silver	Bronze
1896 Athens	Ioannis Mitropoulos (GRE)	Hermann Weingärtner (GER)	Petros Persakis (GRE)
1900 Paris	not included in the Olympic program		
1904 St. Louis	Herman Glass (USA)	William Merz (USA)	Emil Voigt (USA)
1908–1920	not included in the Olympic program		
1924 Paris	Francesco Martino (ITA)	Robert Prazák (TCH)	Ladislav Vácha (TCH)
1928 Amsterdam	Leon Stukelj (YUG)	Ladislav Vácha (TCH)	Emanuel Loffler (TCH)
1932 Los Angeles	George Gulack (USA)	Bill Denton (USA)	Giovanni Lattuada (ITA)
1936 Berlin	Alois Hudec (TCH)	Leon Stukelj (YUG)	Matthias Volz (GER)
1948 London	Karl Frei (SUI)	Michael Reusch (SUI)	Zdenek Ruzicka (TCH)
1952 Helsinki	Grant Shaginyan (URS)	Viktor Chukarin (URS)	Hans Eugster (SUI), Dmitri Leonkin (URS)
1956 Melbourne	Albert Azaryan (URS)	Valentin Muratov (URS)	Masao Takemoto (JPN), Masami Kubota (JPN)
1960 Rome	Albert Azaryan (URS)	Boris Shakhlin (URS)	Velik Kapsazov (BUL), Takashi Ono (JPN)
1964 Tokyo	Takuji Hayata (JPN)	Franco Menichelli (ITA)	Boris Shakhlin (URS)
1968 Mexico City	Akinori Nakayama (JPN)	Mikhail Voronin (URS)	Sawao Kato (JPN)
1972 Munich	Akinori Nakayama (JPN)	Mikhail Voronin (URS)	Mitsuo Tsukahara (JPN)
1976 Montreal	Nikolai Andrianov (URS)	Alexander Dityatin (URS)	Danut Grecu (ROU)
1980 Moscow	Alexander Dityatin (URS)	Alexander Tkachyov (URS)	Jiri Tabak (TCH)
1984 Los Angeles	Koji Gushiken (JPN), Li Ning (CHN)	none awarded	Mitch Gaylord (USA)
1988 Seoul	Holger Behrendt (GDR), Dmitry Bilozerchev (URS)	none awarded	Sven Tippelt (GDR)
1992 Barcelona	Vitaly Scherbo (EUN)	Li Jing (CHN)	Andreas Wecker (GER) Li Xiaoshuang (CHN)
1996 Atlanta	Jury Chechi (ITA)	Dan Burinca (ROU), Szilveszter Csollány (HUN)	none awarded
2000 Sydney	Szilveszter Csollány (HUN)	Dimosthenis Tampakos (GRE)	Jordan Jovtchev (BUL)
2004 Athens	Dimosthenis Tampakos (GRE)	Jordan Jovtchev (BUL)	Jury Chechi (ITA)
2008 Beijing	Chen Yibing (CHN)	Yang Wei (CHN)	Oleksandr Vorobiov (UKR)

Medalists Through the Years: *Gymnastics Vault*

Games	Gold	Silver	Bronze
1896 Athens	Carl Schuhmann (GER)	Louis Zutter (SUI)	Hermann Weingärtner (GER)
1900 Paris	not included in the Olympic program		
1904 St. Louis	George Eyser (USA)	Anton Heida (USA)	William Merz (USA)
1908–1920	not included in the Olympic program		
1924 Paris	Frank Kriz (USA)	Jan Koutny (TCH)	Bohumil Morkovsky (TCH)
1928 Amsterdam	Eugen Mack (SUI)	Emanuel Löffler (TCH)	Stane Derganc (YUG)
1932 Los Angeles	Savino Guglielmetti (ITA)	Al Jochim (USA)	Ed Carmichael (USA)
1936 Berlin	Alfred Schwarzmann (GER)	Eugen Mack (SUI)	Matthias Volz (GER)
1948 London	Paavo Aaltonen (FIN)	Olavi Rove (FIN)	János Mogyorósi-Klencs (HUN), Ferenc Pataki (HUN), Leo Sotornik (TCH)
1952 Helsinki	Viktor Chukarin (URS)	Masao Takemoto (JPN)	Takashi Ono (JPN), Tadao Uesako (JPN)
1956 Melbourne	Helmut Bantz (EUA), Valentin Muratov (URS)	none awarded	Yuri Titov (URS)
1960 Rome	Takashi Ono (JPN), Boris Shakhlin (URS)	none awarded	Vladimir Portnoi (URS)
1964 Tokyo	Haruhiro Yamashita (JPN)	Viktor Lisitsky (URS)	Hannu Rantakari (FIN)
1968 Mexico City	Mikhail Voronin (URS)	Yukio Endo (JPN)	Sergei Diomidov (URS)
1972 Munich	Klaus Köste (GDR)	Viktor Klimenko (URS)	Nikolai Andrianov (URS)
1976 Montreal	Nikolai Andrianov (URS)	Mitsuo Tsukahara (JPN)	Hiroshi Kajiyama (JPN)
1980 Moscow	Nikolai Andrianov (URS)	Alexander Dityatin (URS)	Roland Brückner (GDR)
1984 Los Angeles	Lou Yun (CHN)	Mitch Gaylord (USA), Koji Gushiken (JPN), Li Ning (CHN), Shinji Morisue (JPN)	none awarded
1988 Seoul	Lou Yun (CHN)	Sylvio Kroll (GDR)	Park Jong-Hoon (KOR)
1992 Barcelona	Vitaly Scherbo (EUN)	Grigory Misutin (EUN)	Yoo Ok Ryul (KOR)
1996 Atlanta	Alexei Nemov (RUS)	Yeo Hong-Chul (KOR)	Vitaly Scherbo (BLR)
2000 Sydney	Gervasio Deferr (ESP)	Alexei Bondarenko (RUS)	Leszek Blanik (POL)
2004 Athens	Gervasio Deferr (ESP)	Jevgenijs Sapronenko (LAT)	Marian Dragulescu (ROU)
2008 Beijing	Leszek Blanik (POL)	Thomas Bouhail (FRA)	Anton Golotsutskov (RUS)

Medalists at Beijing 2008

The following section includes a medal table for Beijing 2008 by country and also by athlete, and a list of all the medalists in all the events at the Games. Officially, the International Olympic Committee does not recognise a ranking of participating countries at the Olympic Games, as its position is that *"The Olympic Games are competitions between athletes in individual or team events and not between countries,"* but it does publish medal tables for informational purposes, following a system of sorting by the number of gold medals the athletes from a country have earned as opposed to the total number of medals won by a country.

2008 Olympic Medal Table by National Olympic Committee

Country/NOC	Gold	Silver	Bronze	Total
China (CHN)	51	21	28	100
United States (USA)	36	38	36	110
Russia (RUS)	23	21	29	73
Great Britain (GBR)	19	13	15	47
Germany (GER)	16	10	15	41
Australia (AUS)	14	15	17	46
South Korea (KOR)	13	10	8	31
Japan (JPN)	9	6	10	25
Italy (ITA)	8	9	10	27
France (FRA)	7	16	18	41
Ukraine (UKR)	7	5	15	27
Netherlands (NED)	7	5	4	16
Kenya (KEN)	6	4	4	14
Jamaica (JAM)	6	3	2	11
Spain (ESP)	5	10	3	18
Belarus (BLR)	4	5	10	19
Romania (ROU)	4	1	3	8
Ethiopia (ETH)	4	1	2	7
Canada (CAN)	3	9	6	18
Hungary (HUN)	3	5	2	10
Poland (POL)	3	6	1	10
Norway (NOR)	3	5	1	9
Brazil (BRA)	3	4	8	15
Czech Republic (CZE)	3	3	0	6
New Zealand (NZL)	3	2	4	9
Slovakia (SVK)	3	2	1	6
Georgia (GEO)	3	0	3	6
Cuba (CUB)	2	11	11	24
Kazakhstan (KAZ)	2	4	7	13
Denmark (DEN)	2	2	3	7
Mongolia (MGL)	2	2	0	4
Thailand (THA)	2	2	0	4
Switzerland (SUI)	2	1	4	7
North Korea (PRK)	2	1	3	6
Argentina (ARG)	2	0	4	6
Mexico (MEX)	2	0	1	3
Turkey (TUR)	1	4	3	8
Zimbabwe (ZIM)	1	3	0	4
Azerbaijan (AZE)	1	2	4	7
Uzbekistan (UZB)	1	2	3	6
Slovenia (SLO)	1	2	2	5
Bulgaria (BUL)	1	1	3	5
Indonesia (INA)	1	1	3	5
Finland (FIN)	1	1	2	4

Country/NOC	Gold	Silver	Bronze	Total
Latvia (LAT)	1	1	1	3
Belgium (BEL)	1	1	0	2
Dominican Republic (DOM)	1	1	0	2
Estonia (EST)	1	1	0	2
Portugal (POR)	1	1	0	2
India (IND)	1	0	2	3
Serbia (SRB)	1	0	2	3
Iran (IRI)	1	0	1	2
Cameroon (CMR)	1	0	0	1
Panama (PAN)	1	0	0	1
Tunisia (TUN)	1	0	0	1
Sweden (SWE)	0	4	1	5
Croatia (CRO)	0	2	3	5
Lithuania (LTU)	0	2	3	5
Greece (GRE)	0	2	2	4
Trinidad and Tobago (TRI)	0	2	0	2
Nigeria (NGR)	0	1	3	4
Austria (AUT)	0	1	2	3
Ireland (IRL)	0	1	2	3
Algeria (ALG)	0	1	1	2
Bahamas (BAH)	0	1	1	2
Colombia (COL)	0	1	1	2
Kyrgyzstan (KGZ)	0	1	1	2
Morocco (MAR)	0	1	1	2
Tajikistan (TJK)	0	1	1	2
Chile (CHI)	0	1	0	1
Ecuador (ECU)	0	1	0	1
Iceland (ISL)	0	1	0	1
Malaysia (MAS)	0	1	0	1
South Africa (RSA)	0	1	0	1
Singapore (SIN)	0	1	0	1
Sudan (SUD)	0	1	0	1
Vietnam (VIE)	0	1	0	1
Armenia (ARM)	0	0	6	6
Chinese Taipei (TPE)	0	0	4	4
Afghanistan (AFG)	0	0	1	1
Egypt (EGY)	0	0	1	1
Israel (ISR)	0	0	1	1
Moldova (MDA)	0	0	1	1
Mauritius (MRI)	0	0	1	1
Togo (TOG)	0	0	1	1
Venezuela (VEN)	0	0	1	1
Total	302	303	353	958

2008 Medal Leaders

Athletes who won at least three gold medals or at least four total medals are listed below:

Athlete	Nation	Sport	Gold	Silver	Bronze	Total
Michael Phelps	United States (USA)	Swimming	8	0	0	8
Natalie Coughlin	United States (USA)	Swimming	1	2	3	6
Nastia Liukin	United States (USA)	Gymnastics	1	3	1	5
Libby Trickett	Australia (AUS)	Swimming	2	1	1	4
Ryan Lochte	United States (USA)	Swimming	2	0	2	4
Kirsty Coventry	Zimbabwe (ZIM)	Swimming	1	3	0	4
Shawn Johnson	United States (USA)	Gymnastics	1	3	0	4
Chris Hoy	Great Britain (GBR)	Cycling	3	0	0	3
Usain Bolt	Jamaica (JAM)	Athletics	3	0	0	3
Zou Kai	China (CHN)	Gymnastics	3	0	0	3
Stephanie Rice	Australia (AUS)	Swimming	3	0	0	3

2008 Medalists

Event	Gold	Silver	Bronze
ARCHERY			
Men's individual	Viktor Ruban (UKR)	Park Kyung-Mo (KOR)	Bair Badënov (RUS)
Women's individual	Zhang Juanjuan (CHN)	Park Sung-Hyun (KOR)	Yun Ok-hee (KOR)
Men's team	South Korea (KOR) Im Dong-Hyun, Lee Chang-Hwan, Park Kyung-Mo	Italy (ITA) Mauro Nespoli, Marco Galiazzo, Ilario Di Buò	China (CHN) Jiang Lin, Li Wenquan, Xue Haifeng
Women's team	South Korea (KOR) Park Sung-Hyun, Yun Ok-Hee, Joo Hyun-Jung	China (CHN) Zhang Juanjuan, Chen Ling, Guo Dan	France (FRA) Virginie Arnold, Sophie Dodemont, Bérangère Schuh
ATHLETICS			
Men's 100 m	Usain Bolt (JAM)	Richard Thompson (TRI)	Walter Dix (USA)
Women's 100 m	Shelly-Ann Fraser (JAM)	Sherone Simpson (JAM), Kerron Stewart (JAM)	None
Men's 200 m	Usain Bolt (JAM)	Shawn Crawford (USA)	Walter Dix (USA)
Women's 200 m	Veronica Campbell-Brown (JAM)	Allyson Felix (USA)	Kerron Stewart (JAM)
Men's 400 m	LaShawn Merritt (USA)	Jeremy Wariner (USA)	David Neville (USA)
Women's 400 m	Christine Ohuruogu (GBR)	Shericka Williams (JAM)	Sanya Richards (USA)
Men's 800 m	Wilfred Bungei (KEN)	Ismail Ahmed Ismail (SUD)	Alfred Yego (KEN)
Women's 800 m	Pamela Jelimo (KEN)	Janeth Jepkosgei (KEN)	Hasna Benhassi (MAR)
Men's 1,500 m	Asbel Kipruto Kiprop (KEN)	Nicholas Willis (NZL)	Mehdi Baala (FRA)
Women's 1,500 m	Nancy Jebet Lagat (KEN)	Iryna Lishchynska (UKR)	Nataliya Tobias (UKR)
Men's 5,000 m	Kenenisa Bekele (ETH)	Eliud Kipchoge (KEN)	Edwin Soi (KEN)
Women's 5,000 m	Tirunesh Dibaba (ETH)	Elvan Abeylegesse (TUR)	Meseret Defar (ETH)
Men's 10,000 m	Kenenisa Bekele (ETH)	Sileshi Sihine (ETH)	Micah Kogo (KEN)
Women's 10,000 m	Tirunesh Dibaba (ETH)	Elvan Abeylegesse (TUR)	Shalane Flanagan (USA)
Men's marathon	Samuel Kamau Wanjiru (KEN)	Jaouad Gharib Morocco (MAR)	Tsegay Kebede (ETH)
Women's marathon	Constantina Dita-Tomescu (ROU)	Catherine Ndereba (KEN)	Zhou Chunxiu (CHN)
Men's 110 m hurdles	Dayron Robles (CUB)	David Payne (USA)	David Oliver (USA)
Women's 100 m hurdles	Dawn Harper (USA)	Sally McLellan (AUS)	Priscilla Lopes-Schliep (CAN)
Men's 400 m hurdles	Angelo Taylor (USA)	Kerron Clement (USA)	Bershawn Jackson (USA)
Women's 400 m hurdles	Melaine Walker (JAM)	Sheena Tosta (USA)	Tasha Danvers (GBR)
Men's 3,000 m steeplechase	Brimin Kipruto (KEN)	Mahiedine Mekhissi-Benabbad (FRA)	Richard Mateelong (KEN)
Women's 3,000 m steeplechase	Gulnara Samitova-Galkina (RUS)	Eunice Jepkorir (KEN)	Yekaterina Volkova (RUS)
Men's 4x100 m relay	Jamaica (JAM) Nesta Carter, Michael Frater, Usain Bolt, Asafa Powell, Dwight Thomas	Trinidad and Tobago (TRI) Keston Bledman, Marc Burns, Emmanuel Callender, Richard Thompson, Aaron Armstrong	Japan (JPN) Naoki Tsukahara, Shingo Suetsugu, Shinji Takahira, Nobuharu Asahara
Women's 4x100 m relay	Russia (RUS) Evgeniya Polyakova, Aleksandra Fedoriva, Yulia Gushchina, Yuliya Chermoshanskaya	Belgium (BEL) Olivia Borlée, Hanna Mariën, Élodie Ouédraogo, Kim Gevaert	Nigeria (NGR) Franca Idoko, Gloria Kemasuode, Halimat Ismaila, Oludamola Osayomi, Agnes Osazuwa

2008 Medalists

Event	Gold	Silver	Bronze
Men's 4x400 m relay	United States (USA) LaShawn Merritt, Angelo Taylor, David Neville, Jeremy Wariner, Kerron Clement, Reggie Witherspoon	Bahamas (BAH) Andretti Bain, Michael Mathieu, Andrae Williams, Christopher Brown, Avard Moncur, Ramon Miller	Russia (RUS) Maksim Dyldin, Vladislav Frolov, Anton Kokorin, Denis Alexeev
Women's 4x400 m relay	United States (USA) Mary Wineberg, Allyson Felix, Monique Henderson, Sanya Richards, Natasha Hastings	Russia (RUS) Yulia Gushchina, Lyudmila Litvinova, Tatiana Firova, Anastasia Kapachinskaya, Elena Migunova, Tatyana Veshkurova	Jamaica (JAM) Shericka Williams, Shereefa Lloyd, Rosemarie Whyte, Novelene Williams, Bobby-Gaye Wilkins
Men's 20 km walk	Valeriy Borchin (RUS)	Jefferson Pérez (ECU)	Jared Tallent (AUS)
Women's 20 km walk	Olga Kaniskina (RUS)	Kjersti Plätzer (NOR)	Elisa Rigaudo (ITA)
Men's 50 km walk	Alex Schwazer (ITA)	Jared Tallent (AUS)	Denis Nizhegorodov (RUS)
Men's high jump	Andrey Silnov (RUS)	Germaine Mason (GBR)	Yaroslav Rybakov (RUS)
Women's high jump	Tia Hellebaut (BEL)	Blanka Vlasic (CRO)	Anna Chicherova (RUS)
Men's pole vault	Steven Hooker (AUS)	Yevgeny Lukyanenko (RUS)	Denys Yurchenko (UKR)
Women's pole vault	Yelena Isinbayeva (RUS)	Jennifer Stuczynski (USA)	Svetlana Feofanova (RUS)
Men's long jump	Irving Saladino (PAN)	Godfrey Khotso Mokoena (RSA)	Ibrahim Camejo (CUB)
Women's long jump	Maurren Maggi (BRA)	Tatyana Lebedeva (RUS)	Blessing Okagbare (NGR)
Men's triple jump	Nelson Évora (POR)	Phillips Idowu (GBR)	Leevan Sands (BAH)
Women's triple jump	Françoise Mbango Etone (CMR)	Tatyana Lebedeva (RUS)	Hrysopiyi Devetzi (GRE)
Men's shot put	Tomasz Majewski (POL)	Christian Cantwell (USA)	Andrei Mikhnevich (BLR)
Women's shot put	Valerie Vili (NZL)	Natallia Mikhnevich (BLR)	Nadzeya Astapchuk (BLR)
Men's discus throw	Gerd Kanter (EST)	Piotr Malachowski (POL)	Virgilijus Alekna (LTU)
Women's discus throw	Stephanie Brown Trafton (USA)	Yarelis Barrios (CUB)	Olena Antonova (UKR)
Men's hammer throw	Primoz Kozmus (SLO)	Vadim Devyatovskiy (BLR)	Ivan Tsikhan (BLR)
Women's hammer throw	Aksana Miankova (BLR)	Yipsi Moreno (CUB)	Zhang Wenxiu (CHN)
Men's javelin throw	Andreas Thorkildsen (NOR)	Ainars Kovals (LAT)	Tero Pitkämäki (FIN)
Women's javelin throw	Barbora Spotáková (CZE)	Mariya Abakumova (RUS)	Christina Obergföll (GER)
Men's decathlon	Bryan Clay (USA)	Andrei Krauchanka (BLR)	Leonel Suárez (CUB)
Women's heptathlon	Nataliya Dobrynska (UKR)	Hyleas Fountain (USA)	Tatyana Chernova (RUS)
BADMINTON			
Men's singles	Lin Dan (CHN)	Lee Chong Wei (MAS)	Chen Jin (CHN)
Women's singles	Zhang Ning (CHN)	Xie Xingfang (CHN)	Maria Kristin Yulianti (INA)
Men's doubles	Indonesia (INA) Markis Kido and Hendra Setiawan	China (CHN) Cai Yun and Fu Haifeng	South Korea (KOR) Lee Jae-jin and Hwang Ji-man
Women's doubles	China (CHN) Du Jing and Yu Yang	South Korea (KOR) Lee Kyung-won and Lee Hyo-jung	China (CHN) Zhang Yawen and Wei Yili
Mixed doubles	South Korea (KOR) Lee Yong-dae and Lee Hyo-jung	Indonesia (INA) Nova Widianto and Lilyana Natsir	China (CHN) He Hanbin and Yu Yang
BASEBALL			
Men's team	South Korea Hyun-Jin Ryu, Ki-Joo Han, Jin-Man Park, Hyuk Kwon, Taek-Keun Lee, Dae-Ho Lee, Seung-Hwan Oh, Jung-Keun Bong, Young-Min Ko, Jong-Wook Lee, Keun-Woo Jeong, Min-Jae Kim, Kab-Yong Jin, Jin-Young Lee, Won-Sam Jang, Seung-Jun Song, Kwang-Hyun Kim, Yong-Kyu Lee, Dong-Joo Kim, Min-Ho Kang, Hyun-Soo Kim, Seung-Yeop Lee, Tae-Hyon Chong, Suk-Min Yoon	Cuba Ariel Pestano, Yoandry Urgellés, Alfredo Despaigne, Luis Rodríguez, Alexei Bell, Yadier Pedroso, Jonder Martínez, Adiel Palma, Luis Navas, Giorvis Duvergel, Alexander Mayeta, Eriel Sánchez, Rolando Meriño, Héctor Olivera, Michel Enríquez, Yuliesky Gourriel, Vicyohandry Odelín, Pedro Luis Lazo, Eduardo Paret, Norberto González, Norge Luis Vera, Frederich Cepeda, Elier Sánchez, Miguel La Hera	United States Brett Anderson, Blaine Neal, Matt Brown, Nate Schierholtz, Jeremy Cummings, Michael Koplove, Terry Tiffee, Kevin Jepsen, Brian Duensing, Dexter Fowler, Brandon Knight, Mike Hessman, Casey Weathers, Jason Donald, Jayson Nix, Taylor Teagarden, Stephen Strasburg, Jake Arrieta, Lou Marson, Matt LaPorta, Trevor Cahill, Brian Barden, John Gall, Jeff Stevens
BASKETBALL			
Men's team	United States Carmelo Anthony, Carlos Boozer, Chris Bosh, Kobe Bryant, Lebron James, Dwight Howard, Jason Kidd, Chris Paul, Tayshaun Prince, Michael Redd, Dwyane Wade, Deron Williams	Spain Felipe Reyes, Berni Rodríguez, Ricky Rubio, Álex Mumbrú, Raúl López, Carlos Jiménez, José Calderón, Juan Carlos Navarro, Rudy Fernández, Jorge Garbajosa, Marc Gasol, Pau Gasol	Argentina Manu Ginóbili, Román González, Federico Kammerichs, Leonardo Gutiérrez, Carlos Delfino, Andres Nocioni, Fabricio Oberto, Juan Pedro Gutiérrez, Luis Scola, Paolo Quinteros, Antonio Porta, Pablo Prigioni
Women's team	United States Candace Parker, Cappie Pondexter, Tina Thompson, Katie Smith, Diana Taurasi, Delisha Milton, Kara Lawson, Lisa Leslie, Sylvia Fowles, Sue Bird, Tamika Catchings, Seimone Augustus	Australia Suzy Batkovic, Tully Bevilaqua, Rohanee Cox, Hollie Grima, Lauren Jackson, Kristi Harrower, Penny Taylor, Emma Randall, Laura Summerton, Belinda Snell, Erin Phillips, Jenni Screen	Russia Tatyana Shchelkanova, Oxana Rakhmatulina, Irina Osipova, Irina Sokolovskaya, Maria Stepanova, Natalia Vodopyanova, Becky Hammon, Marina Karpunina, Ilona Korstin, Marina Kuzina, Ekaterina Lisina, Svetlana Abrosimova

2008 Medalists

Event	Gold	Silver	Bronze
BOXING			
Light flyweight	Zou Shiming (CHN)	Pürevdorjiin Serdamba (MGL)	Paddy Barnes (IRL) Yampier Hernández (CUB)
Flyweight	Somjit Jongjohor (THA)	Andry Laffita (CUB)	Georgy Balakshin (RUS) Vincenzo Picardi (ITA)
Bantamweight	Enkhbatyn Badar-Uugan (MGL)	Yankiel León (CUB)	Bruno Julie (MRI) Veaceslav Gojan (MDA)
Featherweight	Vasyl Lomachenko (UKR)	Khedafi Djelkhir (FRA)	Yakup Kılıç (TUR) Shahin Imranov (AZE)
Lightweight	Aleksei Tishchenko (RUS)	Daouda Sow (FRA)	Hrachik Javakhyan (ARM) Yordenis Ugás (CUB)
Light welterweight	Manuel Félix Díaz (DOM)	Manus Boonjumnong (THA)	Roniel Iglesias (CUB) Alexis Vastine (FRA)
Welterweight	Bakhyt Sarsekbayev (KAZ)	Carlos Banteaux (CUB)	Hanati Silamu (CHN) Kim Jung-Joo (KOR)
Middleweight	James DeGale (GBR)	Emilio Correa (CUB)	Darren Sutherland (IRL) Vijender Kumar (IND)
Light heavyweight	Zhang Xiaoping (CHN)	Kenny Egan (IRL)	Tony Jeffries (GBR) Yerkebulan Shynaliyev (KAZ)
Heavyweight	Rakhim Chakkhiev (RUS)	Clemente Russo (ITA)	Osmay Acosta (CUB) Deontay Wilder (USA)
Super heavyweight	Roberto Cammarelle (ITA)	Zhang Zhilei (CHN)	Vyacheslav Glazkov (UKR) David Price (GBR)
CANOEING: FLATWATER			
Men's C-1 500 m	Maxim Opalev (RUS)	David Cal (ESP)	Yuriy Cheban (UKR)
Men's C-1 1,000 m	Attila Vajda (HUN)	David Cal (ESP)	Thomas Hall (CAN)
Men's C-2 500 m	China	Russia	Germany
Men's C-2 1,000 m	Belarus	Germany	Hungary
Men's K-1 500 m	Ken Wallace (AUS)	Adam van Koeverden (CAN)	Tim Brabants (GBR)
Women's K-1 500 m	Inna Osypenko-Radomska (UKR)	Josefa Idem (ITA)	Katrin Wagner-Augustin (GER)
Men's K-1 1,000 m	Tim Brabants (GBR)	Eirik Verås Larsen (NOR)	Ken Wallace (AUS)
Men's K-2 500 m	Spain	Germany	Belarus
Women's K-2 500 m	Hungary	Poland	France
Men's K-2 1,000 m	Germany	Denmark	Italy
Women's K-4 500 m	Germany	Hungary	Australia
Men's K-4 1,000 m	Belarus	Slovakia	Germany
CANOEING: SLALOM			
Men's slalom C-1	Michal Martikán (SVK)	David Florence (GBR)	Robin Bell (AUS)
Men's slalom C-2	Slovakia Pavol Hochschorner, Peter Hochschorner	Czech Republic Ondrej Stepanek, Jaroslav Volf	Russia Mikhail Kuznetsov, Dmitry Larionov
Men's slalom K-1	Alexander Grimm (GER)	Fabien Lefèvre (FRA)	Benjamin Boukpeti (TOG)
Women's slalom K-1	Elena Kaliská (SVK)	Jacqueline Lawrence (AUS)	Violetta Oblinger-Peters (AUT)
CYCLING: ROAD			
Men's road race	Samuel Sánchez (ESP)	Fabian Cancellara (SUI)	Alexandr Kolobnev (RUS)
Women's road race	Nicole Cooke (GBR)	Emma Johansson (SWE)	Tatiana Guderzo (ITA)
Men's time trial	Fabian Cancellara (SUI)	Gustav Larsson (SWE)	Levi Leipheimer (USA)
Women's time trial	Kristin Armstrong (USA)	Emma Pooley (GBR)	Karin Thürig (SUI)
CYCLING: TRACK			
Men's sprint	Chris Hoy (GBR)	Jason Kenny (GBR)	Mickaël Bourgain (FRA)
Women's sprint	Victoria Pendleton (GBR)	Anna Meares (AUS)	Guo Shuang (CHN)
Men's team sprint	Great Britain Chris Hoy, Jason Kenny, Jamie Staff	France Arnaud Tournant, Kevin Sireau, Grégory Baugé	Germany Rene Enders, Maximillian Levy, Stefan Nimke
Men's individual pursuit	Bradley Wiggins (GBR)	Hayden Roulston (NZL)	Steven Burke (GBR)
Women's individual pursuit	Rebecca Romero (GBR)	Wendy Houvenaghel (GBR)	Lesya Kalitovska (UKR)
Men's team pursuit	Great Britain Ed Clancy, Geraint Thomas, Paul Manning, Bradley Wiggins	Denmark Jens-Erik Madsen, Michael Moerkoev, Alex Nicki Rasmussen, Michael Færk Christensen, Casper Jorgensen	New Zealand Westley Gough, Sam Bewley, Hayden Roulston, Marc Ryan, Jesse Sergent
Men's points race	Joan Llaneras (ESP)	Roger Kluge (GER)	Chris Newton (GBR)
Women's points race	Marianne Vos (NED)	Yoanka González (CUB)	Leire Olaberria (ESP)
Men's Keirin	Chris Hoy (GBR)	Ross Edgar (GBR)	Kiyofumi Nagai (JPN)
Men's Madison	Argentina Juan Esteban Curuchet, Walter Fernando Perez	Spain Joan Llaneras, Antonio Tauler	Russia Mikhail Ignatyev, Alexei Markov

2008 Medalists

Event	Gold	Silver	Bronze
CYCLING: MOUNTAIN BIKE			
Men's cross-country	Julien Absalon (FRA)	Jean-Christophe Péraud (FRA)	Nino Schurter (SUI)
Women's cross-country	Sabine Spitz (GER)	Maja Wloszczowska (POL)	Irina Kalentieva (RUS)
CYCLING: BMX			
Men's BMX	Maris Strombergs (LAT)	Mike Day (USA)	Donny Robinson (USA)
Women's BMX	Anne-Caroline Chausson (FRA)	Laëtitia Le Corguillé (FRA)	Jill Kintner (USA)
DIVING			
Men's 3m springboard	He Chong (CHN)	Alexandre Despatie (CAN)	Qin Kai (CHN)
Women's 3m springboard	Guo Jingjing (CHN)	Yuliya Pakhalina (RUS)	Wu Minxia (CHN)
Men's 10m platform	Matthew Mitcham (AUS)	Zhou Lüxin (CHN)	Gleb Galperin (RUS)
Women's 10m platform	Chen Ruolin (CHN)	Émilie Heymans (CAN)	Wang Xin (CHN)
Men's synchronised 3m springboard	China Wang Feng, Qin Kai	Russia Dmitri Sautin, Yuriy Kunakov	Ukraine Illya Kvasha, Oleksiy Prygorov
Women's synchronised 3m springboard	China Guo Jingjing, Wu Minxia	Russia Yuliya Pakhalina, Anastasia Pozdnyakova	Germany Ditte Kotzian, Heike Fischer
Men's synchronised 10m platform	China Lin Yue, Huo Liang	Germany Patrick Hausding, Sascha Klein	Russia Gleb Galperin, Dmitriy Dobroskok
Women's synchronised 10m platform	China Wang Xin, Chen Ruolin	Australia Briony Cole, Melissa Wu	Mexico Paola Espinosa, Tatiana Ortiz
EQUESTRIAN			
Individual dressage	Anky van Grunsven (NED)	Isabell Werth (GER)	Heike Kemmer (GER)
Team dressage	Germany Isabell Werth on Satchmo Heike Kemmer on Bonaparte Nadine Capellmann on Elvis Va	Netherlands Anky van Grunsven on Salinero Hans Peter Minderhoud on Nadine Imke Schellekens-Bartels on Sunrise	Denmark Nathalie Zu Seyn-Wittgenstein on Digby Andreas Helgstrand on Don Schufro Anne van Olst on Clearwater
Individual eventing	Hinrich Romeike (GER)	Gina Miles (USA)	Kristina Cook (GBR)
Team eventing	Germany Peter Thomsen on The Ghost of Hamish Frank Ostholt on Mr. Medicott Andreas Dibowski on Butts Leon Ingrid Klimke on Abraxxas Hinrich Romeike on Marius	Australia Shane Rose on All Luck Sonja Johnson on Ringwould Jaguar Lucinda Fredericks on Headley Britannia Clayton Fredericks on Ben Along Time Megan Jones on Irish Jester	Great Britain Sharon Hunt on Tankers Town Daisy Dick on Spring Along William Fox-Pitt on Parkmore Ed Kristina Cook on Miners Frolic Mary King on Call Again Cavalier
Individual jumping	Eric Lamaze (CAN)	Rolf-Göran Bengtsson (SWE)	Beezie Madden (USA)
Team jumping	United States McLain Ward on Sapphire Laura Kraut on Cedric Will Simpson on Carlsson vom Dach Beezie Madden on Authentic	Canada Jill Henselwood on Special Ed Eric Lamaze on Hickstead Ian Millar on In Style Mac Cone on Ole	Switzerland Christina Liebherr on No Mercy Pius Schwizer on Nobless M Niklaus Schurtenberger on Cantus Steve Guerdat on Jalisca Solier
FENCING			
Men's épée	Matteo Tagliariol (ITA)	Fabrice Jeannet (FRA)	José Luis Abajo Spain (ESP)
Women's épée	Britta Heidemann (GER)	Ana Maria Brânza (ROU)	Ildikó Mincza-Nébald (HUN)
Men's team épée	France Fabrice Jeannet, Jérôme Jeannet, Ulrich Robeiri	Poland Robert Andrzejuk, Tomasz Motyka, Adam Wiercioch, Rados aw Zawrotniak	Italy Stefano Carozzo, Diego Confalonieri, Alfredo Rota, Matteo Tagliariol
Men's foil	Benjamin Kleibrink (GER)	Yuki Ota (JPN)	Salvatore Sanzo (ITA)
Women's foil	Valentina Vezzali (ITA)	Nam Hyun-Hee (KOR)	Margherita Granbassi (ITA)
Women's team foil	Russia Svetlana Boiko, Aida Chanaeva, Victoria Nikichina, Evgenia Lamonova	United States Emily Cross, Hanna Thompson, Erinn Smart	Italy Valentina Vezzali, Giovanna Trillini, Margherita Granbassi, Ilaria Salvatori
Men's sabre	Zhong Man (CHN)	Nicolas Lopez (FRA)	Mihai Covaliu (ROU)
Women's sabre	Mariel Zagunis (USA)	Sada Jacobson (USA)	Rebecca Ward (USA)
Men's team sabre	France Julien Pillet, Boris Sanson, Nicolas Lopez	United States Tim Morehouse, Jason Rogers, Keeth Smart, James Williams	Italy Aldo Montano, Luigi Tarantino, Giampiero Pastore, Diego Occhiuzzi
Women's team sabre	Ukraine Olha Zhovnir, Olga Kharlan, Halyna Pundyk, Olena Khomrova	China Bao Yingying, Huang Haiyang, Ni Hong, Tan Xue	United States Sada Jacobson, Becca Ward, Mariel Zagunis
HOCKEY			
Men's team	Germany Philip Witte, Maximilian Mueller, Sebastian Biederlack, Carlos Nevado, Moritz Fuerste, Jan-Marco Montag, Tobias Hauke, Tibor Weißenborn, Benjamin Weß, Niklas Meinert, Timo Weß, Oliver Korn, Christopher Zeller, Max Weinhold, Matthias Witthaus, Florian Keller, Philipp Zeller	Spain Francisco Cortes, Santiago Freixa, Francisco Fábregas, Victor Sojo, Alex Fabregas, Pablo Amat, Eduardo Tubau, Roc Oliva, Juan Fernandez, Ramon Alegre, Xavier Ribas, Albert Sala, Rodrigo Garza, Sergi Enrique, Eduard Arbos, David Alegre	Australia Jamie Dwyer, Liam de Young, Rob Hammond, Mark Knowles, Eddie Ockenden, David Guest, Luke Doerner, Grant Schubert, Bevan George, Andrew Smith, Stephen Lambert, Eli Matheson, Matthew Wells, Travis Brooks, Kiel Brown, Fergus Kavanagh, Des Abbott

2008 Medalists

Event	Gold	Silver	Bronze
Women's team	Netherlands Maartje Goderie, Maartje Paumen, Naomi van As, Minke Smabers, Marilyn Agliotti, Minke Booij, Wieke Dijkstra, Sophie Polkamp Ellen Hoog, Lidewij Welten, Lisanne de Roever Miek van Geenhuizen, Eva de Goede, Janneke Schopman, Eefke Mulder, Fatima Moreira de Melo	China Ren Ye, Zhang Yimeng, Gao Lihua, Chen Qiuqi, Zhao Yudiao, Li Hongxia, Cheng Hui, Tang Chunling, Zhou Wanfeng, Ma Yibo, Fu Baorong, Pan Fengzhen, Huang Junxia, Song Qungling, Li Shuang, Chen Zhaoxia	Argentina Paola Vukojicic, Belén Succi, Magdalena Aicega, Mercedes Margalot, Mariana Rossi, Noel Barrionuevo, Giselle Kañevsky, Claudia Burkart, Luciana Aymar, Mariné Russo, Mariana González Oliva, Soledad García, Alejandra Gulla, María de la Paz Hernández, Carla Rebecchi, Rosario Luchetti
FOOTBALL			
Men's team	Argentina Oscar Ustari, Ezequiel Garay, Luciano Fabián Monzón, Pablo Zabaleta, Fernando Gago, Federico Fazio, José Ernesto Sosa, Éver Banega, Ezequiel Lavezzi, Juan Román Riquelme, Ángel Di María, Nicolás Pareja, Lautaro Acosta, Javier Mascherano, Lionel Messi, Sergio Agüero, Diego Buonanotte, Sergio Romero, Nicolás Navarro	Nigeria Ambruse Vanzekin, Chibuzor Okonkwo, Onyekachi Apam, Dele Adeleye, Monday James, Chinedu Obasi, Sani Kaita, Victor Nsofor Obinna, Promise Isaac, Solomon Okoronkwo, Oluwafemi Ajilore, Olubayo Adefemi, Peter Odemwingie, Efe Ambrose, Victor Anichebe, Emmanuel Ekpo, Ikechukwu Ezenwa, Oladapo Olufemi	Brazil Diego Alves, Renan, Rafinha, Alex Silva, Thiago Silva, Marcelo, Ilsinho, Breno, Hernanes, Anderson, Lucas, Ronaldinho, Ramires, Diego, Thiago Neves, Alexandre Pato, Rafael Sóbis, Jô
Women's team	United States Hope Solo, Heather Mitts, Christie Rampone, Rachel Buehler, Lindsay Tarpley, Natasha Kai, Shannon Boxx, Amy Rodriguez, Heather O'Reilly, Aly Wagner, Carli Lloyd, Lauren Cheney, Tobin Heath, Stephanie Cox, Kate Markgraf Angela Hucles, Lori Chalupny, Nicole Barnhart	Brazil Andréia, Simone, Andréia Rosa, Tânia, Renata Costa, Maycon, Daniela, Formiga, Ester, Marta, Cristiane, Bárbara, Francielle, Pretinha, Fabiana, Érika, Maurine, Rosana	Germany Nadine Angerer, Kerstin Stegemann, Saskia Bartusiak, Babett Peter, Annike Krahn, Linda Bresonik, Melanie Behringer, Sandra Smisek, Birgit Prinz, Renate Lingor, Anja Mittag, Ursula Holl, Célia Okoyino da Mbabi, Simone Laudehr, Fatmire Bajramaj, Conny Pohlers, Ariane Hingst, Kerstin Garefrekes
GYMNASTICS: ARTISTIC			
Men's individual all-around	Yang Wei (CHN)	Kohei Uchimura (JPN)	Benoît Caranobe (FRA)
Women's individual all-around	Nastia Liukin (USA)	Shawn Johnson (USA)	Yang Yilin (CHN)
Men's team all-around	China Chen Yibing, Huang Xu, Li Xiaopeng, Xiao Qin, Yang Wei, Zou Kai	Japan Takehiro Kashima, Takuya Nakase, Makoto Okiguchi, Koki Sakamoto, Hiroyuki Tomita, K hei Uchimura	United States Alexander Artemev, Raj Bhavsar, Joe Hagerty, Jonathan Horton Justin Spring, Kai Wen Tan
Women's team all-around	China Cheng Fei, Deng Linlin, He Kexin, Jiang Yuyuan, Li Shanshan, Yang Yilin	United States Shawn Johnson, Nastia Liukin, Chellsie Memmel, Samantha Peszek, Alicia Sacramone, Bridget Sloan	Romania Andreea Acatrinei, Gabriela Dragoi, Andreea Grigore, Sandra Izbasa, Steliana Nistor, Anamaria Tamârjan
Women's balance beam	Shawn Johnson (USA)	Nastia Liukin (USA)	Cheng Fei (CHN)
Men's floor	Zou Kai (CHN)	Gervasio Deferr (ESP)	Anton Golotsutskov (RUS)
Women's floor	Sandra Izbasa (ROU)	Shawn Johnson (USA)	Nastia Liukin (USA)
Men's horizontal bar	Zou Kai (CHN)	Jonathan Horton (USA)	Fabian Hambüchen (GER)
Men's parallel bars	Li Xiaopeng (CHN)	Yoo Won-Chul (KOR)	Anton Fokin (UZB)
Men's pommel horse	Xiao Qin (CHN)	Filip Ude (CRO)	Louis Smith (GBR)
Men's rings	Chen Yibing (CHN)	Yang Wei (CHN)	Oleksandr Vorobiov (UKR)
Women's uneven bars	He Kexin (CHN)	Nastia Liukin (USA)	Yang Yilin (CHN)
Men's vault	Leszek Blanik (POL)	Thomas Bouhail (FRA)	Anton Golotsutskov (RUS)
Women's vault	Hong Un Jong (PRK)	Oksana Chusovitina (GER)	Cheng Fei (CHN)
GYMNASTICS: RHYTHMIC			
Women's individual all-around	Yevgeniya Kanayeva (RUS)	Inna Zhukova (BLR)	Anna Bessonova (UKR)
Women's team all-around	Russia Margarita Aliychuk, Anna Gavrilenko, Tatiana Gorbunova, Elena Posevina, Darya Shkurihina, Natalia Zueva	China Cai Tongtong, Chou Tao, Lü Yuanyang, Sui Jianshuang, Sun Dan, Zhang Shuo	Belarus Olesya Babushkina, Anastasia Ivankova, Ksenia Sankovich, Zinaida Lunina, Glafira Martinovich, Alina Tumilovich
GYMNASTICS: TRAMPOLINE			
Men's trampoline	Lu Chunlong (CHN)	Jason Burnett (CAN)	Dong Dong (CHN)
Women's trampoline	He Wenna (CHN)	Karen Cockburn (CAN)	Ekaterina Khilko (UZB)
HANDBALL			
Men's team	France Luc Abalo, Joël Abati, Cédric Burdet, Didier Dinart, Bertrand Gille, Guillaume Gille, Olivier Girault, Michaël Guigou, Jérôme Fernandez, Daouda Karaboué, Nikola Karabatic, Christophe Kempe, Daniel Narcisse, Thierry Omeyer, Cédric Paty	Iceland Alexander Petersson, Ásgeir Örn Hallgríms-son, Björgvin Páll Gústavsson, Ingimundur Ingimundarson, Róbert Gunnarsson, Snorri Guojónsson, Hreioar Guomundsson, Sverre Andreas Jakobsson, Sturla Ásgeirsson, Arnór Atlason, Sigfús Sigurosson, Logi Geirsson, Ólafur Stefánsson, Guojón Valur Sigurosson	Spain Víctor Tomás, David Barrufet, Jon Belaustegui, David Davis, José Javier Hombrados, Rubén Garabaya, Juanín García, Alberto Entrerríos, Raúl Entrerríos, Carlos Prieto, Albert Rocas, Iker Romero, Cristian Malmagro, Demetrio Lozano
Women's team	Norway Katrine Lunde Haraldsen, Kristine Lunde, Tonje Larsen, Gro Hammerseng, Marit Malm Frafjord, Tonje Nøstvold, Katarina Nyberg, Kari Mette, Linn-Kristin Riegelhuth, Karoline Dyhre Breivang, Kari Aalvik Grimsbø, Ragnhild Aamodt, Else-Marthe Sørlie Lybekk, Gøril Snorroeggen	Russia Emilia Turey, Yana Uskova, Inna Suslina, Elena Dmitrieva, Irina Bliznova, Ekaterina Andryushina, Oxana Romenskaya, Natalia Shipilova, Maria Sidorova, Yelena Polenova, Irina Poltoratskaya, Liudmila Postnova, Ekaterina Marennikova, Anna Kareeva	South Korea Choi Im-Jeong, Bae Min-Hee, Lee Min-Hee, Kim Nam-Sun, Moon Pil-Hee, Kim O-Na, Oh Seong-Ok, Kim Cha-Youn, Park Chung-Hee, Hong Jeong-Ho, An Jung-Hwa, Song Hai-Rim, Huh Soon-Young, Oh Yong-Ran

2008 Medalists

Event	Gold	Silver	Bronze
JUDO			
Men's 60 kg	Choi Min-Ho (KOR)	Ludwig Paischer (AUT)	Rishod Sobirov (UZB) Ruben Houkes (NED)
Men's 66 kg	Masato Uchishiba (JPN)	Benjamin Darbelet (FRA)	Yordanis Arencibia (CUB) Pak Chol Min (PRK)
Men's 73 kg	Elnur Mammadli (AZE)	Wang Ki-Chun (KOR)	Rasul Boqiev (TJK) Leandro Guilheiro (BRA)
Men's 81 kg	Ole Bischof (GER)	Kim Jae-Bum (KOR)	Tiago Camilo (BRA) Roman Gontiuk (UKR)
Men's 90 kg	Irakli Tsirekidze (GEO)	Amar Benikhlef (ALG)	Hesham Mesbah (EGY) Sergei Aschwanden (SUI)
Men's 100 kg	Naidangiin Tüvshinbayar (MGL)	Askhat Zhitkeyev (KAZ)	Movlud Miraliyev (AZE) Henk Grol (NED)
Men's +100 kg	Satoshi Ishii (JPN)	Abdullo Tangriev (UZB)	Oscar Braison (CUB) Teddy Riner (FRA)
Women's 48 kg	Alina Alexandra Dumitru (ROU)	Yanet Bermoy (CUB)	Paula Pareto (ARG) Ryoko Tani (JPN)
Women's 52 kg	Xian Dongmei (CHN)	An Kum-Ae (PRK)	Soraya Haddad (ALG) Misato Nakamura (JPN)
Women's 57 kg	Giulia Quintavalle (ITA)	Deborah Gravenstijn (NED)	Xu Yan (CHN) Ketleyn Quadros (BRA)
Women's 63 kg	Ayumi Tanimoto (JPN)	Lucie Décosse (FRA)	Elisabeth Willeboordse (NED) Won Ok-Im (PRK)
Women's 70 kg	Masae Ueno (JPN)	Anaysi Hernández (CUB)	Ronda Rousey (USA) Edith Bosch (NED)
Women's 78 kg	Yang Xiuli (CHN)	Yalennis Castillo (CUB)	Jeong Gyeong-Mi (KOR) Stéphanie Possamaï (FRA)
Women's +78 kg	Tong Wen (CHN)	Maki Tsukada (JPN)	Lucija Polavder (SLO) Idalys Ortiz (CUB)
MODERN PENTATHLON			
Men's individual	Andrey Moiseyev (RUS)	Edvinas Krungolcas (LTU)	Andrejus Zadneprovskis (LTU)
Women's individual	Lena Schöneborn (GER)	Heather Fell (GBR)	Victoria Tereshuk (UKR)
ROWING			
Men's single sculls	Olaf Tufte (NOR)	Ondrej Synek (CZE)	Mahé Drysdale (NZL)
Women's single sculls	Rumyana Neykova (BUL)	Michelle Guerette (USA)	Ekaterina Karsten (BLR)
Men's double sculls	Australia David Crawshay, Scott Brennan	Estonia Tõnu Endrekson, Jüri Jaanson	Great Britain Matthew Wells, Stephen Rowbotham
Women's double sculls	New Zealand Georgina Evers-Swindell, Caroline Evers-Swindell	Germany Annekatrin Thiele, Christiane Huth	Great Britain Elise Laverick, Anna Bebington
Men's lightweight double sculls	Great Britain Zac Purchase, Mark Hunter	Greece Dimitrios Mougios, Vasileios Polymeros	Denmark Mads Reinholdt Rasmussen, Rasmus Nicholai Quist Hansen
Women's lightweight double sculls	Netherlands Kirsten van der Kolk, Marit van Eupen	Finland Sanna Stén, Minna Nieminen	Canada Melanie Kok, Tracy Cameron
Men's quadruple sculls	Poland Konrad Wasielewski, Marek Kolbowicz, Micha Jeli ski, Adam Korol	Italy Luca Agamennoni, Simone Venier, Rossano Galtarossa, Simone Raineri	France Jonathan Coeffic, Pierre-Jean Peltier, Julien Bahain, Cédric Berrest
Women's quadruple sculls	China Tang Bin, Jin Ziwei, Xi Aihua, Zhang Yangyang	Great Britain Annie Vernon, Debbie Flood, Frances Houghton, Katherine Grainger	Germany Britta Oppelt, Manuela Lutze, Kathrin Boron, Stephanie Schiller
Men's coxless pair	Australia Drew Ginn, Duncan Free	Canada David Calder, Scott Frandsen	New Zealand Nathan Twaddle, George Bridgewater
Women's coxless pair	Romania Georgeta Andrunache, Viorica Susanu	China Wu You, Gao Yulan	Belarus Yuliya Bichyk, Natallia Helakh
Men's coxless four	Great Britain Tom James, Steve Williams, Pete Reed, Andrew Triggs-Hodge	Australia Matt Ryan, James Marburg, Cameron McKenzie-McHarg, Francis Hegerty	France Julien Desprès, Benjamin Rondeau, Germain Chardin, Dorian Mortelette
Men's lightweight coxless four	Denmark Thomas Ebert, Morten Jørgensen, Mads Christian Kruse Andersen, Eskild Ebbesen	Poland Lukasz Pawlowski, Bartlomiej Pawelczak, Milosz Bernatajtys, Pawel Randa	Canada Iain Brambell, Jon Beare, Mike Lewis, Liam Parsons
Men's eight	Canada Kevin Light, Ben Rutledge, Andrew Byrnes, Jake Wetzel, Malcolm Howard, Dominic Seiterle, Adam Kreek, Kyle Hamilton, Brian Price (cox)	Great Britain Alex Partridge, Tom Stallard, Tom Lucy, Richard Egington, Josh West, Alastair Heathcote, Matthew Langridge, Colin Smith, Acer Nethercott (cox)	United States Beau Hoopman, Matt Schnobrich, Micah Boyd, Wyatt Allen, Daniel Walsh, Steven Coppola, Josh Inman, Bryan Volpenhein, Marcus McElhenney (cox)
Women's eight	United States Erin Cafaro, Lindsay Shoop, Anna Goodale, Elle Logan, Anna Cummins, Susan Francia, Caroline Lind, Caryn Davies, Mary Whipple (cox)	Netherlands Femke Dekker, Marlies Smulders, Nienke Kingma, Roline Repelaer van Driel, Annemarieke van Rumpt, Helen Tanger, Sarah Siegelaar, Annemiek de Haan, Ester Workel (cox)	Romania Constanta Burcic , Viorica Susanu, Rodica Serban, Eniko Barabás, Simona Musat, Ioana Papuc, Georgeta Andrunache, Doina Ignat, Elena Georgescu (cox)

2008 Medalists

Event	Gold	Silver	Bronze
SAILING			
Men's sailboard	Tom Ashley (NZL)	Julien Bontemps (FRA)	Shahar Zubari (ISR)
Women's sailboard	Yin Jian (CHN)	Alessandra Sensini (ITA)	Bryony Shaw (GBR)
Men's Laser	Paul Goodison (GBR)	Vasilij Zbogar (SLO)	Diego Romero (ITA)
Women's Laser Radial	Anna Tunnicliffe (USA)	Gintare Volungeviciute (LTU)	Xu Lijia (CHN)
Men's 470	Australia Nathan Wilmot, Malcolm Page	Great Britain Nick Rogers, Joe Glanfield	France Nicolas Charbonnier, Olivier Bausset
Women's 470	Australia Elise Rechichi, Tessa Parkinson	Netherlands Marcelien de Koning, Lobke Berkhout	Brazil Fernanda Oliveira, Isabel Swan
49er	Denmark Jonas Warrer, Martin Kirketerp	Spain Iker Martínez de Lizarduy, Xabier Fernández	Germany Jan-Peter Peckolt, Hannes Peckolt
Finn	Ben Ainslie (GBR)	Zach Railey (USA)	Guillaume Florent (FRA)
Star	Great Britain Iain Percy, Andrew Simpson	Brazil Robert Scheidt, Bruno Prada	Sweden Fredrik Lööf, Anders Ekström
Tornado	Spain Antón Paz, Fernando Echavarri	Australia Darren Bundock, Glenn Ashby	Argentina Santiago Lange, Carlos Espínola
Yngling	Great Britain Sarah Ayton, Sarah Webb, Pippa Wilson	Netherlands Mandy Mulder, Annemieke Bes, Merel Witteveen	Greece Sofia Bekatorou, Sofia Papadopoulou, Virginia Kravarioti
SHOOTING			
Men's 10 m air pistol	Pang Wei (CHN)	Jin Jong-oh (KOR)	Jason Turner (USA)
Women's 10 m air pistol	Guo Wenjun (CHN)	Natalia Paderina (RUS)	Nino Salukvadze (GEO)
Men's 10 m air rifle	Abhinav Bindra (IND)	Zhu Qinan (CHN)	Henri Häkkinen (FIN)
Women's 10 m air rifle	Katerina Emmons (CZE)	Lioubov Galkina (RUS)	Snjezana Pejcic (CRO)
Women's 25 m pistol	Chen Ying (CHN)	Otryadyn Gündegmaa (MGL)	Munkhbayar Dorjsuren (GER)
Men's 25 m rapid fire pistol	Oleksandr Petriv (UKR)	Ralf Schumann (GER)	Christian Reitz (GER)
Men's 50 m pistol	Jin Jong-oh (KOR)	Tan Zongliang (CHN)	Vladimir Isakov (RUS)
Men's 50 m rifle three positions	Qiu Jian (CHN)	Jury Sukhorukov (UKR)	Rajmond Debevec (SLO)
Women's 50 m rifle three positions	Du Li (CHN)	Katerina Emmons (CZE)	Eglis Yaima Cruz (CUB)
Men's 50 m rifle prone	Artur Ayvazian (UKR)	Matthew Emmons (USA)	Warren Potent (AUS)
Men's skeet	Vincent Hancock (USA)	Tore Brovold (NOR)	Anthony Terras (FRA)
Women's skeet	Chiara Cainero (ITA)	Kim Rhode (USA)	Christine Brinker (GER)
Men's trap	David Kostelecky (CZE)	Giovanni Pellielo (ITA)	Aleksei Alipov (RUS)
Women's trap	Satu Mäkelä-Nummela (FIN)	Zuzana Stefeceková (SVK)	Corey Cogdell (USA)
Men's double trap	Walton Eller (USA)	Francesco D'Aniello (ITA)	Hu Binyuan (CHN)
SOFTBALL			
Women's team	Japan Naho Emoto, Motoko Fujimoto, Megu Hirose, Emi Inui, Sachiko Ito, Ayumi Karino, Satoko Mabuchi, Yukiyo Mine, Masumi Mishina, Rei Nishiyama, Hiroko Sakai, Rie Sato, Mika Someya, Yukiko Ueno, Eri Yamada	United States Monica Abbott, Stacey Nuveman, Crystl Bustos, Jennie Finch, Laura Berg, Lauren Lappin, Lovieanne Jung, Cat Osterman, Tairia Flowers, Andrea Duran, Jessica Mendoza Victoria Galindo, Kelly Kretschman, Caitlin Lowe, Natasha Watley	Australia Jodie Bowering, Kylie Cronk, Kelly Hardie, Tanya Harding, Sandy Lewis, Simmone Morrow, Tracey Mosley, Stacey Porter, Melanie Roche, Justine Smethurst, Danielle Stewart, Natalie Titcume, Natalie Ward, Belinda Wright, Kerry Wyborn
SWIMMING			
Men's 50 m freestyle	César Cielo Filho (BRA)	Amaury Leveaux (FRA)	Alain Bernard (FRA)
Women's 50 m freestyle	Britta Steffen (GER)	Dara Torres (USA)	Cate Campbell (AUS)
Men's 100 m freestyle	Alain Bernard (FRA)	Eamon Sullivan (AUS)	Jason Lezak (USA), César Cielo Filho (BRA)
Women's 100 m freestyle	Britta Steffen (GER)	Libby Trickett (AUS)	Natalie Coughlin (USA)
Men's 200 m freestyle	Michael Phelps (USA)	Park Tae-Hwan (KOR)	Peter Vanderkaay (USA)
Women's 200 m freestyle	Federica Pellegrini (ITA)	Sara Isakovic (SLO)	Pang Jiaying (CHN)
Men's 400 m freestyle	Park Tae-Hwan (KOR)	Zhang Lin (CHN)	Larsen Jensen (USA)
Women's 400 m freestyle	Rebecca Adlington (GBR)	Katie Hoff (USA)	Joanne Jackson (GBR)
Women's 800 m freestyle	Rebecca Adlington (GBR)	Alessia Filippi (ITA)	Lotte Friis (DEN)
Men's 1,500 m freestyle	Oussama Mellouli (TUN)	Grant Hackett (AUS)	Ryan Cochrane (CAN)
Men's 100 m backstroke	Aaron Peirsol (USA)	Matt Grevers (USA)	Hayden Stoeckel (AUS), Arkady Vyatchanin (RUS)
Women's 100 m backstroke	Natalie Coughlin (USA)	Kirsty Coventry (ZIM)	Margaret Hoelzer (USA)
Men's 200 m backstroke	Ryan Lochte (USA)	Aaron Peirsol (USA)	Arkady Vyatchanin (RUS)
Women's 200 m backstroke	Kirsty Coventry (ZIM)	Margaret Hoelzer (USA)	Reiko Nakamura (JPN)
Men's 100 m breaststroke	Kosuke Kitajima (JPN)	Alexander Dale Oen (NOR)	Hugues Duboscq (FRA)
Women's 100 m breaststroke	Leisel Jones (AUS)	Rebecca Soni (USA)	Mirna Jukic (AUT)

2008 Medalists

Event	Gold	Silver	Bronze
Men's 200 m breaststroke	Kosuke Kitajima (JPN)	Brenton Rickard (AUS)	Hugues Duboscq (FRA)
Women's 200 m breaststroke	Rebecca Soni (USA)	Leisel Jones (AUS)	Sara Nordenstam (NOR)
Men's 100 m butterfly	Michael Phelps (USA)	Milorad Cavic (SRB)	Andrew Lauterstein (AUS)
Women's 100 m butterfly	Libby Trickett (AUS)	Christine Magnuson (USA)	Jessicah Schipper (AUS)
Men's 200 m butterfly	Michael Phelps (USA)	László Cseh (HUN)	Takeshi Matsuda (JPN)
Women's 200 m butterfly	Liu Zige (CHN)	Jiao Liuyang (CHN)	Jessicah Schipper (AUS)
Men's 200 m individual medley	Michael Phelps (USA)	László Cseh (HUN)	Ryan Lochte (USA)
Women's 200 m individual medley	Stephanie Rice (AUS)	Kirsty Coventry (ZIM)	Natalie Coughlin (USA)
Men's 400 m individual medley	Michael Phelps (USA)	László Cseh (HUN)	Ryan Lochte (USA)
Women's 400 m individual medley	Stephanie Rice (AUS)	Kirsty Coventry (ZIM)	Katie Hoff (USA)
Men's 4x100 m freestyle relay	United States Michael Phelps, Garrett Weber-Gale, Cullen Jones, Jason Lezak, Nathan Adrian, Benjamin Wildman-Tobriner, Matt Grevers	France Amaury Leveaux, Fabien Gilot, Frédérick Bousquet, Alain Bernard, Grégory Mallet, Boris Steimetz	Australia Eamon Sullivan, Andrew Lauterstein, Ashley Callus, Matt Targett, Leith Brodie, Patrick Murphy
Women's 4x100 m freestyle relay	Netherlands Inge Dekker, Ranomi Kromowidjojo, Femke Heemskerk, Marleen Veldhuis, Hinkelien Schreuder, Manon van Rooijen	United States Natalie Coughlin, Lacey Nymeyer, Kara Lynn Joyce, Dara Torres, Emily Silver, Julia Smit	Australia Cate Campbell, Alice Mills, Melanie Schlanger, Lisbeth Trickett, Shayne Reese
Men's 4x200 m freestyle relay	United States Michael Phelps, Ryan Lochte, Ricky Berens, Peter Vanderkaay, Klete Keller, Erik Vendt, David Walters	Russia Nikita Lobintsev, Evgeny Lagunov, Danila Izotov, Alexander Sukhorukov, Mikhail Polishchuk	Australia Patrick Murphy, Grant Hackett, Grant Brits, Nick Ffrost, Leith Brodie, Kirk Palmer
Women's 4x200 m freestyle relay	Australia Stephanie Rice, Bronte Barratt, Kylie Palmer, Linda Mackenzie, Lara Davenport, Felicity Galvez, Angie Bainbridge, Melanie Schlanger	China Yang Yu, Zhu Qianwei, Tan Miao, Pang Jiaying, Tang Jingzhi	United States Allison Schmitt, Natalie Coughlin, Caroline Burckle, Katie Hoff, Christine Marshall, Kim Vandenberg, Julia Smit
Men's 4x100 m medley relay	United States Aaron Peirsol, Brendan Hansen, Michael Phelps, Jason Lezak, Matt Grevers, Mark Gangloff, Ian Crocker, Garrett Weber-Gale	Australia Hayden Stoeckel, Brenton Rickard, Andrew Lauterstein, Eamon Sullivan, Ashley Delaney, Christian Sprenger, Adam Pine, Matt Targett	Japan Junichi Miyashita, Kosuke Kitajima, Takuro Fujii, Hisayoshi Sato
Women's 4x100 m medley relay	Australia Emily Seebohm, Leisel Jones, Jessicah Schipper, Lisbeth Trickett, Tarnee White, Felicity Galvez, Shayne Reese	United States Natalie Coughlin, Rebecca Soni, Christine Magnuson, Dara Torres, Margaret Hoelzer, Megan Jendrick, Elaine Breeden, Kara Lynn Joyce	China Zhao Jing, Sun Ye, Zhou Yafei, Pang Jiaying, Xu Tianlongzi
Men's 10 km marathon	Maarten van der Weijden (NED)	David Davies (GBR)	Thomas Lurz (GER)
Women's 10 km marathon	Larisa Ilchenko (RUS)	Keri-Anne Payne (GBR)	Cassandra Patten (GBR)
SYNCHRONISED SWIMMING			
Women's duet	Russia (RUS) Andrea Davydova, Anastasia Ermakova	Spain (ESP) Andrea Fuentes, Gemma Mengual	Japan (JPN) Saho Harada, Emiko Suzuki
Women's team	Russia (RUS) Anastasia Davydova, Anastasia Ermakova, Maria Gromova, Natalia Ishchenko, Elvira Khasyanova, Olga Kuzhela, Yelena Ovchinnikova, Anna Shorina, Svetlana Romashina	Spain (ESP) Alba María Cabello, Raquel Corral, Andrea Fuentes, Gemma Mengual, Thaïs Henríquez, Laura López, Gisela Morón, Irina Rodríguez, Paola Tirados	China (CHN) Gu Beibei, Huang Xuechen, Jiang Tingting, Jiang Wenwen, Liu Ou, Luo Qian, Sun Qiuting, Wang Na, Zhang Xiaohuan
TABLE TENNIS			
Men's singles	Ma Lin (CHN)	Wang Hao (CHN)	Wang Liqin (CHN)
Women's singles	Zhang Yining (CHN)	Wang Nan (CHN)	Guo Yue (CHN)
Men's team	China (CHN) Wang Hao, Ma Lin, Wang Liqin	Germany (GER) Dimitrij Ovtcharov, Timo Boll, Christian Suss	South Korea (KOR) Oh Sang-Eun, Ryu Seung-Min, Yoon Jae-Young
Women's team	China (CHN) Guo Yue, Wang Nan, Zhang Yining	Singapore (SIN) Feng Tianwei, Li Jiawei, Wang Yuegu	South Korea (KOR) Dang Ye-Seo, Kim Kyung-Ah, Park Mi-Young
TAEKWONDO			
Men's 58 kg	Guillermo Pérez (MEX)	Gabriel Mercedes (DOM)	Chu Mu-yen (TPE) Rohullah Nikpai (AFG)
Men's 68 kg	Son Tae-Jin (KOR)	Mark López (USA)	Servet Tazegül (TUR) Sung Yu-Chi (TPE)
Men's 80 kg	Hadi Saei (IRI)	Mauro Sarmiento (ITA)	Zhu Guo (CHN) Steven López (USA)
Men's +80 kg	Cha Dong-Min (KOR)	Alexandros Nikolaidis (GRE)	Chika Chukwumerije (NGR) Arman Chilmanov (KAZ)
Women's 49 kg	Wu Jingyu (CHN)	Buttree Puedpong (THA)	Daynellis Montejo (CUB) Dalia Contreras (VEN)
Women's 57 kg	Lim Su-Jeong (KOR)	Azize Tanrıkulu (TUR)	Diana López (USA) Martina Zubcic (CRO)
Women's 67 kg	Hwang Kyung-Seon (KOR)	Karine Sergerie (CAN)	Gwladys Épangue (FRA) Sandra Saric (CRO)
Women's +67 kg	Maria Espinoza (MEX)	Nina Solheim (NOR)	Sarah Stevenson (GBR) Natália Falavigna (BRA)

2008 Medalists

Event	Gold	Silver	Bronze
TENNIS			
Men's singles	Rafael Nadal (ESP)	Fernando González (CHI)	Novak Djokovic (SRB)
Women's singles	Elena Dementieva (RUS)	Dinara Safina (RUS)	Vera Zvonareva (RUS)
Men's doubles	Switzerland Roger Federer and Stanislas Wawrinka	Sweden Simon Aspelin and Thomas Johansson	United States Bob Bryan and Mike Bryan
Women's doubles	United States Serena Williams and Venus Williams	Spain Anabel Medina Garrigues and Virginia Ruano Pascual	China Yan Zi and Zheng Jie
TRIATHLON			
Men's triathlon	Jan Frodeno (GER)	Simon Whitfield (CAN)	Bevan Docherty (NZL)
Women's triathlon	Emma Snowsill (AUS)	Vanessa Fernandes (POR)	Emma Moffatt (AUS)
VOLLEYBALL: BEACH			
Men's beach volleyball	United States Todd Rogers and Phil Dalhausser	Brazil Fabio Luiz Magalhães and Marcio Araujo	Brazil Ricardo Santos and Emanuel Rego
Women's beach volleyball	United States Kerri Walsh and Misty May-Treanor	China Wang Jie and Tian Jia	China Zhang Xi and Xue Chen
VOLLEYBALL: INDOOR			
Men's team	United States Lloy Ball, Sean Rooney, David Lee, Richard Lambourne, William Priddy, Ryan Millar, Riley Salmon, Thomas Hoff, Clayton Stanley, Kevin Hansen, Gabriel Gardner, Scott Touzinsky	Brazil Bruno Rezende, Marcelo Elgarten, Andre Heller, Samuel Fuchs, Gilberto Godoy Filho, Murilo Endres, Andre Nascimento, Sergio Santos, Anderson Rodrigues, Gustavo Endres, Rodrigo Santana, Dante Amaral	Russia Alexander Korneev, Semen Poltavskiy, Alexander Kosarev, Sergey Grankin, Sergey Tetyukhin, Vadim Khamuttskikh, Yury Berezhko, Alexey Ostapenko, Alexander Volkov, Alexey Verbov, Maxim Mikhaylov, Alexey Kuleshov
Women's team	Brazil Walewska Oliveira, Carolina Albuquerque, Marianne Steinbrecher, Paula Pequeno, Thaisa Menezes, Hélia Souza, Valeska Menezes, Fabiana Claudino, Welissa Gonzaga, Jaqueline Carvalho, Sheilla Castro, Fabiana de Oliveira	United States Ogonna Nnamani, Danielle Scott-Arruda, Tayyiba Haneef-Park, Lindsey Berg, Stacy Sykora, Nicole Davis, Heather Bown, Jennifer Joines, Kim Glass, Robyn Ah Mow-Santos, Kim Willoughby, Logan Tom	China Wang Yimei, Feng Kun, Yang Hao, Liu Yanan, Wei Qiuyue, Xu Yunli, Zhou Suhong Zhao Ruirui, Xue Ming, Li Juan, Zhang Na, Ma Yunwen
WATER POLO			
Men's team	Hungary Zoltán Szécsi, Tamás Varga, Norbert Madaras, Dénes Varga, Tamás Kásás, Norbert Hosnyánszky, Gergely Kiss, Tibor Benedek, Dániel Varga, Péter Biros, Gábor Kis, Tamás Molnár, István Gergely	United States Merrill Moses, Peter Varellas, Peter Hudnut, Jeff Powers, Adam Wright, Rick Merlo, Layne Beaubien, Tony Azevedo, Ryan Bailey, Tim Hutten, Jesse Smith, J. W. Krumpholz, Brandon Brooks	Serbia Denis Sefik, Zivko Gocic, Andrija Prlainovic, Vanja Udovicic, Dejan Savic, Dusko Pijetlovic, Nikola Raden, Filip Filipovic, Aleksandar Ciric, Aleksandar Sapic, Vladimir Vujasinovic, Branko Pekovic, Slobodan Soro
Women's team	Netherlands Ilse van der Meijden, Yasemin Smit, Mieke Cabout, Biurakn Hakhverdian, Marieke van den Ham, Daniëlle de Bruijn, Iefke van Belkum, Noeki Klein, Gillian van den Berg, Alette Sijbring, Rianne Guichelaar, Simone Koot, Meike de Nooy	United States Elizabeth Armstrong, Heather Petri, Brittany Hayes, Brenda Villa, Lauren Wenger, Natalie Golda, Patty Cardenas, Jessica Steffens, Elsie Windes, Alison Gregorka, Moriah van Norman, Kami Craig, Jaime Hipp	Australia Emma Knox, Gemma Beadsworth, Nikita Cuffe, Rebecca Rippon, Suzie Fraser, Bronwen Knox, Taniele Gofers, Kate Gynther, Jenna Santoromito, Mia Santoromito, Melissa Rippon, Amy Hetzel, Alicia McCormack
WEIGHTLIFTING			
Men's 56 kg	Long Qingquan (CHN)	Hoang Anh Tuan (VIE)	Eko Yuli Irawan (INA)
Men's 62 kg	Zhang Xiangxiang (CHN)	Diego Fernando Salazar (COL)	Triyatno (INA)
Men's 69 kg	Liao Hui (CHN)	Vencelas Dabaya (FRA)	Tigran Martirosyan (ARM)
Men's 77 kg	Sa Jae-Hyouk (KOR)	Li Hongli (CHN)	Gevorg Davtyan (ARM)
Men's 85 kg	Lu Yong (CHN)	Andrei Rybakou (BLR)	Tigran Martirosyan (ARM)
Men's 94 kg	Ilya Ilin (KAZ)	Szymon Kolecki (POL)	Khadjimourad Akkayev (RUS)
Men's 105 kg	Andrei Aramnau (BLR)	Dmitry Klokov (RUS)	Dmitry Lapikov (RUS)
Men's +105 kg	Matthias Steiner (GER)	Evgeny Chigishev (RUS)	Viktors Scerbatihs (LAT)
Women's 48 kg	Chen Xiexia (CHN)	Sibel Özkan (TUR)	Chen Wei-ling (TPE)
Women's 53 kg	Prapawadee Jaroenrattanatarakoon (THA)	Yoon Jin-Hee (KOR)	Nastassia Novikava (BLR)
Women's 58 kg	Chen Yanqing (CHN)	Marina Shainova (RUS)	O Jong Ae (PRK)
Women's 63 kg	Pak Hyon Suk (PRK)	Irina Nekrassova (KAZ)	Lu Ying-chi (TPE)
Women's 69 kg	Liu Chunhong (CHN)	Oxana Slivenko (RUS)	Natalya Davydova (UKR)
Women's 75 kg	Cao Lei (CHN)	Alla Vazhenina (KAZ)	Nadezhda Yevstyukhina (RUS)
Women's +75 kg	Jang Mi-Ran (KOR)	Olha Korobka (UKR)	Mariya Grabovetskaya (KAZ)

2008 Medalists

Event	Gold	Silver	Bronze
WRESTLING: FREESTYLE			
Men's 55 kg	Henry Cejudo (USA)	Tomohiro Matsunaga (JPN)	Besik Kudukhov (RUS) Radoslav Velikov (BUL)
Men's 60 kg	Mavlet Batirov (RUS)	Vasyl Fedoryshyn (UKR)	Morad Mohammadi (IRI) Kenichi Yumoto (JPN)
Men's 66 kg	Ramazan Sahin (TUR)	Andriy Stadnik (UKR)	Sushil Kumar (IND) Otar Tushishvili (GEO)
Men's 74 kg	Buvaisar Saitiev (RUS)	Soslan Tigiev (UZB)	Murad Gaidarov (BLR) Kiril Terziev (BUL)
Men's 84 kg	Revaz Mindorashvili (GEO)	Yusup Abdusalomov (TJK)	Taras Danko (UKR) Georgy Ketoyev (RUS)
Men's 96 kg	Shirvani Muradov (RUS)	Taimuraz Tigiyev(KAZ)	Georgi Gogshelidze (GEO) Khetag Gazyumov (AZE)
Men's 120 kg	Artur Taymazov (UZB)	Bakhtiyar Akhmedov (RUS)	David Musulbes (SVK) Marid Mutalimov (KAZ)
Women's 48 kg	Carol Huynh (CAN)	Chiharu Icho (JPN)	Mariya Stadnik (AZE) Irina Merleni (UKR)
Women's 55 kg	Saori Yoshida (JPN)	Xu Li (CHN)	Tonya Verbeek (CAN) Jackeline Rentería (COL)
Women's 63 kg	Kaori Icho (JPN)	Alena Kartashova (RUS)	Yelena Shalygina (KAZ) Randi Miller (USA)
Women's 72 kg	Wang Jiao (CHN)	Stanka Zlateva (BUL)	Kyoko Hamaguchi (JPN) Agnieszka Wieszczek (POL)
WRESTLING: GRECO-ROMAN			
Men's 55 kg	Nazyr Mankiev (RUS)	Rovshan Bayramov (AZE)	Park Eun-Chul (KOR) Roman Amoyan (ARM)
Men's 60 kg	Islam-Beka Albiev (RUS)	Vitaliy Rahimov (AZE)	Nurbakyt Tengizbayev (KAZ) Ruslan Tumenbaev (KGZ)
Men's 66 kg	Steeve Guenot (FRA)	Kanatbek Begaliev (KGZ)	Armen Vardanyan (UKR) Mikhail Siamionau (BLR)
Men's 74 kg	Manuchar Kvirkelia (GEO)	Chang Yongxiang (CHN)	Yavor Yanakiev (BUL) Christophe Guenot (FRA)
Men's 84 kg	Andrea Minguzzi (ITA)	Zoltán Fodor (HUN)	Nazmi Avluca (TUR) Vacant
Men's 96 kg	Aslanbek Khushtov (RUS)	Mirko Englich (GER)	Adam Wheeler (USA) Asset Mambetov (KAZ)
Men's 120 kg	Mijaín López (CUB)	Khasan Baroyev (RUS)	Mindaugas Mizgaitis (LIU) Yuri Patrikeyev (ARM)

Glossary

470: a double-handed, single-hulled dinghy named for its length in centimetres (470 cm). It is the class of boat used for both the men's and women's two persons dinghy events

49er: a one-design class of small sailing dinghy. It is a double handed twin trapeze boat, meaning that it is sailed by a helm and a crew

Aborigine: a member of a dark-skinned hunting and gathering people who were living in Australia when European settlers arrived (also called native Australian)

accolade: strong praise or approval; an award or honour

aggregate: sum total

amateur: an athlete who has never competed for money, or who accepts money under restrictions specified by a regulatory body, for participating in a competition

anti-Semitism: hostility toward or prejudice against Jews or Judaism

apartheid: racial segregation between Whites and non-Whites, enforced by the South African government between 1948 and 1993

applicant city: a city which has received approval from their NOC and has submitted an application to the IOC to be considered for a candidate aity

archaeologist: someone who studies man's past by scientific analysis of the material remains of his cultures (artifacts, inscriptions, monuments etc), especially those that have been excavated

Aryan: (in Nazi ideology) a Caucasian (white person) of non-Jewish descent, esp of the Nordic type

austerity: being austere (stern, severe); a reduced availability of luxuries and consumer goods

autopsy: dissection and examination of a dead body to determine the cause of death

Basque pelota: the name for a variety of court sports played with a ball using one's hand, a racket, a bat or a basket, against a wall

biathlon: a term used to describe any sporting event made up of two disciplines, but usually refers specifically to the winter sport that combines cross-country skiing and rifle shooting

bid city: any city that has announced it will bid to host the Olympic Games

Black Power Salute: a clenched fist salute in which the arm is held straight, used among Black Americans to show racial pride and social equality

Tommie Smith and John Carlos raise their fists in a Black Power salute at the 1968 Games

BMX: a bicycle race over a rough cross-country course, usually consisting of jumps, obstacles, and turns; also the bike used for this type of sport

budo: the ethical code on which all martial arts are based

butterfly stroke: a swimming stroke in which the arms are thrown forward together out of the water while the feet kick up and down

candidate city: a city bidding for the opportunity to host an Olympic Games. The city has already received the approval of their NOC, has submitted an application and questionnaire to the IOC and has been selected to the short-list

canoe: a long, narrow, pointed lightweight paddle boat which floats on the surface of water

concentration camp: a guarded prison camp in which non-military prisoners are held, especially one of those in Nazi Germany in which millions were exterminated (killed)

constitutional: relating to the fundamental political principles on which a state or country is governed

contingency fund: money or securities set aside to cover unexpected conditions or losses in business

coxswain (cox): the oarless crew-member, usually included, who is responsible for steering and race strategy. The cox either sits in the stern or lies in the bows of the boat

decathlon: an athletic contest consisting of ten track and field events: 100 m, 400 m and 1,500 m runs, 110 m high hurdles, discus and javelin throws, shot put, pole vault, high jump and long jump

defect: to desert one's country or allegiance, especially in order to join the opposing forces

delegation: a person or group chosen to represent another or others

demonstration sport: a sport performed to promote itself in the Olympic Games and other sporting events. Some demonstration sports gain popularity and become a part of the official programme

discipline: in the Olympics the IOC makes a distinction between sports and disciplines. A sport, in Olympic terms, is a single or group of disciplines as represented by an international governing body. For example, aquatics, represented at the Olympic level by the International Swimming Federation, is a sport at the Summer Olympics that includes four disciplines: swimming, diving, synchronized swimming and water polo

dobok: the uniform worn by practitioners of Korean martial arts. Usually white, with wide sleeves and pants tied together with a coloured belt denoting the rank of the wearer

Dream Team: the first American Olympic team to feature active professional basketball players which won the gold medal in the 1992 Games. Sometimes considered the greatest team assembled in any sport, it defeated its opponents by an average of almost 44 points

dressage: an equestrian event where the horse performs a series of trained movements on the rider's command. They perform in a prescribed arena, where they are judged on the finesse of their movement

echidna: a spine covered primitive Australian mammal with a long snout and claws for hunting ants and termites

Elliot 6m: an Olympic-class keelboat, selected for the women's match racing event for the 2012 Olympics

épée: this sword is slightly heavier than the foil sword, with a stiffer three sided blade, and has the hardest blade of the three fencing swords. In the Olympic discipline, fencers may touch the point of the sword on any part of the opponent's body

Finn: the Finn dinghy is the men's single-handed, cat-rigged (single mast, positioned well forward) Olympic class for sailing and has been used in every summer Olympics since 1952

foil: a type of sword used in fencing. In the Olympic discipline, fencers are allowed to touch the point of the foil on the back and front of the opponents' torso and belly area

Fosbury Flop: a modern high-jumping technique whereby the jumper clears the bar headfirst and backwards, named after Dick Fosbury, the US winner of the men's high jump at the 1968 Olympics

freestyle: a race, particularly in swimming, where the participant can use any style that he or she prefers (usually front crawl is selected)

Golden Slam: winning the four Majors and a gold medal in tennis at the Summer Olympics has been called a 'Golden Slam' since 1988 when Steffi Graf became the only person to accomplish that feat in a single calendar year

Grand Slam: a tennis player or team which wins all the four Major tournaments in one year (the Australian Open, the French Open, Wimbledon and the US Open)

Graves Disease: an illness caused by excessive production of the thyroid hormone, characterised by protrusion of the eyeballs, a rapid heartbeat, and nervous excitability

half-pipe: a half-moon-shaped chute or ramp used by snowboarders and skateboarders to provide a takeoff for a jump

heavyweight: a weight division in sports like boxing. Boxers who participate in this category generally weigh over 90 kg

heptathlon: an athletic contest usually for women consisting of the following seven track and field events: 200 m and 800 m runs, 100 m hurdles, shot put, javelin throw, high jump and long jump

Heraia: festival in ancient Greece for unmarried women

hieromenia: sacred truce held to allow contestants and spectators of the ancient Olympic Games to travel safely to the Games and home again

Holocaust: the mass murder by the Nazis of the Jews of continental Europe between 1940 and 1945

hoplite: a heavily armed infantry (foot) soldier in ancient Greece

hoplitodromos: race in ancient Games which was as much a military training exercise as an athletic contest. Competitors had to run wearing the helmet and greaves (armour to protect the shins) of the hoplite infantryman from which the race took its name. Runners also carried a bronze-covered wood shield, bringing the total encumbrance to at least 50 pounds

host city: the city responsible for organising and funding the Games according to the Olympic Charter humanism: a system of thought that is non-religious and centres on humans and their values and worth

humanitarian: someone devoted to the promotion of human welfare and to social reforms; someone devoted to helping others

Intercalated Games: International Games that were to be held in Athens every four years half-way between the Games of the Olympiad. The only such games were held in 1906.

International Olympic Committee (IOC): an international, non-governmental, non-profit organisation and the supreme authority of the Olympic Movement. Its major responsibility is to supervise the Summer and Winter Olympic Games

jade: a semi-precious stone varying in colour from white to green

jeu de paume: a French precursor of tennis originally played without racquets. The players hit the ball with their hands. Later, bats and then raquets were used

jujitsu: a Japanese system of wrestling that uses throws, holds and blows, and derives added power from the attacker's own weight and strength

kayak: a long, narrow, lightweight paddle boat with pointed ends, like a canoe. However, unlike canoes, which float on the surface, kayaks float just below the surface, forcing the water to be pushed aside as they move

keirin: a form of track cycling originating in Japan, where riders must race in heats behind a motorised pace-setter which leaves the track a few laps before the end

kendo: a modern Japanese martial art of sword-fighting based on traditional samurai swordsmanship, or kenjutsu

kookaburra: a large kingfisher of southern and eastern Australia, with brown and white plumage and a call resembling raucous laughter

korfball: a mixed gender team sport originating from the Netherlands, with similarities to netball and basketball. A team consists of eight players: four female and four male

kyudo: a modern Japanese martial art meaning 'way of the bow,' used as a technique of concentration and spiritual discipline

laser radial: a variant of the laser standard, with shorter mast and reduced sail area, allowing a single light sailor to sail in heavy winds

laser: a popular one-design class of small sailing dinghy, usually sailed by one person

luge: a small one- or two-person sled on which one sleds extremely fast face up and feet-first

Martin Luther King Jr: a prominent American leader of the African-American civil rights movement and Nobel Peace Prize laureate, who was a powerful speaker and who advocated social change through non-violent means. He was assassinated in Memphis, Tennessee, on April 4, 1968

mascot: a symbol of an animal, human or thing that represents a group or event and is supposed to bring good luck. Olympic mascots also represent the culture of the place where the Games are held

medley: a swimming race in which a different stroke is used for each length; or in athletics, a relay race in which each leg has a different distance

merchandise: goods or products sold

migrant: a person who moves from one region or country to another

modern pentathlon: a competition (not to be confused with the pentathlon) in which each participant competes in five events: running, swimming, horseback riding, fencing and pistol shooting

Andrey Moiseev of Russia competes in the men's Modern Pentathlon Riding Show Jumping at the Beijing Games

moguls: a series of bumps on a ski trail formed when skiers push the snow into mounds or piles as they execute short-radius turns

nationalise: convert from private to government ownership and control

Nazi: a member of the fascist National Socialist German Worker's Party which seized political control in Germany in 1933 under Adolf Hitler

Nike: ancient Greek Goddess of Victory

In Greek mythology, the winged goddess Nike personifies speed, strength and victory. Her image was first used on an Olympic medal in 1900

National Olympic Committee (NOC): an organisation authorised by the IOC to oversee Olympic activities within a particular country such as organising national teams, hosting Games, marketing and sponsorships

New Emerging Forces Games: Games held in Jakarta in 1963 — set up in competition to the Olympics by Indonesia with the philosophy that politics and sport were interlinked

nom de plume: a pseudonym or 'pen name' used by a writer wishing to conceal his or her true identity

Nordic: native or inhabitant of one of the Scandinavian countries — Iceland, Norway, Denmark, Sweden or Finland — or something relating to Scandinavia. In sport, it refers

to a ski competition featuring ski jumping and cross-country racing

Olympiad: a period of four years, beginning in a year divisible by four

Olympic Charter: a set of rules and guidelines for the organisation of the Olympic Games, and for governing the Olympic Movement

pagan: a member of a group who worships or believes in more than one god, or a person without religion

pankration: an all-in wrestling competition in the ancient Games almost without rules — only biting and gouging with the fingers were forbidden

Parkinson's Disease: a disease which attacks the central nervous system and causes poor muscular coordination and shaking

patron: someone who supports, protects or champions someone or something

pentathlon: an athletic contest, generally for women, in which each participant competes in five track and field events: usually the 200 m and 1,500 m runs, long jump, and discus and javelin throws

pictogram: a symbol which is a picture that represents an object or concept

platypus: an amphibious (able to live on both land and in water) egg-laying mammal of eastern Australia with dense fur, a broad bill and tail, and webbed feet

podium: a small raised platform

pole vault: a track and field event where a person jumps over a high crossbar with the aid of a long, flexible pole

polio: a disease that chiefly affects children and, in its acute forms, can lead to paralysis, muscular atrophy, and often deformity

political asylum: refuge given by one

country to a citizen of another country to protect that person from arrest or persecution

pommel horse: a gymnastic apparatus that has a metal frame, a leather cover and two handles for support. It is used by male athletes in gymnastic events

professional: a person who earns a living in a sport or other occupation frequently engaged in by amateurs

Prohibition: a period (1920-33) when the manufacture, sale and transportation of intoxicating liquors (alcohol) was banned by constitutional amendment in the US

protocol: forms of ceremony and etiquette; a code of conduct

puck: a disk used in ice hockey and certain other games serving the same functions as a ball does in ball games

quarantine: a period of isolation, especially of people or animals arriving from abroad, to prevent the spread of disease

relay: a race between two or more teams, in which each team member participates in part of the race and is then relieved by another member of the team

repechage: a heat (especially in fencing and rowing) in which runners-up in the eliminating heats compete for a place in the final race

rhythmic gymnastics: a style of gymnastics in which an individual or a team performs with props

sabre: a sword used in fencing, with a narrow V-shaped blade, a semicircular guard, and a slightly curved hand. It is a very light weight and flexible weapon which is commonly used for thrusting and cutting. A fencer is allowed to touch the opponent's body with the point and edges of this fencing sword, above the hip line, including arms and excluding hands

sailboard: a modified surfboard with a single sail which pivots, ridden while standing up

satellite: a man-made object in orbit around the earth which contains electronic devices for originating or relaying communications and data

sculler: a rower who rows with two oars, one in each hand

sculling: propelling a boat with oars

silver iodide: a yellow powder which becomes dark when exposed to light, used in photography, medicine and in seeding clouds to make rain

ski cross: a skiing competition where skiers race in a group of four on a course of bumps and turns, progressing to the final through a series of heats. The name is derived from motocross

slalom: a timed Alpine race downhill over a zigzag course marked by flag-topped poles, or gates; also in canoeing, contestants must navigate a decked canoe or kayak through a course of hanging gates on river rapids in the fastest time

sponsor: someone who supports or champions something, especially financially

springboard: a flexible board for jumping upward, used by gymnasts when vaulting and by divers

stanozolol: a banned performance-enhancing steroid which gives users increased strength and allows them to recover faster from exercise. Ben Johnson was stripped of his gold medal in the 100 m sprint at the 1988 Summer Olympics when he tested positive for stanozolol after winning the final

Star: a racing keelboat for two people. It has been an Olympic sailing class since 1932

steeplechase: a 3,000-m track footrace with obstacles and a water jump. The race derives its name from steeplechase in horse racing

strychnine: a poisonous alkaloid drug that can act as a stimulant, boosting athletic performance when used in small doses, but can be fatal if used in high doses

Suez Crisis: an international crisis that arose in 1956 when Egypt nationalised the Suez Canal, (owned by the Suez Canal

Company, which was controlled by French and British interests) after Western countries failed to help finance the construction of the Aswan High Dam as they had previously promised

sumo: a form of wrestling in Japan in which a contestant wins by forcing his opponent out of the ring or by causing him to touch the ground with any part of his body other than the soles of his feet

synchronised swimming: a form of swimming where solo swimmers or teams perform elaborate movements in water accompanied by music

synthetic: relating to compounds formed by man through a chemical process, as opposed to those of natural origin

taekwondo: a Korean martial art, similar to karate, that utilizes punches, jabs, chops, blocking and choking moves, and especially powerful, leaping kicks

Taliban: a fundamentalist (strictly religious) Islamic militia in Afghanistan

tartan: a synthetic track surface which gives greater cushioning for running

triathlon: a competition in which athletes compete without stopping in three successive events: usually long-distance swimming, cycling and running

uneven bars: an artistic gymnastics apparatus, used only by female gymnasts. It is made of a metal or steel frame, with two bars set at different heights

vault: (or vaulting horse) a piece of gymnastic equipment with an upholstered body over which the gymnast will jump with the help of a springboard

Slalom canoeing and kayaking made their first appearance (on an artificial river) at the Munich Olympics in 1972

Index

The Olympic flag unfurled at the Beijing Olympics 2008